OTHER
HOOD

OTHER HOOD

Essays on being
childless, childfree
and child-adjacent

Edited by
ALIE BENGE,
LIL O'BRIEN &
KATHRYN VAN BEEK

MASSEY UNIVERSITY PRESS

To all the 'others'

There is something threatening about
a woman who is not occupied with children.
There is something at-loose-ends feeling about
such a woman. What is she going to do instead?
What sort of trouble will she make?

— Sheila Heti, *Motherhood*

Whenever boring old men went,
'What? No children? Well, you'd better get
on with it, old girl,' I'd say 'No! Fuck off!'

— Helen Mirren

Contents

Famous last words

On 3 July 2022, a link to Kate Camp's essay 'No Miracle Baby To See Here' was shared on Twitter, where the following conversation soon appeared:

@LilOBrienWrites: I'm also a failed IVFer and this essay's captured so many feelings. Brilliant. Petition to add this to @aliebenge3's essay 'Mother Of' about making peace with not wanting children, and creating an anthology (I would SO contribute).

@KathrynvanBeek: I've just written an essay about this too. Glad it's in the zeitgeist!

@LilOBrienWrites: Okay so we have 4 essays. There's something in this!

@aliebenge3: Someone make this happen!

Making it happen

We soon realised that 'we' were that someone. Sure, we'd never met before and we lived in different parts of the world, but we weren't going to let that hold us back. By the end of the day, we'd drafted a pitch letter for publishers.

We thought about what Kate Camp's essay had given us: 10 minutes of feeling her grief and frustration, of giggling at all the things she voiced that you kinda aren't supposed to say out loud. And most importantly, a feeling of being seen. That's what we wanted to try to create with this book.

It seems that one of the lovely things about motherhood is that when you become a mother, you join a community. You have a shared experience that can be drawn upon in any situation, from playground small talk to deep conversations. But we 'others' don't get that community, unless we seek it out — or, create it ourselves.

If you've ever felt like you're on the outside looking in, have lived an unexpected life, or given the finger to social expectations, we hope that you'll find your people inside the pages of this book.

Why us?

It turns out that each of us has a tendency to throw ourselves into causes or projects we really believe in — such as Alie in her former volunteer role for Child Rescue New Zealand, Lil as an LGBTQ+ advocate, and Kathryn as a champion for miscarriage support; in 2021, Kathryn's work with MPs Ginny Andersen and Clare Curran led to a change in the law to ensure that people who experience pregnancy loss can take bereavement leave.

The three of us were drawn to this project because we knew it would help to reduce the stigma that people who don't become parents still face. We also wanted to provide a counter-argument to some of the bullshit mythologies out there, like that people without children are inherently unfulfilled, that they will always be missing something, are selfish, or can't truly know love in the fullest sense. Why, we asked ourselves, is no relationship — no matter how meaningful and fulfilling — considered anywhere close to the lofty parent–child relationship?

We each have our own 'otherhood' stories, too. While Alie has embraced the DINK (double income, no kids) lifestyle, Kathryn and Lil both went through IVF treatment and pregnancy loss — Lil with the added complexity of navigating the fertility industrial complex as a queer person.

Engaging with reproductive healthcare in our beleaguered health system was a lesson in how the patriarchal roots of Western medicine still tangle the care we receive today. Terms such as 'geriatric pregnancy' (to describe pregnant people aged 35+), and structural issues such as midwives not being financially incentivised to provide first-trimester care meant our fertility journeys were filled with wrong turns, dead ends, traps, delays and sinkholes.

Our kaupapa

Thanks, in part, to the advocacy of early 'mommy bloggers' who carved out a space for their communities, there are now so many books, podcasts and online spaces dedicated to parenting and motherhood. Parents can read about each other's experiences and find comfort and solidarity. But there aren't many stories for the rest of us.

Our aim is for this collection to contribute to a more inclusive conversation. We want anyone who resonates with the term 'otherhood' to be able to pick up this book and relate to the multiplicity of stories within it — stories that intersect with race, disability, sexuality and gender identity, and that cover everything from IVF to foster care.

(M)otherhood

When we began working on *Otherhood*, we hadn't planned to include any essays by mothers. After all, part of the inspiration behind this collection was the desire to push back against common narratives around infertility, including the stories that end with a 'miracle baby' — which, as we know, not everyone gets.

But two women with living children did sneak into these pages — Janie Smith, who writes about being an egg donor in 'Benevolent deadbeat baby-daddy', and Nicola Brown, who speaks from her unique perspective of navigating secondary infertility as an infertility counsellor in 'Synchronicity'. There are other mothers in this collection, too. Iona Winter, in 'Stranded on a shore I never wanted to visit', and Linda Collins, in 'Departure from the motherland', write about the pain of losing their only children to suicide.

Some of our contributors write about the slipperiness between being an 'other' and a mother. Jazial Crossley ponders terminology and responsibility as she gets to know her partner's daughter, while other contributors — such as foster carer Melanie Newfield and Jackie Clark of The Aunties — explore forms of care that aren't easy to categorise.

It's clear that 'motherhood' and 'otherhood' are shifting terms, and there's not necessarily a clear distinction between the two. As Feby Idrus alludes to in her essay, 'How to not be a mother', people who are perceived or socialised as women are always brushing up against motherhood — even if only in societal expectation. We wanted to explore this nuance.

The Barrennesses group chat

With Kathryn and Lil living in Aotearoa and Alie living in London, Alie would wake up to 156 unread messages and find herself volunteered for all sorts of schemes via what we dubbed the Barrennesses group chat.

Kathryn: I am currently of the opinion that Alie should write all the essays.

Lil: I reckon. Maybe then we won't need funding for the contributors. She can just write them for free. As different personas.

Kathryn: Love this idea.

Our professional relationship soon morphed into friendship — and a source of support.

Kathryn: Was just in a work meeting and everyone went around the table and introduced themselves by saying how many kids they have! I was so mad I couldn't even trot out my usual 'I have cats' line.

Alie: Ugghhh that is the worst.

Lil: Missed opportunity to answer 'I'm currently editing a book about the stigma faced by women without children.'

Kathryn: OK got the right response now, just 90 minutes too late: 'I've got three dead babies but I did successfully change the law to have miscarriage recognised as bereavement.'

Alie: That would have been SO GOOD.

Turning an idea into a book

From our first Zoom with the Massey University Press team, we knew we'd found our dream publisher. Based on only a small selection of writing samples, they immediately saw how special this book was going to be.

We put out a call for submissions and wrote the funding application that would enable us to pay our contributors. Too easy! Essays began flooding in.

It quickly became clear how strongly the term 'otherhood' resonated with people. We expected we would hear from people who had unsuccessfully tried fertility treatment, hadn't found the right partner at the right time, had concerns about finances or climate change, or had simply never wanted children. We heard all those stories — and more.

For some people the topic of otherhood was too painful, and they weren't ready to go there, but many writers expressed a sense of relief that someone was giving them an outlet to write about their experiences.

When we didn't get Creative New Zealand funding to pay our contributors, we braced ourselves to run a Boosted crowdfunding campaign. We weren't sure if we'd get much backing, but by the end of the first day we'd raised half our goal. One of Alie's childfree friends told her how moved she felt watching the incredible support for our project. As our crowdfunding campaign barrelled along, we greedily consumed every essay submission, getting more and more excited as the book began to gain form. Then we got worried again — too many amazing essays! How on earth could we choose just 30?

Submissions were printed out, scribbled on, and hotly debated. We told the writers whose work we weren't able to include that every essay we received had something important to say, that every essay was fought for, and that we were gutted we couldn't share more of them. It was true. The quality of submissions was so high that we've published 36 — instead of the planned 30 — essays (including a comic). And we would have picked even more if we could have squeezed them in.

Looking back, we wouldn't recommend crowdfunding, selecting essays and editing them pretty much simultaneously, but that's what ended up having to happen. At times it was only our group chat — where we dreamed up increasingly ridiculous ideas for the book launch — that kept us going.

Kathryn: New book launch idea . . . driving motorbikes into the venue while a band plays. Also, glitter cannons.

Lil: I love all these ideas. Gender reveal confetti colours for the glitter cannons. Pink and blue cupcakes that say 'It's a book!'

Kathryn: I ride in like Meat Loaf. Behind me I drag a hospital bed and on it Alie dramatically gives birth to a book.

We edited through the Auckland floods, a residency in Budapest, Alie's move to London, and the deaths of pets. As we travelled around different parts of the world we woke up early and stayed up late to Zoom with one another. And we — mostly — did the editing around our other responsibilities.

Lil: I am so supposed to be working on my life insurance client rn.

Alie: I'm supposed to be writing a page on bruises and sprains for St John.

Kathryn: I'm writing about the new Mosgiel pool facility.

We edited on the run, in bars, on trains, and from beneath foils at the hairdresser. We spent so much time at our desks that Lil ended up buying weird-looking products from Instagram to help stretch her cervical spine. And just when our energy was flagging, we were revived by reading Helen Rickerby's essay in which a friend implored her to finish writing her *Otherhood* submission, saying 'Women must know that there is a choice.'

Gonna try to ask this genuinely . . .

At some point a man whom none of us knows took to social media to ask us the following question:

> Gonna try to ask this genuinely since I'm also childfree and plan to stay that way for the foreseeable future. What is there to say about living without kids? Isn't that the default? Can't see not having kids having any challenges or similar.

Our hunch was that there's a lot to say about living without kids, because for various reasons, otherhood stories get silenced. Pregnancy loss isn't spoken about because it touches on the twin taboos of sex and death, and because there's implicit pressure for the bereaved not to bum other people out. Infertility isn't spoken about because it can be so painful, because it can elicit such unhelpful reactions, and because other people just don't want to hear about it. And choosing not to have children isn't spoken about openly because it flies in the face of social norms.

But a genuine question deserves a genuine answer, so we spoke with health psychology expert Dr Tracy Morison, who specialises in reproductive decision-making, to see if she thought there was any value in speaking about living without kids.

'Nobody questions why people want to have children — it's just taken for granted,' Dr Morison said. 'But if you don't have children, the three stigma positions are that you're sad, you're mad or you're bad. If you can't have children, that's very sad. If you're deliberately not having children, there's an assumption of deviance — of being mad. Or that you're bad — you're incredibly selfish and materialistic. These stereotypes are worse for women, because women are supposed to have a maternal instinct.'

As Dr Morison spoke, we reflected on the essays in our collection, such as Raina Ng's 'The happy wanderer', that grapple with these stereotypes and assumptions.

'Sexuality and reproduction are very attached to people's different morals and values, so these topics are loaded,' she continued. 'There's a degree of judgement on the part of the people who think that having children is the right and normal way to live based on their religion or politics.'

In their essays 'The feminist shelf' and 'Another good year', Hazel Phillips and Michaela Tempany describe the fundamentalist childhoods they had to break free from, and the pronatalist expectations they overturned in order to forge the lives they wanted.

'Pronatalism is the taken-for-granted worldview that having children is something that you should do, and will bring life fulfilment and happiness,' Dr Morison explained. 'There's a strong religious influence, and strong nation-state influence, where people must have — white — babies to bolster the nation. Certain people are encouraged to have children, and people who are seen as "unfit" are discouraged,' she continued, adding that pronatalism goes hand-in-hand with rigid expectations around gender.

'Another reason for the push-back some women might experience as "non-mothers" — I hate that term, but there's no other word for it — is because they've stepped out of the traditional gender roles.'

These roles are explored in several essays, particularly those by Golriz Ghahraman and Lucy O'Connor. Lucy's essay 'Atmosphere' points out the irony in our Twitter commenter's message — 'I'm also child free and plan to stay that way for the foreseeable future'. Inherent in that statement is the knowledge that he has years in which to weigh his options. As Lucy writes, 'How differently men and women must perceive time.'

'Selfish' by Donelle McKinley speaks eloquently about the decision to prioritise her own life over the life of an imagined future child, and the judgement that comes when you swim against the tide. The use of third person in her essay expresses the self-stigma of choosing to be childfree.

'Some of the research I've done is looking at how people handle stigma,' Dr Morison said. 'One of the things we look at in health psychology is called minority stress — the stress that comes from constantly living in a marginalised position and having to cope with the comments that are made. The more socially marginalised categories you occupy, the more it compounds.'

There's a one-sided glorification of parenthood in which non-parenthood is diminished, as Dr Morison explained. 'A dynamic is created when people who haven't had children have to defend their positions. This potentially creates hostility — but you can't really blame people who are on the back foot and trying to defend their choices in the face of the norm.'

This hostility goes both ways, as Lily Duval explores in her essay 'The Addington house', in which she's accused by a mother of having 'childfree privilege'. But worse than hostility can be the silence.

'Society is very set up towards people with children. When you don't have that commonality, people don't know what to talk to you about,' Dr Morison said. 'People [without children] who have flocked to online communities and "found their people" there talk about how that's helped them manage and cope.'

Our contributor Linda Rooney, who set up an early blog about living with infertility, has helped countless others by creating such a supportive space. As Dr Morison pointed out, it's also important to share otherhood stories more widely.

'Having people tell their own stories brings different types of being into the cultural imagination,' she said. 'It opens up space for what it means to be a woman.'

We told Dr Morison about the Twitter comment. She rolled her eyes.

Here's to the others

Inside this collection we hope you'll find stories you may not have even realised were missing, hear people voicing the thoughts you've had too, or living lives that more closely represent yours. As romance writer Steff Green comments in her essay, there's more than one way to have a happy ending.

More schlongs, more cats

STEFF GREEN

'm Steff, a 30-something cishet woman with a doting husband, too many cats and a penchant for overpriced cocktails. And I'm in love with a fictional man. OK, OK. I should be honest here — he's not a man, but several men, each one taller than the last. Each with a deep, gloomy voice, piercing, fathomless eyes, and a schlong that has to be checked as oversized luggage on aeroplanes. My fictional boyfriends are all brooding and protective, with a relentless appetite for pleasing a woman over and over and over . . .

I am a romance reader. I love nothing more than curling up on the sofa with a block of Whittaker's Dark Salted Caramel and a sexy book boyfriend. I'm particularly drawn to paranormal and fantasy stories where the heroine is hurled into a secret part of the modern world where magic, vampires, werewolves and other supernatural creatures exist. The heroes in these books aren't just handsome and brooding and possessive — they also drink blood, howl at the moon, and possess superhuman strength (perfect for opening relish jars) and 'interesting' appendages.

I'm so in love with these fictional men that I made a career out of writing them — I am also a romance writer. Under my pen name, Steffanie Holmes,

I've independently published over 50 romance novels, sold hundreds of thousands of copies, and have fans all over the world. I've joined an incredible female-led industry, and I'm proud to have penned some of the broodiest, most tattooed, schlongiest men in the business.

The readers, writers and publishers of romance have worked hard to cast aside the 'bodice-ripper' image of the 1960s and '70s. The discourse around romance novels and the people who love them is finally changing. For the longest time, romance was ignored by the publishing elite, despite the fact that the genre is the powerhouse of publishing. A 2018 study showed that 25 per cent of all books and 50 per cent of all mass-market paperbacks sold are romance novels. We romance readers are voracious, devouring books faster than Elon Musk can tank a company, desperate for our fix of falling in love.

And is it any wonder that romance novels are enduringly popular? In the real world, women are still forced to fight for reproductive rights and autonomy over our own bodies. We've got piles of laundry and a work report due and we haven't had an orgasm in six months. We have the wage gap and the thigh gap and the pleasure gap and the gaping chasm of our own existential angst. We all just lived through a global pandemic, and we are tired.

So why not escape for a few hours to a world where a hot prince crashes into our lives like a tousled-haired freight train and solves all our problems? Why not enjoy a happy bubble where our voices shape the narrative and our desires are placed front and centre for once?

Maya Rodale, author of a history of the romance novel industry, writes that they are enduring because they are 'dangerous books for girls that show women again and again that they're worth it', where 'women's voices predominantly shape the narrative about themselves in the world', and where 'real, good love doesn't ask you to lose weight, change your hair, get a different job, silence your feelings or in some way shrink yourself to fit into a box society has labelled "desirable"'.[1]

And yet, not even a woman's free time is truly free. If she dares to spend her Sunday afternoon between the pages with the Four Horsemen of the Apocalypse, who descend upon earth to give the heroine multiple orgasms (the actual plot of an actual series I read recently, and I highly recommend it),[2]

1   Maya Rodale, *Dangerous Books for Girls: The bad reputation of romance novels explained* (Maya Rodale, 2015), www.fairobserver.com/culture/romance-novels-womens-rights-donald-trump-misogyny-culture-news-79544
2   Laura Thalassa, The Four Horsemen series.

she will be mocked. The terms 'mommy porn' and 'trash books' are commonly used to describe romance novels. I use the word 'smut' lovingly, but some use it derisively. 'What if these books give women unhealthy expectations about men?' cries the ubiquitous male commenter on every article about the industry.

What if, indeed.

☀

The romance audience no longer wishes to be silenced about their choice of reading material. Instead, fans proudly take to BookTok and Instagram to show off their 'smutty bookshelves' and TBR (to-be-read) piles, and swoon over their favourite fictional boyfriends.

And romance novels are changing with them. The modern romance novel promises not only a swoony romance (and, usually, panty-meltingly good smut), but also a commentary on the changing roles of women, contraception, sexual harassment and rape culture, climate change, women in the workplace, family drama . . . you name it.

But in the centuries since the first love story was penned, one thing about the romance novel hasn't changed: the happily-ever-after.

In industry shorthand, we call the happily-ever-after the HEA. And the HEA means specific things to romance readers, no matter the gender, race, sexual identity or background of their preferred pairing. A grand gesture to show the characters have grown and changed. A wedding ring. A perfectly planned proposal. A scintillating kiss. And then, one or two or five years later, in the epilogue, the couple get down to making babies.

Readers adore the babies. Some of them skip to the last chapter to read the HEA before they even begin the book, just to make sure the characters get a satisfying ending.

As a childfree woman and an avid reader and author, this both fascinates and infuriates me.

Why is a happily-ever-after not complete without babies?

Why are we not satisfied until the heroine conforms to the traditional gender roles of wife and mother?

What does this say about the way we view romance, love, sex and family?

In books and films and TV, the modern romance heroine is a strong, funny, successful, fierce woman, in charge of and aware of her own sexuality. She does not wait around in a flimsy nightgown for a man to kidnap and ravish her. She makes her desires clear and she builds a connection with her chosen partner as an equal. She is me. She is my friends. And yet . . .

And yet, for her to have her happily-ever-after, she must have children.

Romance novels, like all media, hold up a twisted mirror to the real world. They say a lot of fascinating, nuanced things about feminine desire and agency, and about the changing attitudes toward contraception and a woman's role in society. Romance novels enable women to have conversations about sex and desire and fantasy they'd normally be too afraid to have . . . even if those conversations are only with themselves.

The genre — which, as all genres do, must continue to reckon with its heteronormative, patriarchal, ableist and white supremacy narratives — is at the forefront of diversity within the publishing industry. Queer romance, polyamorous romance, and romance between characters of colour and characters with disabilities are becoming more common and more celebrated, with networks and industry bodies working hard to lift the voices of marginalised authors and their experiences. As a blind woman who always longed to see myself in my favourite heroines, I'm thrilled by the progress we have made.

Modern romance novels have thrown off so many of their outdated norms. And yet, they still propagate a traditional notion of what it means to live happily ever after as a woman.

This might be why abortion is rarely discussed in romance. It's not a 'sexy' subject, for sure, but where writers are willing to wade in on all kinds of dark and upsetting topics, in some cases making romantic heroes out of serial killers and gang leaders, they shy away from this one. In most stories when a woman encounters an unplanned pregnancy, she decides to keep it.

✹

So what? You might ask. Does it matter? Romance novels deal in fantasy. The heroine's fucking a vampire. Every second guy is a young, hot, kinky heir to a chocolate empire with a heart of gold. No man is that good in bed and *also* a top chef and *also* a secret assassin. Like our concerned male internet commenter above, there's a narrative that runs alongside media made for women by women: that we wouldn't want to give women false expectations of what the real world is like. As if women can't tell the difference between reality and fantasy.

Personally, if asking to be treated like a goddess in and out of bed is considered an unrealistic fantasy for women, then excuse me while I retreat to my boudoir to be with Geralt of Rivia.

We want our media — the books we read, the movies and TV shows we enjoy, the music and podcasts we listen to — to reflect the beautiful variety of our collective experience as women. We have progressed in so many ways (the fact that I have a bestselling series with a blind heroine, who isn't magically healed at the end, says so much to me about how far we've come) but we are not yet ready to give up on this outdated notion of the happily-ever-after.

Is asking for the happily-ever-after to change unreasonable? Is this the exchange we must make in order to have our smut cake and eat it too?

I've wrestled with this question in my own career. What does a happily-ever-after look like if your characters don't want, or can't have, children?

My way through this has been to allow my characters to lead this decision. I don't begin a story with an end goal of babies, or even marriage. I write a lot of polyamorous romance — where marriage in a traditional sense isn't an option for the characters. This is challenging, but it also acts as a permission slip to write a more nuanced depiction of the HEA.

George, the nerdy, true-crime-obsessed heroine of my Dark Academia duet, falls in love with both a Catholic priest and a minor royal, as well as falling afoul of a dangerous secret society. She has her HEA when she accepts a job as a trainee medical examiner while her two men set up a house together and argue over soft furnishings. The final scene is a wedding, but it's not her wedding. I enjoyed playing with this expectation.

The two most badass, blood-soaked women I've ever written in my crime family Stonehurst Prep series — Claudia August and Fergie Munroe — both have children. This felt right for their characters, though the focus in Claudia's HEA isn't about pregnancy, but the animal shelter she set up with her hero. Readers love kittens almost as much as they love babies.

And Mina, the heroine of my popular Nevermore Bookshop Mysteries series, is a blind woman who solves murder mysteries with her three boyfriends, who are all famous villains from classic literature. I am writing the final book in her series right now, in which her wedding day is interrupted when the celebrant is found dead. I have decided that Mina will not be having children. Her reasons are many and nuanced, and they are her own to explore.

❄

Will readers be angry about the lack of babies? Maybe. But so many are grateful, too. I receive fan mail from readers, mostly about the schlongs, but sometimes expressing how grateful they are to read a happily-ever-after that aligns with their own experiences. These readers want to celebrate love and blissful, beautiful lives that don't require the addition of children to be complete.

My friend Devyn Sinclair writes paranormal romance and goes one step further. It is part of her brand that her characters will never have children.

'"You'll change your mind one day!" is the most common response to a woman not wanting children,' Devyn says. 'No matter if it's family, coworkers or strangers on the internet, few people believe that women can be happy and fulfilled in a childless life. It's coded into the fabric of our society. As a writer in a genre for women, and as a childfree woman myself, I choose to keep my books childfree as well. Romance is a safe space for women to explore, and every type of woman deserves that space.'

I agree with Devyn completely. Childless and childfree women already face incredible pressure from the real world. They don't need that same pressure from their fantasy worlds, too. But I've decided not to take so strong a stance in my books — I may not want kids, but not all my characters share my views. Their relationships with motherhood are as complicated as the writers in this collection. I want to give my heroines the freedom to discover their own HEA, whatever that may look like.

Romance novels may be becoming more inclusive and feminist, but they are also a product of the society that created them. Romance writers have more freedom and agency than ever to react to, reflect and subvert the rhetoric of the world we live in, and it warms my heart to see the happily-ever-after becoming more inclusive and nuanced.

I hope that when next I snuggle up on the couch on a Sunday morning with a block of Whittaker's and my latest read, I'll turn the pages to find more broody, schlongy men, more women who take control of their destinies, a few fewer babies and many more cats.

Mother issues

KERRY SUNDERLAND

While other people his age were experimenting with psychedelic drugs, Dad spent most of the 1970s inhaling glue in his workshop in our backyard — an occupational hazard as he designed and then built a 15-metre wingspan sailplane glider. He called it MOBA, short for 'my own bloody aeroplane'.

Dad was obsessed with aviation his entire life: he built model aeroplanes as a kid, went solo at 16 and qualified as an aeronautical engineer. After hours, he spent every waking moment either on the airfield, in his workshop or talking about flying.

Mum and Dad first met on the gliding field. He admired her for many reasons, including the fact she'd built her own model aeroplane. They married four months after their first date. Mum was just 23 when she had me; Dad was 34.

Much of my childhood was spent on rural aerodromes. In many ways, the dusty gliding field felt more like home than our little suburban house. Most weekends, my parents made the four-hour-return road trip from our house in Melbourne's south-eastern suburbs to Bacchus Marsh, about 60 kilometres west of the city, and took to the sky. Left to my own devices on the airfield, I became a gliding 'orphan'.

I coped with any sense of abandonment by reading, seeking out surrogate families, and creating imaginary worlds wherever I could. A voracious reader, I imagined myself being part of fictitious families — the child in other people's families, never the mother. Being a mother didn't look like very much fun.

And I told tales about my parents. They weren't always true. But the underlying theme of all of them was this: my parents were extraordinary people who had met in very extraordinary circumstances. This was my way of compensating for the fact that my family didn't operate the way other families did. We only socialised with those who flew. We never went on normal holidays.

※

I am the eldest of two daughters. I was the 'golden child'. My sister, Clare, two years younger than me, was the 'black sheep'. That's what infant colic and post-natal depression will do to the mother–daughter relationship. And Mum never really recovered. She was often indisposed, shut away in my parents' bedroom with the curtains drawn.

Being left to your own devices wasn't uncommon for children growing up in the seventies and eighties. Yet unlike many other Generation X children, I wasn't a latch-key kid. Mum didn't work, so she was always home — but she was often unavailable, physically and emotionally.

When other Gen X kids grew up, realising their needs hadn't been met, they vowed to do parenting differently. Sometimes they succeeded, although occasionally they swung to the polar opposite: becoming helicopter parents who kept their children wrapped in cotton wool.

I didn't trust myself to do parenting better. For the next 20 years, I wore the label 'feminist' like armour, oblivious that it was masking the fear and sadness I was carrying.

※

During my first year at university, I finally began to develop some womanly curves. I put myself on a strict diet and discovered I was very good at dieting, although starving myself was less about body image and more about wanting to feel like I had some control over my life, when everything else felt so out of control. Within three months, I lost so much weight that I stopped menstruating for almost a year.

Perhaps it was tokophobia, a pathological fear of getting pregnant.

Not long after my eighteenth birthday, someone very close to me had gotten pregnant. A decision was made to adopt out the child. This had horrified me for many reasons, not least because I realised: *This could happen to me.* My fears jumbled together; I was afraid of the pain of giving birth, the shame of an unwanted pregnancy, the fear of losing the child, the fear of the child being taken from me.

Then my anorexia morphed into bulimia and I rounded out, and started bleeding again. I began taking the pill and did so for the next five years, before I realised it was making me crazy, so I stopped.

҉

When I was living in London in my late twenties, I got pregnant, which astonished me; by then I'd convinced myself that I was infertile. After going off the pill, I hadn't been very careful with contraception, but until then it hadn't mattered. When my period was late, my breasts started hurting and I began feeling queasy, I took myself off to the doctor for a pregnancy test. When the test came back positive, I thought it was *very bad news.*

That night, I met my boyfriend for dinner in Covent Garden. When I told him the news, tears welled in his eyes. He jumped off his seat and knelt beside me, with one of his hands on my belly, his words bursting with pride as he said: 'I'm having dinner with the mother of my child.' This wasn't the reaction I expected, and I immediately felt very alone.

Over the next few weeks we discussed every possible scenario, but a big 'yes' eluded me. One night, I stepped outside onto our small patio and stared at the sky, willing the unseeable stars to give me the answer. When I walked back inside, my boyfriend told me how he'd seen me 'talking to our baby'.

Wow, I thought to myself, *I had no idea I was doing that.* But I had stopped smoking cigarettes, just in case I decided to go ahead with the pregnancy.

A few nights later, I arrived home to discover my boyfriend had found a loose page I thought was safely tucked away in my personal belongings. On one side, I'd listed all the reasons he would make a good father, on the other side all the reasons he wouldn't. The negatives far outweighed the positives. He was predictably very hurt. I cried for most of the evening. In the end, he said he would understand if I wanted to terminate the pregnancy.

Turns out I'd prevaricated for too long. I was almost 12 weeks pregnant. Now that I'd decided to have an abortion I felt a sense of urgency that the public health system couldn't accommodate. The following day, I rang a private hospital on the edge of the metropolitan area. I caught the train to the hospital by myself. My boyfriend had offered to come with me but I thought it was my responsibility alone to bear.

I elected to have a general anaesthetic. For this reason, I was supposed to stay in hospital overnight, but when I woke up I desperately wanted to leave. I called my boyfriend and asked him to come and get me. We caught a taxi all the way back into London, arriving just before midnight, the driver sneering at me whenever I caught his eye in the rear vision mirror.

Our relationship never recovered.

✳

In 2001, I moved to the Byron Shire on the far north coast of New South Wales. That year, Australia had recorded its lowest overall fertility rate in history to date — only 1.779 births per woman. But you wouldn't have known this in Byron, which as well as being Australia's counterculture capital, was also known as the Land of the Goddess. I found myself surrounded by young families. As a childless woman, I felt both contrary and alien. My closest female friends were my mother's age. I tried to socialise with women my age but their conversations, which revolved around their children, bored me. I never dared tell anyone this. Instead, I threw myself into my work and built a thriving custom publishing business. And I fell in love with Steve, my tai chi teacher.

Not long after we bought a house together, Steve and I adopted a puppy, a Lhasa Apso Maltese X we called Lappie. My life soon revolved around this small, white bundle of fur. I poured all my love and attention into him. In contrast, I didn't know quite what to do with Steve's son, who was seven when we met and occasionally stayed the night.

A few years later, Steve, his son (by then 10) and I went camping with two other couples, along with their respective children.

We scored the last remaining camping spots beside the river and pitched our tents, prepared an evening meal and then settled in around a roaring campfire to drink wine, sing songs and share tales. By nightfall, I'd already had too much to drink. All my suppressed sorrow sprang to the surface; for some reason, I only ever contemplated having children when drunk. I remember sobbing in a small huddle with my girlfriends, as the full moon shone above us. At some stage, I became vaguely aware of Steve pulling aside one of them to find out what was distressing me so much.

Back home on the Sunday evening — tired and still a little seedy, with piles of camping gear around us and a cooler bin yet to unpack — Steve sat at the end of the dining table and asked me to join him. I was wary; sitting down for a talk inside was something we hadn't done in years. The busyness of life always got in the way. We usually just made small talk on the deck outside, fighting for attention among the cacophony of magpies during the day, or numbed by our respective self-medicating ways at night. I'd rattle on about my day, but focused on what I was doing or thinking rather than what I was feeling. Steve preferred to smoke a joint in silence.

When I sat, I felt self-conscious, so I stood and rearranged the chair, then tucked one leg under my bum and turned to him. He waited for me to settle and give him my full attention.

'Kerry,' he said, as he put aside the cigarette he'd just rolled, 'I'm wondering why you don't feel like you can talk to me about wanting to have children?'

I told him I didn't know what I wanted. This was inching close to the truth, as I was struggling with the Kerry who was trying to make herself heard in the haze of drunkenness but who vanished in the longer hours of sobriety.

But I didn't tell Steve why I couldn't talk to him. Although I couldn't express it then, I was unprepared to test his love. Deep down, part of me hoped that, if he truly loved me, he would tell me he wanted to have children with me. But even deeper down, I worried he hadn't been a very good father to the two children he already had, with two different women. For much of the time we were together, he and his daughter were estranged.

So when Steve said, 'If you really want children, I will support you,' it still wasn't enough for me.

The decision whether or not to have children soon became an intellectual exercise. I resolved to think it through thoroughly.

A truth-telling friend told me, 'For fuck's sake, Kerry, most people don't think about it, they just do it and worry about it later.'

But not me. I grappled with the external considerations (an over-populated world, the challenges of being a mum while self-employed) and, in quieter moments, the more distressing internal considerations (my doubts about Steve as a father, my doubts about myself being a good mother).

At that time, my biggest fear was that choosing not to have children made me selfish. Could I admit to myself, let alone others, that my work was more important to me than children? To feel better, I just had to remind myself there were already too many people on the planet.

I decided to redirect my energy into creating a book about women who had chosen not to have children — not the 'Oops, I forgot to have children' types, but those who had, like me, deliberated. I called it *Pro-creation*. On an individual level, it would be about choosing creative pursuits instead of procreation. On a global level, it would be about choosing not to procreate for the good of the planet, for the good of all creation. I submitted a proposal with a chapter outline to a publisher and they expressed interest, asking me to send them the first few chapters.

It was a great distraction from the deep need inside me; to feel both worthy of being nurtured myself and capable of nurturing others. In many small ways throughout my life I had learnt to repress my fears and suppress my emotions. But it wasn't until I reached my late thirties that I discovered this predisposition comes at a great cost. When Steve, by then my partner of seven years, was diagnosed with colorectal cancer, I found myself ill-equipped to initiate the difficult conversations we needed to have.

※

For a whole bunch of complex reasons, including being raised by a conspiracy theorist, Steve decided against any mainstream medical treatment and instead pursued one alternative therapy after another: fasting, radical dietary changes, vitamin C infusions, juicing, laetrile infusions, enemas, bicarb soda. I deferred to him and set about doing everything I could to keep him alive. I shelved the book project.

More than anything else, Steve believed in the power of belief; we never discussed the possibility he would die. I found myself incapable of speaking honestly, incapable of expressing my fears. Instead, I did everything I could to support his pursuit of a cure.

If my buried desire to have children had been a repressed need to feel nurtured and to nurture another, I had found my place, but caring for Steve was a lonely and unglamorous role. It involved a lot of waiting in my car while he used the toilets at McDonalds or at roadside rest areas. It involved carting 20-kilogram bags of carrots to the fridge. It involved hours and hours at the juicer. There were no mothers' groups, no chance meetings at the school gate, no playground dates. If Steve had chosen the conventional cancer treatment route, I suspect we both would have found more support.

With no agency in the decisions Steve was making, I redirected my energy into what I believed I *could* control. Although I was in complete denial, right up to the end — so much so that his death came as a shock to me — for a short time, I got what I subconsciously wanted: the opportunity to care for someone else.

I am grateful I made one good decision. When Steve suggested we get married, I said yes. Our wedding gave everyone there a chance to celebrate Steve's life. He died 73 days later.

※

Forty-three years old and in the euphoric stages of a new relationship, I flew to Melbourne to catch up with some old friends and to spend a few days at my parents' home, where we would celebrate an early Christmas.

But I was preoccupied; my period was late. On the flight, I agonised about what to do if I was pregnant. And what to say to my (very new) boyfriend, David, if I was.

I didn't feel pregnant. Or did I? I'd felt mild cramps, which I didn't normally get, but there was still no sign of bleeding. Perhaps, I concluded, it was just the anxiety about being pregnant keeping my period at bay.

Then the fearful thoughts arrived: *What if David is upset, or angry, or doesn't want our child? What if there are complications, given my age? What if David's feelings towards me change in some fundamental way? What if he leaves me and I have to struggle as a single mother for the next 20 years? What if he's delighted that we're pregnant but we agree to have all the intrusive tests and find out the baby has Down's syndrome?* I suspected I would choose to continue the pregnancy. *But if we went ahead, would I ever be able to work again?*

And then: *What if I miscarry late or the baby dies?* That was my worst nightmare, having just spent the past two years mourning the death of Steve.

I felt frustrated being 30,000 feet above sea level, contemplating all of this for the first time but unable to discuss it with David. And I didn't want to tell him over the phone that I was pregnant. I needed to see his face, his eyes, his body language. I was so absorbed in my worries that the plane landing took me by surprise.

As I waited for my bag, I remembered how, a few days before, David and I had dropped into end-of-year drinks at my friend's art gallery. I ended up speaking with a woman I had only met a handful of times. During the conversation she told me that she didn't think parents chose to have children. Instead, children chose their parents. David, who I didn't know had been listening, agreed immediately, telling us both that his daughter Jess had definitely chosen him and her mother. They had broken up but ended up in bed together on New Year's Eve, when Jess was conceived. Their relationship didn't last but David played a key role in her upbringing, solo parenting her on and off over the years. He adored his daughter.

When I got to my accommodation, I unpacked my journal and began to list all the fears I had tallied up on the plane. And I added a new one: ectopic pregnancy.

Writing down my fears helped me let go of them, at least a little bit. Eventually I was able to get to sleep.

The following morning, I tried to let go of the idea that being pregnant meant I would necessarily have a baby. I'd had a termination before and could again. This time I wouldn't be alone. Or should I say I wouldn't be keeping myself alone. I trusted David and knew it would be a decision we'd make together, whichever way. And all of those doubts I'd had last time — that my then boyfriend would be a lousy father — didn't apply. David was a wonderful father.

That night, just before I turned out the lights, I realised I couldn't kid myself anymore that I wasn't pregnant. For the past hour, I'd been experiencing powerful (but mercifully short-lived) waves of nausea.

The following day, I caught the train to Footscray. My friend Kim picked me up at the station, on her way home from work. As we were driving, she glanced sideways at me.

'It's good to see you,' she said. 'You look really well. Almost like you're pregnant?'

I looked at her with amazement, then felt confusion and a hint of fear wash over me. 'What makes you say that?'

'I don't know, you're kind of glowing.'

'Well, actually, it's possible that I am.' I felt my breasts. 'And my boobs are sore. Oh God, Kim, what if I am?'

'Don't you want to be pregnant?'

'I don't know, I don't think so. But maybe I do.'

'If it were me, I'd be really happy,' Kim, who also didn't have children, said. 'I would have the baby. I don't have any doubts about that at all.'

I couldn't say the same.

When we got to her house, we busied ourselves cleaning up in preparation for the dinner party she was hosting the following evening. I was in the middle of vacuuming the dining room when I realised I had started bleeding, ferociously. This wasn't a typical period; I had miscarried. I felt sad and immensely relieved, all at the same time. But, most of all, I felt drained, weary, like I wanted to sleep for weeks.

When I flew home a few nights later, I was finally able to share everything with David. He responded in a way that made me feel loved and heard. While he told me he didn't want to have any more children, he didn't bombard me with his own relief.

❊

Almost three years after Steve died, I moved to Aotearoa with David. He'd been desperate to move back to his beloved South Island for years and now that Jess had finished high school, he could. I was ready to start a new chapter in my life; I saw it as an opportunity to reinvent myself in a place where people didn't know me as 'Steve's widow'.

Not long after we arrived, David and I went camping for a week at a gathering called Convergence, held annually over the New Year near Rangiora.

Every day, we sat in a circle to 'heart share'; to be vulnerable and speak openly and honestly about our lives. All the big life challenges were aired: abuse, addiction, mental illness. As were all the emotions: jealousy, envy, anger, sadness, grief, joy, relief.

In the beginning, I didn't even know how to identify the sensations I felt in my body when I was activated or triggered, let alone how to express them as feelings. My first Convergence set me off on a journey of discovery, learning how to express my inner life; eventually, it felt like I'd acquired a new language.

I also learnt about the Jungian concept of the 'shadow self'. I had grown up resenting what I perceived to be my mother's neglect, resenting the fact that we never talked about anything important. I learnt to recognise the little girl inside me who'd felt abandoned by my aviation-obsessed father, and my chronically ill mother. I remembered how I'd spent most of my life constructing tales, for the amusement of others, about this little abandoned girl, as if to say, 'This was what made me who I am today.' I realised my abandonment stories were my way of shouting: 'Look at me, how independent I was at only five years of age. Look at me, how I survived parental neglect.'

Until I articulated my frustrations about Mum's physical and emotional absence, I hadn't even realised I had mother issues.

It also dawned on me how little I knew about my matrilineal line. My mother, Robyn, was an only child. Her mother, Eva, had died when I was three years old. I wondered who my grandmother had been as a person, what sort of mother she'd been to my mum. What had little Robyn learnt from Eva about being a mother? Deep down, part of me didn't feel equipped to be a parent. I had decided to break the cycle. My sister broke the cycle, too, by becoming a wonderful mother to my niece.

※

The second wave of feminists had paved the way for Gen X women to prioritise their career. My generation was also the first to have the privilege to genuinely choose whether we wanted to have children.

If Mum had been born five years later, would she have taken the pill, chosen not to have children herself? After all, in the beginning, she was a trained teacher and she loved flying just as much as Dad did.

While the contraceptive pill had been introduced in Australia in 1961, it came with a hefty 27.5 per cent luxury tax, which made it financially — if not morally — beyond most women. By the time Gough Whitlam was elected prime minister in 1972 and abolished the luxury tax — thus reducing its cost to $1 per month — I was four years old. When my parents married in 1967, they did so with the expectation that they would immediately start a family. Perhaps Mum had no choice.

Nowadays, Mum and I have a tender new relationship. She is in Melbourne in dementia care. My sister takes her on a weekly outing, oversees her daily needs. I call her every couple of days, having the same conversation each time, in slightly different ways.

And I've come to realise that for most of my life, I simply hadn't understood Mum's love language: her gift-giving and acts of service.

Now that Mum is completely reliant on others, I notice the absence of her many offerings to me — the elaborate costumes she made me for school dress-up days, the quilts it took her more than a year to hand-stitch, the thoughtful care packages that appeared in the mail at unexpected times, the many phone calls that began with 'It's your mother here.'

For the love of aiga

AMIE TAUA

limb two flights of stairs and you will find my attic room, complete with an en suite, a wall of wardrobe space and a half-slanted ceiling. Beige and benign, my room is the tree-hut among the terraced homes that line London's Glengall Road. My bed is a large single, centred under windows that look down to the rows of back-squares where people grow things and play and listen for birdsong. My bathroom is tiled with turquoise and has a skylight that opens out.

Before, I listened to planes overhead, music, sirens and footfalls on concrete broken by burgeoning cherry tree roots. Now, it is still; an unnerving quiet interjected with sirens. I never really feel lonely here; but in this lockdown experience, with my aiga at home in Aotearoa, I am alone — mostly. I wander within the 5-kilometre radius of my house — sometimes with one of the girls on my back. When we do go to Hampstead Heath or along the canals via Warwick Avenue, I always stop and let them touch things — the tree trunk, the wall, the bush — and ask, 'Is it rough, or soft?'

On my solitary weekend walks I listen to podcasts so I don't think about those details that I can't control or influence (the list is mounting). I can't leave the house without wearing activewear and a firm I-have-things-to-do expression, defying the very real threat of serious illness and possibly death (yesterday's national Covid-19 death toll was 1122), and the ongoing anxiety that I may lose a family member — or they might lose me — and we would have to mourn from a distance.

Every outing with the girls needs to count. Where we once ventured via the underground to the British Museum, or to that fancy art gallery on New Bond Street with the digital floral still-life images that wilted when we touched them, we now visit the swans that have nested next to the Hampstead entrance, and use sticks to prod and dig and climb up and off the main walking track. But, even through lockdowns, the girls I'm nannying still have things, experiences, freedoms that my parents could never give us.

✷

We have enough, growing up. Just enough. We don't have craft materials, a playroom, or regular art gallery visits. We have trees with branches for sword-making, a yellow and blue swing set to jump off, a VHS player to record and then tape over TV-movies and a nearby school court to ride bikes. When dinner is ready, Mum yells across the expanse of the school grounds through the lounge window. What we lack in resources we make up for with imagination and ingenuity. My little brother and sister and I record home movies, re-enacting the tropes of action films, foreign language films.

And we make up games. I dig extravagantly into my pocket and pull out a fist. 'I have some lollies, would you like one?' I ask my brother. 'Oh yes please, I'd love one.' He takes the invisible treat and unwraps it, before dropping it into his mouth. 'What flavour is it?' I ask. 'Ughh!' he gasps, 'Cabbage!' My sister and I giggle, before he buries his empty fist deep into his trouser pocket, fossicking for another imaginary sweet.

During school holidays, we take long walks under orange street lights to meet Mum when she finishes her shift at midnight. When she walks out of the Cadbury factory, she smells like the milk chocolate she's spent eight hours wrapping and packing. Stepping through the purple door into the still night air, on rare occasions she carries a paper bag full of caramel, toffee and fudge-centred chocolates — the ones that haven't made it into the Favourites box, the Roses box or the Continental box.

Growing up in 1990s Ōtepoti in a working-class, bicultural family, the Samoan and New Zealand European identities and cultural norms are uneven but present. Two vastly different worldviews under one roof leads to competing and complementary priorities, ideas of success and simmering ambition.

Mum and Dad are always at our rugby games. On the sideline Mum yells in support; she lets us know that she's there and doesn't care so much about the outcome as the experience. Dad occasionally pipes up, but is generally quiet and observant, less likely to draw attention in the moment and more likely to have words to share about passing technique on the car ride home.

When Mum and Dad separate and we welcome my stepmum and stepdad into our family, we also welcome seven stepsiblings into the fold. My parents had a child each before having us, and my dad and stepmum soon have one more, bringing the grand total to 13 children. As our family expands, it becomes more complex — and better. I go from two to four to six parents, with the addition of chosen aiga who live on Waimea Ave and provide love and support that is integral to our upbringing. The agility of this structure illustrates the capacity for forgiveness, support, laughter and tears. It also prepares me to be able to slip in and out — largely unseen — of any given family portrait.

Between the six parents who give me life and then shape my adolescence and early adulthood, I'm fed stories of both independent and family migration, from Sāmoa as well as the Netherlands; of diverse cultural norms and traditions; as well as the childhood stories of being born and raised in New Zealand in the 1960s and '70s. This overlap of alternate childhoods also helps me to understand that my parents learnt life's lessons differently; Dad's plantation in Pata Falelatai was Mum's backyard in Forfar Street, Mornington.

※

As a 'mature' first-year university student in 2012, I sign up for papers in media and film studies, philosophy, English and classical studies, and interrogate daily whether I am really the type of person who finds romantic love. I spend traffic-light stops and those minutes of lucidity before sleep figuring out how I will become the fun auntie with all the tropes — cool clothes, great gifts and always slightly buzzed — if romantic love isn't meant for me. Reconciling what I would like in this lifetime versus what is actually on offer helps me cope with the reality that romantic love isn't a given, or an entitlement. I have a healthy respect for its nice-to-have status and make decisions knowing that this nice-to-have may be just a nice-for-*you*.

On top of university papers and existential crises, I become a part-time nanny to a five-year-old called Hannah. This opportunity falls into my lap through the tangled grapevine that is Ōtepoti. Two months turns into four months, and enquiries from other parents come in regarding my availability over semester and summer breaks. What's initially a stopgap turns into almost seven years. From Broad Bay to Belleknowes, I get to know and deeply care for almost 20 children, ranging in age from five months to 12 years old. I develop small friendships, new pasta recipes and a deep appreciation for the grief palate of children. I manage the anxiety of carrying an EpiPen, conjure considered responses to the gag reflex that comes with having to eat pumpkin in order to get dessert, and collect a few degrees.

In 2019, I move to London and become a full-time, live-in nanny. I do this to start again, to be challenged. Ōtepoti is familiar and comfortable; at 29, I feel the undertow to try something I haven't tried before — moving to a foreign place and beginning again — because I know my days to live this type of adventure are numbered. As years pass I will crave a particular routine, a particular seat on the number 10 bus and those shoestring fries from Woof every other Friday. There is also that small detail of children; where and how and why they would fit into this routine.

From April 2019 until May 2021, I work from 8 a.m. to 6 p.m., plus two late finishes, five days a week. I work for two families, who each have a baby girl. I become a primary carer for the first time. Being able to do the everyday, like going to the bathroom alone, is no longer the norm. For some reason, the bathroom door always spills open with toddler climbs and jabber and squabbles, just as I sit down.

As they grow, the girls sing 'māhunga, pakihiwi, puku, hope, waewae' and jump in puddles with wetsuits on. I read *Goodnight Moon* to them before every nap and play music I think is equal parts quality and calm, like Nadia Reid and Edith Piaf. There is an immense power in creating a child's reality, and such heavy responsibility.

Unlike my time as a nanny in New Zealand, I'm central in the implementation of how the girls are supported as they become small people and develop their love of strawberries and intense dislike of frittata. There is a vulnerability to allowing someone into your home, to see you and your children in moments of weakness and bewilderment. But it's not lost on me that my parents could not have afforded the support I'm now paid to provide. The remuneration is on par with other 'pink-collar' work and reflects many of the luxuries afforded to the white middle and upper-middle class.

It is also not lost on me that I have exclusively worked for white families — therefore continuing the pattern of this sort of labour being consistently deferred to women of colour by affluent white communities throughout history. It is an unfortunate outcome of this industry that respect is not inherent in the relationship, but the parents I work for, I feel, value my contributions. I respond to and challenge both my employers' worldview on the role of parenthood and the parameters set in place for their children.

Their questions about my own family reveal the alternative ways a family can function: the cyclical nature of resources like time and money; regular family meals where sometimes the baby does cry when handed to Granddad (and it's OK); and sharing the joy and responsibility of child-rearing.

In the midst of nap routines, underground tube rides to the Natural History Museum and micro-chopping 5-plus a day into lunch, dinner and snacks, the terrain dramatically changes with the arrival of Covid-19. I support the mums and dads to alleviate the tension of lockdown. Together we create a new normal of spectacularly ordinary adventures in extraordinary circumstances. Zoom music classes, Wiggles hour, planting sunflowers in elevated garden beds in the unusually long backyard. While I carry my aiga in New Zealand with me every day, I navigate this new, unfamiliar world together with my UK family. This profound experience means that, long after leaving an empty Heathrow airport, I keep my UK aiga in my periphery. It will also indelibly alter what I know to be true when it comes to raising children, valuing children and who I am to the children I love.

※

In the 11 years since I began working as a part-time nanny, I think about all the children and parents that I have met — so many different familial dynamics and ideologies at play, and alternative notions of what the division of parental labour looks like or should be. I get asked a lot if I'm 'clucky', if I have the desire to have children or when that might happen. I don't begrudge these enquiries; they largely come from a place of love and curiosity — I have, after all, spent the majority of my adult life looking after little ones. But I like to sleep in and cook spicy food and only occasionally share my ice cream. My body is, for now, mine.

Nannying reinforced the value and privilege of having more than parents on hand to raise a child; the value of incorporating different socioeconomic backgrounds, cultural heritage and lived experiences into conversations; creating a chosen aiga that can inform how we teach our children to be kind, brave and carry themselves with integrity.

I'm not a nanny anymore — I'm a public servant, an advocate for the arts and a volunteer at arts events, a proud union member . . . and, of course, an auntie. My partner and I recently bought a house, which we're slowly making into our home. I write this while she sands our rimu floors. The dust finds its way to my keyboard. I sit on the crooked floor in the conservatory, where we'll put a couch for when we have sweet drinks and long yarns with friends in the summer. Eventually, there'll be a woodburner for the winter, and images we collected overseas on the walls. We also want little hooks in the hallway for little coats, which will complement the items we already have: drop-proof crockery, a suitcase of toys, and a spare room for visiting children.

I don't know if we will have a child. Being a nanny highlighted for me the deep, in-your-belly joy that comes from raising kids: watching her search for you at her first assembly; watching her develop a love of the Harry Potter series; hearing him recognise letters for the first time. I was also witness to the heartache, the lingering questions and the reality of this life-long commitment.

Children have always been in my life; what I didn't know was whether I would fall in love with a person who would love me back. Now, several years and a first home later, I live with the love of my life, who is cooler, calmer, more clever and more beautiful than I ever could've imagined.

Nannying complicated my idea of being a parent on a fundamental level, and I am thankful for that because I appreciate what is traded when that new baby is handed to you. There is also the financial hurdle we'd have to overcome before we would even hold our child for the first time. If this womb and our bank balance allow it, then a child could be in our future . . . perhaps.

❋

Last Thursday I went to see a film at Rialto, and I saw a familiar face by the ticket counter. My first girl, Hannah, all 16 years and seven months of her, was there with her high school media class. She gave me a big cuddle, we watched the film and then we went out for a cold drink afterwards. We talked about school and the movie, about her womanhood and my experiences of growing into my body. It felt like a full-circle moment and the beginning all in one.

No masturbation allowed

LIL O'BRIEN

When she heard why I was visiting New York, she responded via email, 'Oh gosh, well it is SUCH a fertile apartment.' I was subletting her place for a couple of weeks. 'You know the fish that you're feeding?'

I'd looked at the tank, gurgling away on the bedroom dresser. There were about 40 tiny translucent fish in it, each one shot through with electric red.

'Well, when we bought the fish there were only THREE of them! Everyone who stays in the apartment will spawn! Ha-ha.'

I was on day seven of the nine-day wait between an IVF cycle's embryo transfer and the day I could test to see if I was pregnant. What a bitch those nine days are. You're exhausted. You veer between positivity and berating yourself for daring to hope. You're probably also broke, you'd quite like a large glass of wine or maybe half a bottle, and then on top of everything else, they say: *no masturbation allowed*. Please, no orgasms — lest you dislodge the blastocyst trying to burrow its way into your uterine lining. And so you wait. To find out if you're pregnant, but also until you can get yourself off again. Not that you feel like getting yourself off, but you want to be allowed to. There are many cruelties on the treacherous road that is IVF, but this is the one that felt like a real 'fuck you'. It reeks of the patriarchy. I don't know how that's to blame, but somehow it must be.

※

A couple of days later another email arrived from the well-meaning woman while I was lying on her bed, wiping tears into her bedding. The embryo transfer had failed.

'I forgot to tell you, more evidence of the fertile apartment,' the woman's follow-up email read. 'Our son was both conceived and given birth to in that very bed! So you'll definitely have success this time, I can just feel it!'

We were now down to our last embryo, which my wife and I had left here in New York on ice when we moved back to New Zealand. We'd had two years of fertility treatments, getting pregnant, losing the pregnancies — the last one had a particularly brutal ending that left me bleeding and leaking breast milk for weeks afterwards.

People don't talk about how when you lose a pregnancy after a certain number of weeks, there's no procedure to remove the tissue. You have to go through all the pain and trauma of delivering, knowing that a baby won't be placed into your arms at the end. The doctor who'd tried to save the foetus had done an operation that no one in New Zealand had ever done before, including her. What had gone wrong in my pregnancy was so rare that most doctors have never heard of it: a form of TRAP sequence. When we were told the operation to try to fix the problem had failed and there was subsequently no longer a heartbeat, my grief was overshadowed by the terror of having to go through a birthing process, although you probably can't call it that.

※

I was desperately homesick that last time in New York, but not for my home in New Zealand or even for my wife, who hadn't been able to join me due to the financial costs. I was homesick for the New York I used to love; the one that made me feel like I'd found my place in the world, and all the other gushing clichés the city provokes. That feeling was being wiped out by the grind of this trip, which would now be a month longer than we'd hoped, because I had to wait for my body to pull itself back together for one last attempt.

It also meant I had to find accommodation to cover that extra time, on a limited budget. That long wait in New York would include two nights in a hoarder's apartment hidden behind a respectable brownstone front, where the pillows on the bed made me sneeze and where I slept fitfully, watched by the eyes of more than a hundred stuffed toys.

I've always been good at actively managing my happiness, believing you can build on your resting happiness level by doing things you enjoy every day, and consciously appreciating them. And so, during those long weeks in New York while waiting to do the final embryo transfer, I'd tried doing the things that used to make me happy when I lived in that crazy place: sickly sweet iced chai lattes from Black Star on Metropolitan Ave, walking through Union Square to author talks at Strand Books, live storytelling events at Housing Works in Soho, or just walking around, waiting for things to happen.

During our first week in New York in 2015, my wife and I were walking to brunch when we saw a collection of people coming out of a church near our new apartment.

'Look how beautiful that woman looks in her Sunday best,' I'd said.

'Errrr.'

My wife's mouth was hanging open, and there was the woman with her pink frilly dress hoisted around her waist, pissing right there on the pavement. That's the brilliant thing about New York. You don't need to be doing anything interesting when you live there. Interesting things just happen to you.

But on that trip, trying to get pregnant again, I was miserable, despite my efforts towards mindfulness. Perhaps it was all the fertility drugs my clinic had prescribed me. I was on a double dose of progesterone because the pills they'd given me at Fertility Associates in Auckland hadn't raised my levels enough. When I'd made it to New York the doctor had tutted and prescribed the injectable progesterone I was supposed to be on — which wasn't available in New Zealand — on top of the pills. Every morning I managed breakfast, a shower and an injection in the soft flesh of my hip before I crashed into unconsciousness, finally surfacing from a dreamless, black sleep around noon.

※

Buying sperm in the US is much like searching for an apartment online. You create an account on the website and add your credit card. You input your filters to see a tailored selection of results, then read the short blurbs to see if you want to click into the listing to learn more. It's just that instead of number of bedrooms or bathrooms, you're selecting hair colour, ethnicity, education level, religion, height — or even who the donor's lookalikes are, just in case you're looking for a donor who bears a similarity to Jake Gyllenhaal (the one man I would consider sleeping with). Actually, this is a silly analogy. There are far more filters on California Cryobank than on Trade Me, or Apartments.com. Eighteen, in fact. So, perhaps it's actually more like Airbnb? But without the pretty pictures. You have to pay to see the pictures.

☀

As a lesbian couple, deciding to have a baby is the first step in a journey of research, organisation and, often, money. Romance? Pah. Sex? Not relevant. It's a list of decisions. Who will carry the baby? How will you get sperm? Will you ask someone you know, or join the list of queers and unlucky straights suffering through the long wait for sperm at Fertility Associates?

Most queer mums I've known have pretty firm ideas about whether they want to use a known donor or an anonymous one. For my wife and me, it was very firmly the latter. I personally wanted to cede the smallest possible part of creating this child to a man. There was no dad in this equation, just as there was no man in my relationship. In fact, if the technology where scientists can grow sperm from your female partner's stem cells was further along and available, I would have been first in line. For me, there is a small grief baked into having a baby as a same-sex couple. Creating a person out of biological input from both of you just isn't available to most of us. I wished that my child could inherit my wife's creativity, or her broad shoulders. I wished that we could put their baby photos side by side and laugh about how they had the same squishy nose. And I wish more people understood that being able to produce a child between you and your partner, with no interventions, is a privilege, not a given.

Trying for a baby while we were in America was a no-brainer because of the opportunities living in the States gave us. Most of that is to do with the fact that with credit card in hand we could have sperm in the space of two minutes, rather than two years or more, which is what the wait for sperm can be when you're going through Fertility Associates, one of the few clinical sources of sperm in New Zealand. More than two years, and then you may be given as few as three or four options to choose from, due to the ongoing sperm shortage.

'Ninety per cent of them being an absolute "no",' says my friend who has had an adorable son through Fertility Associates. A fairly important consideration for me was also the population size of New Zealand. Now, I'm no statistician, but surely our choice of sperm donor would have also been used by at least one if not a number of the lesbians we know. I didn't want any part in that situation if I could help it.

Couples learn a lot about each other when they're travelling, when they see each other in their work environments and, it turns out, also when trying to select a sperm donor from about 250 options. My approach was to painstakingly comb through the profiles, making a shortlist, adding notes about what I found appealing based on a single photograph of each dude as a baby — as well as their profile, personal essay or staff impressions. However, when my wife looked at my shortlist, she was like, 'Meh'.

And then I was like, 'OK. Yeah. I guess I'm meh, too.'

How do you choose such a huge thing with so little information? But then again, is it really that important? Because you never know how the kid is going to come out — they could end up being someone who tortures small animals for fun, no matter what you do.

We decided to pay US$145 to reach Level 2 on the Cryobank website. This would give us access to a few more photos for each person, including possibly an adult photo depending on what the donor had uploaded. There can be quite a gulf between what people look like as a toddler (cute as shit) and an adult (Republican-looking motherfucker), so a few more photos was quite an appealing option. It also gave us access to something called Express Yourself, with an icon of a paintbrush and a musical note. People's expressing of themselves subsequently cancelled out about 80 per cent of my shortlist, so I guess that was money well spent. Paying for Level 2 also gives you access to a 'Donor Keepsake: when you tell us you are pregnant', which gave me terrifying thoughts of a lock of hair turning up in our letterbox one day.

Still none of the options jumped out at us, so my wife decided she'd have a go at looking, and in her typical way of bettering me with little effort (the few things I could beat her at included speed-walking and that game where you try to hit a tennis ball tied to a pole with string), she came up with a great option within minutes.

The main thing I remember about the donor we chose is that he looked a little bit like Prince William at 12 years old, when he was toothy in an adorable way. The donor was also tall, six-foot plus, which is a requirement I see come up for straight women again and again on reality TV shows such as *Indian Matchmaker* and *Love Island*. (But like, maybe you should worry about whether he's a toxic, gaslighting misogynist, rather than how tall he is?)

Our height preference came from the fact that my wife was tall, and she already felt like a giant whenever she was around the rest of my family, who all hover around five feet three to five feet six. She wanted to have at least the chance of a tall child, so that she and they could be connected physically in some way.

The donor we chose was also a rocket scientist. This would obviously be a great story to tell at parties when I was pregnant. We had our donor, and forked out US$5225 to get five vials of sperm.

✳

Our fertility clinic was on Madison Avenue in Manhattan's Upper East Side, surrounded by shops like Givenchy and Balenciaga in case you felt like pretending to be Julia Roberts in *Pretty Woman* after being in stirrups. The first time we went to the clinic, we thought, *Are we allowed to be here?* Surely they should check if we were in any way famous, or influential, but no, we were rich enough to pay for fertility treatments, and that's all that seemed to matter. (We achieved this with the help of my wife's US health insurance — we were very lucky that it had a fertility treatment clause in there, and even more lucky that it allowed us to utilise it as a same-sex couple, which was rare.)

The waiting room was always 90 per cent women with a few men scattered about, including the occasional Hasidic Jewish couple who I noticed would sit as far away from everyone else as possible — the men aren't allowed to sit next to a woman who isn't their wife. The dominant number of women at the clinic might seem obvious on first thought. But, given the assumption that most people accessing fertility treatments would be coupled up, and most of those couples were opposite sex, why were there so few men?

Here's a list of some of the reasons why you might be at the clinic: initial consultation, men jacking off for various reasons, IUI insemination, blood tests, meetings to discuss results, ultrasounds to see how your ovaries are responding to fertility drugs, ultrasounds to check in on a foetus' progress and so on. Now, how many of those do you *need* the man to be there for?

As I type this, I'm imagining a white American man. He's dressed head to toe in Nike, and he wants to get in five miles on the Peloton before work, but his wife needs to go to the fertility clinic to get her weekly blood test, or maybe to discuss the results of her test to see if her fallopian tubes are blocked.

'Babe,' he'd say, drinking his kale smoothie. 'Do I *need* to be there for this visit? Like, I am fully here to support you, but this is just a routine appointment, right? You can handle it yourself, can't you? You're a big girl.'

I imagine that this man will be there for the ultrasound to see the baby's heartbeat, though. That's when he can say, 'Babe, look what *we* made.'

✳

The guy in charge of getting me pregnant had at one time been voted America's Top Fertility Doctor, whatever that means. Most successful pregnancies? Best quality babies? It's unclear. I googled 'America's-top-fertility-doctor-reality-tv-show' as I was writing this essay, certain that the concept would have been capitalised on by now. It hasn't, but surely it's only a matter of time. Either way, this doctor had seen a lot of vaginas, and that was comforting, as someone who had only had her first pap smear a year earlier due to being deeply uncomfortable with health professionals putting things 'up there'. Oh, how quickly you get used to people rummaging around in your vagina when you undergo fertility treatments.

My doctor looked scarily like Dr Spaceman from *30 Rock*, so I'll call him that. Dr Spaceman had also been named a New York 'Super Doctor', and despite the marketing aligning fertility doctors with superheroes he was a low-key dude.

Dr Spaceman reckoned my egg count was looking good and we were definitely going to help him keep his spot as America's Top Fertility Doctor. I should have no problem getting pregnant through intrauterine insemination (IUI), aka 'the turkey baster method', which is a lot less involved than in vitro fertilisation (IVF). But this being America they threw a whole bunch of drugs at me anyway. Things to make my ovaries glisten with preparedness and the lining of my womb grow thick and welcoming. It took a few goes and more than a few thousand US dollars, but once Dr Spaceman realised one of my fallopian tubes was blocked and squirted the sperm towards the other one, I got pregnant pretty fast.

✳

An early-stage miscarriage is something that happens to so many pregnant people, but has different effects on everyone. For me, when we were told there was no longer a heartbeat at the 12-week scan, my initial reaction of sadness was replaced by reasoning: *Of course this happened. You were so fucking naïve to think it would be this easy. In fact, thinking 'Wow, that was not too difficult after all' is probably what* made *the pregnancy fail!*

But I'm someone who's pretty good at compartmentalising, and I soon brushed off that setback. It was just part of the process, I saw now, and I adjusted my expectations. I began a single-minded, pig-headed pursuit towards 'success'. That's how I cope with bad shit in general: I just keep going, sometimes at a maniacal pace. When you're still going, you can focus on the plan and the practicalities — and not the feelings. The things you do have control over, when so much of trying to have a baby is out of your control.

My wife, on the other hand, seemed devastated, and she's not like me — she didn't shake things off (and then write an essay about it for closure five years later). By the time I was eventually pregnant again, she couldn't bring herself to touch my growing bump. I felt like she didn't dare to believe that this one would work; to become too attached.

When we started IVF, I was fairly confident. I wasn't infertile, after all. It was simply a matter of logistics. By then, a year or so had passed and we only had one of the rocket scientist's vials of sperm left after four rounds of IUI, with no more available. On top of that, we had to leave the country soon. IVF was our best chance at making another pregnancy happen, and we could potentially get multiple embryos from one shot of white gold. If we didn't have success during the time we had left in the States, it could mean having embryos to come back to.

It's hard to articulate how the pressure started ramping up at that point.

I remember being wheeled into the recovery room after my egg retrieval and hearing another woman arrive not long after as I was lying in a hospital bed behind a privacy curtain.

'How many eggs did you get?' she'd asked the nurse.

'The doctor was able to collect three viable eggs,' I'd heard the nurse reply gently.

'Is that good?'

I could hear the hopeful tremor in the woman's voice, but my heart had sunk for her. In comparison, they'd gotten 23 of my eggs. From there, 19 survived to be fertilised, and 15 were successfully fertilised. And from those, we ended up with five surviving 'Day 5' blastocysts, which is when they're frozen. Given the way those numbers dropped, what were her chances? It's such a cruel game of luck, the trying to have a child thing, with very clear winners and losers.

※

The best part about undergoing fertility treatments in New York, after the access to sperm, was being treated equally to straight couples. As a queer person I go into many new settings with my guard slightly up, particularly medical ones, where heteronormativity is rife. I'm waiting to see if I'll be treated differently, or if there will be that tiny pause people make when they click that I'm not straight. But we were able to very quickly relax in New York. There was not one millisecond of awkwardness, or incorrect pronouns or assumptions. Perhaps that's partly why our experience with a Sydney fertility clinic was so shocking.

It was about nine months after our final embryo transfer had failed, and we'd given up on our American fertility dream. We were back to square one, no sperm, no embryos, nothing. When I started making enquiries into sperm access and how the system worked in Australia, the fertility clinic told us that the first thing we had to do was meet with a counsellor. This in itself is pretty fucked — that people who need help getting pregnant have to prove themselves fit in some way, whereas people who can get pregnant with the old P in V can do what they want (as they should).

But when you've been through fertility treatment you're used to bending yourself into knots to reach your goal, and so we went into the session without too much thought. Just tired resignation. What could this therapist possibly say that we hadn't thought of before?

What she said, near the end of the session, was: 'Have you got many straight friends?'

My wife and I glanced at each other, both thinking, *Is she saying what we think she's saying?*

'Um, yeah, we have straight friends.'

'Oh good,' she said. 'It's important for a child to be exposed to a diverse range of people.'

I don't remember how we managed to get through the rest of the session, but I know that we were too shocked to say anything and I remember the feeling it gave me, because I have it now even just writing about it. My breathing is shallow and my skin feels too tight around my ribcage. I wish I could go back to that moment and let rip on her. There's so much I want to say to her, like how even if we kept our child locked in our gay-ass house for their whole life, or only ever exposed them to our queer friends, they would still have heterosexuality in their face nearly every day. Heteronormativity would still do its sinister ideological work, and that is far more influential than whether we had straight friends or not. I want to know if she asks straight couples if they have gay friends.

We didn't go any further with the clinic. And when six months after that my wife and I separated amicably, for a variety of complicated reasons, something strange happened. I didn't want it anymore. All that drive and desire and stubbornness just drained out of me.

At first I didn't believe it, and I kept testing myself. With every mum I drove past on the street pulling a toddler behind her, or parent shushing a baby to sleep in a pram, I measured how I felt against that scenario, putting myself in their shoes, and the overwhelming feeling was: yuck. I realised just how much of wanting a child was about wanting to have one with my wife specifically — when I imagined having a child it was about the family we would build together, not so much about having one itself.

And so, I just . . . let it go, and I felt a strange but welcome relief. Because by letting go of the idea of having a baby it felt like I was also stepping outside of a system of oppression. The people who can birth children are tied to a timeline of what we must do and when we must do it, all centred around when we are fertile. When you take that consideration away, life opens up. You can do what you like, whenever.

I didn't realise how much I had felt the societal pressure to have children until I chucked the ticking biological clock in the bin — I'd honestly thought that I was outside of that pressure because I was queer. After all, people didn't ask me when I was going to have kids the way they did with my straight friends.

✻

It's been about five years since I stopped trying to have children, but I have ended up with them in my life, including my partner's teenage kids. They joke that my partner and I are just roommates, who share a bed because we can only afford one. They also call me 'bonus mom', which feels nice.

I feel so lucky to be queer; part of a community that I believe has a healthier, less stifling concept of what family is, beyond who you're born to — or who is born to you. My family is those I've found, and those who've found me, and it's a joy to think that there's more family out there I just haven't met yet.

Send her back

MELANIE NEWFIELD

Someone said 'Happy Mother's Day' to me today, and I cried. It was just a brief, random conversation with another person walking their dog. He had one of those well-behaved, chilled-out dogs, the sort of dog that people think they'll have before they actually get one. I've got a bundle of nerves who can't wait to get to the next smell and barks like a monster every time she sees another dog; the sort people judge you for. He offered a few words of advice and then moved on, tossing out that phrase as if it were nothing.

I say those words to my own mother, but they are not words I hear said to me. Why would anyone wish me a happy Mother's Day? I'm not a real mother.

＊

My journey to not-real motherhood began when I was in my early forties, single, childless and facing the realities of time and biology. I knew that fostering wouldn't be the same, but it seemed right to me. I was adopted, and I understand better than most that it's not a lack of love that prevents some parents from raising their own children. But I didn't make a hasty decision. I read. I thought things through. I talked it over with people I thought might understand.

And then I applied. It wasn't a short process. There was an introductory session, where I was given a pile of application forms, to be filled out by me, my GP and two referees. There was a police and criminal justice check. There were three all-day training sessions. There was a home visit by two social workers.

The whole process took more than six months. Then . . . the waiting. I didn't really know what would happen next. When I'd met with the social workers, they said I'd be doing weekend respite care for primary school-aged children. I was so naïve about the system, I really thought that was what I'd be doing.

My first call came at 4 p.m. one Friday afternoon. *Would I take a girl for six weeks?* I said that I only did weekend respite care, as I had a full-time job. *Would I take her for the weekend, then?*

I said yes.

And that's all I'm going to say about this child. When you foster, your children aren't your own, and you don't get to talk about them as if they are. You don't share their photos or mention their names on social media. You don't talk about them with your friends. You don't write about them and publish what you've written.

This was one of a thousand ways I knew I was not a real mother when I fostered. In fact, I wasn't any type of mother. These days, the term 'foster mother' isn't used. The official terminology is 'caregiver'. I was always watching my words, conscious I wasn't supposed to be talking about the children I cared for, protecting their privacy, their dignity and their safety. People learnt names if they met the children, but under those circumstances, I wasn't to mention that they were in foster care. People joined the dots, of course, but it wasn't like I was becoming a real mother, announcing it to the world with excitement and having people congratulate me.

As someone who wanted but didn't have children, I noticed things like that. Telling people that I had signed up to do foster care was quite different from when someone announced they were having a baby. Mostly, the reaction was positive, but it wasn't something that many people related to. Quite often, people said 'Oh, I couldn't do that', as if they needed to emphasise the difference between them and me.

Occasionally, the response was more direct. Someone from my work's human resources department told me that fostering was considered secondary employment. I needed to be sure it wasn't going to affect my work, I was told — if it did, they had the right to stop me doing it. I made sure to never mention fostering in front of anyone from HR ever again.

For the first couple of years I did a mix of weekend respite and emergency care. One girl came to me regularly. In between, children and teenagers came to me when they needed somewhere for a few nights. The youngest was three, the eldest 17. I don't fool myself that they enjoyed staying with me — being left in the home of a stranger is no child or teenager's idea of a good time. But I tried to give them some positive memories. I read them bedtime stories (even a couple of the teenagers). I cooked with them. I took them to the local playground, or out walking with my neighbour's dog.

The social workers figured out that I wasn't easily fazed. One day, they asked me to take two children. I said I couldn't, as I had only one bed in my spare room. But after that I bought an air bed that blew up to the size of a full single bed, and said yes the next time I was asked.

Looking back on that time, I know it was hard, but that's not what I remember. What I remember is this: I loved what I was doing. I wasn't a mother, but that no longer mattered. In fact, it became a strength. Because I didn't have children of my own, there was no need for the children I cared for to fit in with their routines or compare their experiences. I tried, as much as possible, to adapt to them rather than forcing them to adapt to me.

I discovered that the foster care system was not what I thought it was. I imagined a lot of care and thought would go into finding the right place for a child, not the frantic scramble to find somebody, anybody, who was available immediately. I imagined that when a child went to a 'permanent' caregiver, they had a permanent home. That was true for the lucky ones, but it seemed to be a lottery. Too often, things didn't work out and caregivers said that they'd had enough. I don't know how many homes some of the children I met had lived in.

As time went on, children came into my home for longer and longer periods. I found ways to work around the fact that I had a full-time job. I had some flexibility in my work, and I had a laptop. Then, with three hours' notice, two girls came for 'a couple of weeks'. They stayed for five months.

There was a lot going on with those girls and their lives. I can't say what any of that was, but I can say I look back and wonder where I found the energy. It was unrelenting. And yet, I can remember a point, when they were at school and I was at work, when I took a moment to reflect. By that time, it was unclear where they would go after being in my care. I was contemplating whether they could stay with me permanently.

I realised, then, that in the months they'd been with me, I'd never once thought, *I want my old life back.* Sure, a bit of time to myself would have been nice. But I couldn't imagine going back to doing just weekend respite and emergencies, or having no children at all. I loved my role as not-quite-a-mother to those girls.

It was no longer enough for me to offer a temporary home. And so, before long, I went from an emergency and respite caregiver to a permanent caregiver with a teenager. I was a different kind of not-quite-a-mother. It all happened without ceremony. There's no celebration or cultural marker; it just happens.

It's something that seems wrong to celebrate, anyway. Even if, for you, becoming not-quite-a-mother is a long-anticipated dream, it's not a dream for the child who comes into your home, nor for their family. When I signed up to foster, I didn't fully comprehend how much the fostering relationship is built on trauma. I knew that the events that resulted in them needing foster care would be traumatic. But I didn't appreciate how damaging the act of being brought into foster care was in itself.

It's entirely possible that the day a child comes to you is the worst day of someone's life. It might be the worst day for the child, for their parents, or for all of them. Even if a child goes to someone in their wider family, someone they know, it's still a trauma, still a loss. And for some, the losses compound. Some children live in home after home — close relatives, distant relatives, strangers. How can you celebrate that?

※

Knowing all that, it seems wrong to say I was never happier than during those first few years I was fostering. But it's true.

Bringing a teen into your home is not the same as bringing a younger child. You bond differently. I've heard foster parents say that they regard their foster children as no different from their biological children. Perhaps that is the case for them, but I always thought it must be different, especially with a teen. You're trying to bond at the same time as they're trying to establish independence.

I wouldn't exactly say that things went smoothly. I had a full-time job as well as a teenager. Life was intense. I carried my laptop in my bag when I took her places and used quiet moments to catch up on work. But things were going in the right direction.

As a caregiver, love and maternal instinct won't take you far. I once heard fostering described as 'more head-parenting than heart-parenting', and that's a good way to explain it. The heart is important, but there's also a huge amount to learn and apply when your child is not your own and has been through the things they've been through. I did a lot of training.

A caregiver also needs to be able to deal with bureaucracy — first and foremost, social workers. Having their trust and cooperation will make things better for both you and the child you care for. But it's not just one social worker, because the system churns through staff like it churns through photocopy paper. There's a constant cycle of restructuring, in a series of hasty reactions to the latest crisis and the ideology of the day. There are multiple organisations, too. Schools. Health services. Police. Courts. Non-governmental organisations. I've lost track of them now.

There's one more thing that's essential to being a good caregiver — dealing with your child's family. Our foster care system, quite rightly, aims to keep children with their families as much as possible. If they can't be with their families, it still aims to keep the connections. How well it achieves that aim is debatable. But it's not like the American system, where there is such a thing as 'terminating parental rights' (which means terminating certain rights of the child, as well).

So, fostering a child isn't just about connecting with that child. Think about what happens when parents separate, and how their ongoing relationship affects their children. That's kind of what it's like being a caregiver — your relationship with your child's biological family affects them. Judge the family, and the child will feel it.

※

For a while, I juggled the relationships with my girl, her family and the bureaucracy with my full-time job as a manager and took everything in my stride. I was good at dealing with difficult situations calmly and compassionately and my life put this ability to good use. But, somewhere along the way, things changed direction. I began to feel the stress of the situations I was dealing with.

And then, it was as if the system began to give up on me.

The first time I remember it coming up, it was a comment made by one of the professionals involved with my girl to the main social worker. She passed it on to me, probably because she wanted my reassurance it wasn't true. Apparently, according to this professional, I was about to give up and say I didn't want to care for my girl anymore.

I wasn't even close to giving up on her. But I suppose it was a valid concern, because if you're a caregiver it's built into the system. You're expected to give up when it gets hard. The social workers expect it. The teachers expect it. The police and mental health professionals expect it. Your friends and family and co-workers expect it. And the kids expect it.

'Send her back.' Someone actually said those words to me. You know you're not a real mother when people tell you that getting rid of your child is the solution to your problems.

'Let someone else do it.' 'Can't they find someone else to look after her?' The comments weren't overly frequent, but they were frequent enough. Some came from professionals, others from people around me who saw some of what I was dealing with. I felt as if people thought I could end my struggle simply by walking away. Not just that I *could*, but that I *should*.

No way was I giving up. How devastating must it be for a child to be given up on? I'd done emergency care, seeing situations where long-term homes had broken down. I was determined not to be one of those homes.

We stumbled from crisis to crisis. There were moments when I felt as if I was doing some good, where the bond I'd built with her made a difference. But I was struggling.

Professionals came and went. It seemed to me that most of them found her too much trouble. Things that were supposed to happen didn't. Support that was meant to be there wasn't. I needed help to keep her with me, help that wasn't there.

I felt as if I couldn't take any more, not one more crisis, not one more demand, not one more reminder that I wasn't a real mother. But I kept going. After a while, I got used to the feeling that I couldn't take any more.

The constant crises I couldn't share began to make me feel isolated. I started to feel as if I was failing. I paid a kind woman to listen to me once a week — I was allowed to speak to a therapist about what was going on. But I couldn't hold everything in for a whole week without falling apart. At work, I would lock myself in a bathroom cubicle and cry. When I got control back, I'd return to my desk. It happened nearly every day, and nobody ever commented.

I thought people must have noticed I wasn't OK. Surely it was obvious? But perhaps it wasn't. After all, people were assuming I would give up if it got too hard. I wondered if people thought I brought it all on myself. I don't think they understood what giving up truly meant.

There weren't many people lining up to foster teenagers. And by that time

I'd realised how traumatising the foster system was to those in its supposed care. It wasn't just the circumstances that had brought them into foster care. It was being in the claws of a system that was meant to help them — as one social worker said, being moved from one home to another, again and again, was abuse in itself.

I started to wonder — just how bad did a child's home have to be to justify bringing them into such a system?

I didn't know what would happen to my girl if I wasn't there. So I kept going. I kept passing thresholds where I thought I couldn't take any more. There was always more and I always took it.

The moments that told me I was making a difference stopped coming. I was staring down a chasm into which I poured love and care, and I never knew whether any of it reached her. I lost any belief that I was doing her any good. But I still recognised that I could do her harm. Walking away, abandoning her — I still knew that would hurt her.

But I realised that when I reached the end of my journey with this girl, I wouldn't foster again. It had taken too much. And that realisation crushed me.

※

Eventually, circumstances arose that meant she was no longer in my home. I can't explain, but I can say that I didn't walk away.

And then it was just me alone again, with a job that continued to ask more and more of me, and a life that had lost its meaning. Nothing had ever made me happier than fostering. It was the best thing I ever did, until it wasn't. I couldn't imagine anything taking its place.

My story of fostering should have ended there, but it didn't. I was trying to put myself back together when I was contacted by the family of a girl I had looked after regularly in the past. She needed somewhere for the night, would I take her?

Had it been any other child, I would have said no — but not this girl. Even though I was burned out and thought I had nothing left, what was I going to say?

That 'one night' turned into more than two years. She didn't get the best of me. Where I'd once been an anchor of calm, now I was a cork tossed on the waves. I felt as if I had nothing left and yet was still expected to give. I gave at work and I gave at home and still more was extracted from me.

I did what I could. My girl didn't want to be with me, but she didn't have anywhere else to go. It became a matter of enduring. One foot in front of the other, home and work.

✻

t's been two years now since she decided to move out. I've changed jobs. The bedroom I once dedicated to children is now an office.

I got a dog. I hoped I'd take her places and have adventures and meet other dog owners, but her reactivity has meant I can't. I feel as if there's something wrong with me, that I invite these difficulties on myself. Still, I persist. When I'm feeling brave, I take her to busier places and feed her treats for ignoring other dogs. We have more setbacks than forward progress, but she loves me, in the way that dogs do. I'm not giving up.

When Mother's Day comes around, I know it doesn't apply to me. It hurts, but the grief isn't raw in the way it used to be.

If I stretch my brain, I can remember the woman I was in those first few years, when I wasn't quite a mother. But the memories feel unreal. It's as if I borrowed them from someone else, someone stronger and braver, with a heart full of love and hope.

Sometimes I hear from my girls. I've helped them during some difficult times. I've taken them out for birthdays. I don't see a lot of them, but they know I'm here.

I don't regret the love and care I gave to those girls and the other children who passed through my home.

I wasn't a mother, but I was something.

How to not be a mother

FEBY IDRUS

- Birth control. Follow the policy of both anaesthetists and Mad-Eye Moody: *constant vigilance.*
- Don't marry someone who already has kids. This is more difficult than it seems. The problem, obviously, is limerence. You meet a guy, he has pretty eyes and pretty abs and he says he's not looking for anything serious, and, well, that's perfect because neither are you, and in any case he has kids and you already know you don't want to be a mother, not even of the 'step' variety. And then: Bam! Limerence. Dictionary.com defines this as 'The state of being obsessively infatuated with someone, usually accompanied by delusions of or a desire for an intense romantic relationship with that person.' The pivotal word here is 'delusions'. He tells you he doesn't want anything serious; he tells you he's not looking for another mother for his kids; he tells you that you can be as involved with them as you want — and, deluded, you believe him.
- If you're going to ignore the above advice, then at least don't marry someone who has kids of a different ethnicity, class or social background to you. Make sure the kids are exactly the same as you.

(How like a parent.) Otherwise, you will find yourself to be a stranger. That's what you always were anyway. It's just that you were so good at passing in white society that you even fooled yourself into thinking you were one of them, or at least that you mostly were. But kids will prove that you are not. They leave their shoes on inside the house, they think Chinese restaurants are weird because they never go to them, they refuse to eat their dinner and their parents capitulate to their tantrums and bring them tomato sauce sandwiches instead. Their real parents let them shriek at them when they're angry. Their real parents don't mention the word 'homework', ever. You are not their parent and you never could be. You are not them. You will never feel more un-owned by society, more un-belonging, than when you are boiling mini saveloys in a silver pot, watching red leak into the water, for kids who are actually looking forward to eating the crimson sausages because they're just not being raised the way you were. Thanks to kids, the corners of your own strangeness will gouge ruts into your skin.

- Write a retelling of the *Cinderella* fairy tale, in the voice of Angela Carter and from the point of view of the stepmother. Send it to a sci-fi and fantasy journal. Receive a nice rejection letter that says, 'I wish the stepmother could have been a bit more sympathetic.' Jesus, *why*? Why does she need to be sympathetic for my story to get published? She's a stepmother. She's fed up. She has all the responsibilities of parenting but none of the rights, powers or benefits.
- Reread that rejection letter six weeks later. Realise it actually says, 'The story could have been strengthened by a more sympathetic tone towards the stepmother and her situation.' Recognise your own knee-jerk defensiveness.
- Write an extremely thinly veiled autobiographical short story with an initial title of 'How to be an Asian mother'. Rejoice when it is selected for publication in an anthology. At this anthology's launch, read out the beginning of this story. Hide your shock at the peals of laughter your story generates. They're not just tittering. They are *laughing*. Raucously, side-splittingly, *belly* laughing. As if they think you wrote a comedy or something. Like — a *good* comedy. Remain stumped, to this day, as to why your story — your life — was so fucking hilarious.
- You know that whole 'don't marry a guy with kids' thing? Actually, just don't marry a guy.

'Babe, where are my keys?'

'Babe, do you know where my hat is?'

'Babe, have you seen my phone? Can you ring it? OK, I got it. OK, hang up. Fuck! I dropped it.'

'Babe, do you want to have dinner? I'll have whatever you want. Oh, you want that? But I don't like that.'

'Babe, are you coming home? When are you coming home?'

'Babe, I don't know what to do. Can *you* do it?'

If you do not want to be a parent, do not marry.

- Don't let your father die. If you do, then you will find yourself driving your mother to the lawyer's (and speaking for her when she can't) and to the bank (and speaking for her when she can't) and to the city council (and speaking for her when she can't). You'll drive her to the grocery store and to her friend's house and to the cemetery. You will have to teach her how to do internet banking and how to set up her tablet. You will have to comfort her when she cries because she's afraid of being alone. And slowly you will discover that your mother is sometimes unnecessarily judgemental; doesn't really listen or pay attention; is sometimes flighty; doesn't really think things through; and is unsentimental not out of emotional brutality but simply because she lacks nuance, her emotions and opinions pumping like pistons instead of tinkling like ivories. You will discover that this person, who you've known your whole life, is blossoming into a person you do not completely recognise. (Again: how like a parent.) And you will be so run down and run off your feet parenting your parent that you will forget to grieve.

- Consider Jennifer Aniston, who said around or perhaps just before her break up with Brad Pitt that no, she had not planned to have children but she felt she'd birthed a lot of things. By this, she must have meant creative projects, either as lead actor or producer. Consider also Virginia Woolf, who wrote in her diary regarding her work that she thought she had set her statues against the sky, which is to say that she felt her writing left enough of a legacy to last her down the ages. Consider also your own stories. You've never thought of your stories as truly equivalent to children, though both are sometimes unruly and uncontrollable. No, stories are not children; making art is not making humans or raising them to be adults. But both unruly things are made to be set against the sky — to be legacies. 'Who will remember you when you are gone?' is often a question asked of childless people, as if the only people capable of forming memories of you are the people made by banging your hips with another human. If someone asks you that, hand them a collection of your stories, or that PhD thesis someone wrote on your paintings, or point at that armchair you lovingly restored, or that garden you tend, or the house you built or that school full of children you taught, and say, 'These tell me that I'll be remembered anyway.'

- Consider Jennifer Aniston, who revealed last year that around or just after her break up with Brad Pitt she attempted to get pregnant via IVF, and it just wouldn't work.

- You know that whole 'don't marry a guy with kids', 'don't marry a guy', 'don't parent a parent', thing? Nah. Scrap that. Scrap all of that. Instead, just don't be a woman. Go on. Be a dude! Grow a beard! If you remain a woman, motherhood will just follow you around like a perpetually hungry cat (which is to say: like a cat). That annoying motherfucker will keep yowling at you, no matter what you do. So just *give up*. Give up entirely! Cut your breast off like an Amazon and become a dude.

- Look up 'Nacho Kids' on Facebook. The name is from the American founders of both the page and the philosophy (say 'not your kids' in a thick American accent to explain the name). Basically, let the actual parent be the actual parent, and let yourself . . . not be. Step away from the saveloy pot. Step well back. And watch your husband cook his kids — *his* kids — their tea instead. He wants to, anyway. He loves his kids. He says they are a part of him; says he's rearranged his work hours so he can do school pick-ups; looks at his daughters and says they are the most beautiful girls in the world. And, clear-eyed, you believe him. So let him do this strange alien parenting thing. Go do what you want to do. Go . . . write an essay.

- Consider these two final thoughts:
  * There are words for most things, but not all things. A cat with no owner is a stray. A wife with no husband is a widow. A child with no parent is an orphan. But there's no word for a mother who has lost a child. Such a loss reveals words to be too small a container for a void so big. There's also no word for a woman who has no child and doesn't want one. At least, there's no flattering words.
  * David Graeber writes in his short book *Pirate Enlightenment, or*

The Real Libertalia that today's radical historians do not 'somehow notic[e] that a four-hundred-page book attacking Rousseau is still a four-hundred-page book about Rousseau.'[1] Realise, with a grudging sigh, that this essay about not being Rousseau was always, eternally, about Rousseau. At the faded edge of your hearing, discern a muffled yowl.

---

1   David Graeber, *Pirate Enlightenment, or The Real Libertalia* (London: Penguin Books, 2023), xi.

Kingfisher

HINEMOANA BAKER

O ur family does funerals in a variety of ways. I couldn't say that one resembles any other except in the most basic details: someone has died, their loved ones are gathering, and there will probably be slightly underheated sausage rolls at the afternoon tea. If it's the Māori side, there will at least be plenty else to choose from. Maybe eel or raw fish, definitely scones and almost always frybread.

My Pākehā stepfather was a magician for a while when he was young. At his funeral, my mother draped his coffin with a special length of black cloth, and on top of it she laid his magician's wand, his white gloves and a hand of cards — a Royal Flush — fixed together with clear nail polish. When I first saw this, I choked up. It seemed so poignant, symbolic. Where was his magic now?, etc. Then my sister and I started our terrible, dark laughter. We had both had the same thought at the same time: any minute now, some guy in a sequined tux would walk in waving a huge blade and slice the coffin in half.

If the funeral is for someone from my father's side, there is usually a mix of Pākehā and Māori protocols, language and proceedings. There might be a prayer in Māori, hymns, even a karanga. Or not: these things may have been pre-disapproved of by a key member of the close family. Often that person is themselves Māori, but not keen on the trappings. 'I don't want things taken over by Māori stuff,' they might say. 'But I'd like you to sing that song you did for Auntie E. That was nice, that one.' It's interesting to observe these things in one's own family — how the wider context of living in a colonised country plays out in microcosm in your aunties and uncles, your parents, yourself.

※

Birds can give us a language for grief. Apart from the original one — I mean Hine-nui-te-pō and the pīwakawaka — there's so many stories of strange behaviour from ruru or sparrows, blackbirds, ducks even.

When a relative dies in Taranaki I am visited that afternoon by two tūī who fly at the window of the lounge again and again. A friend who is grieving her teenage niece finds a seagull in her lounge for the third day in a row, and watches dumbstruck while it flies and hops calmly around. Eventually it leaves the lounge and swoops its way into their bedroom. She finds it sitting, legs tucked under and almost asleep, on the bookshelf beside the framed picture of her niece as a baby.

My bird was a kingfisher.

※

It's 2011 and I am 43 years old.

My partner, Christine, and I got together when I was 36. We had been friends for about 10 years before that. One of the first things I asked Christine was whether she wanted to have kids.

I had just come out of a relationship with another woman who had desperately wanted children, but was newly and unreliably in recovery from drug and alcohol addiction, and therefore so was our relationship. We weren't able to pay for inseminations so it would have to be a friend. She would say let's do it, let's just go for it, but then the minute we sat down to talk about a possible donor, she would find fault with all of them. Every guy we knew was unsuitable because, basically, he wasn't her. She was also (legitimately) anxious about the legal situation for queer couples and her rights as a non-biological parent. Every time we tried to talk about having children, we would end up having a hideous fight, and often I'd have to leave the house to get away from her anger.

That relationship eventually blew apart. This new one with Christine, precisely because it was so much healthier and safer and more fun, made me want to have children even more. It was becoming unlike any other feeling I'd ever had. Christine, for her part, was ambivalent, having no parental instincts whatsoever, except when it came to her phlegmatic yet undeniably handsome black-and-white tomcat, Maverick. The thought of being pregnant made her feel physically ill, terrified even. For me, having that big pregnant belly was all I wanted.

Yes, I was also scared — depression and PTSD told me I would be a terrible mother. My constant anxiety told me that I'd never be able to get pregnant and I would destroy myself in the process of trying. It told me I was too poor, too old, too unwell. But unlike Christine, my burning need to be a mum bypassed all of those blockades, arguably all rationality. It bypassed my love for Christine at times, though I so wanted her to come on the parenthood journey with me.

We fought about it a lot. She isn't one to make a decision fast, and she prevaricated for months before finally telling me, after another awful screaming argument, that no, she really truly didn't want to have children, and never would. Full stop. I was devastated. I knew enough of my own mental health that I was certain I couldn't do this alone. Our relationship was still relatively new at this point, but I also knew I didn't have it in me to break up with Chris, meet someone else and do this all again from scratch. So this was it for me: Chris was my only hope, and she was out.

Perhaps we should have left it there. But over the following year Christine kind of, well, sort of changed her mind. It was a combination of seeing my sadness, and being encouraged by her own family to see that parenting wasn't the terrifying thing she thought it would be. She began to see that she could achieve her own dreams as well as have a child — that the two weren't mutually exclusive. She connected with her brand-new baby niece in a different way, and her other niece and nephew, too. We started to see ourselves as a family: we didn't have all our ducks in a row financially and we wouldn't be like other, more conventional family constellations, but she began to see it was possible. That it could even be something magical, rewarding.

I don't want to paint this as a smooth transition on her part. She was still unsure by the time we started trying. When early attempts failed month after month, she was the nearest target, and there was no end to my manipulations and anger. I told her she was trying to sabotage me. That she should go and find some 20-year-old who only wants to watch soccer games and do the door at her gigs. I am ashamed of some of the things I said to her. I am ashamed of how blinding my own desperation was. But as I'm sure many of you know, that's how this thing rolls. And by 'rolls' I mean, of course, rolls through your life like a malevolent juggernaut.

※

F inding a donor took about a year. As soon as we started trying, I was consumed by the machinations of monthly insemination cycles and the scrutiny they entailed. To be clear, not everyone would have been so, erm, conscientious about keeping track to the level I did. But I wanted to leave as little as possible to chance. Each morning I shoved a thermometer in my mouth as soon as my eyes opened. Every afternoon, sitting on the bed propped up with pillows, wearing a head torch and balancing a hand-mirror between my heels, I cranked open my vagina with a plastic speculum my doctor had given me. I charted the colour, texture and amount of my cervical fluid, as well as the position and appearance of the cervix itself. Around the middle of my cycle each month I would spit on a small rectangle of glass and slide it under a microscope, to see if my saliva was forming a 'fern-like' pattern — an indication of imminent ovulation.

I spent hundreds of dollars (we didn't have thousands) on supplements, acupuncture, homoeopathy, cranial osteopathy, pregnancy tests, ovulation tests. My father loaned me the thousands it cost to have two IUI procedures at Fertility Associates (we couldn't afford IVF; this was a lower-cost alternative). As the months dragged on, any change in protocols took on an intoxicating power in my imagination. Surely this session of bodywork, or this mineral, or this mantra would make all the difference.

But these things did not make a difference. I would find myself bleeding when I wanted anything but, heaving with grief and writing DAY 1 in red biro in my cycle chart. It felt like I'd wandered into some hellish casino, where each loss meant I was somehow more locked in to trying again, and then again, because otherwise, what would all this effort have been for? 'Sunk cost', I think they call it.

I had to keep going because how else could I justify the amount of time, tears, money, energy, sanity and goodwill this whole thing had already eaten through? It was hundred-watt hope and six-fathom disappointment. Nothing much in between.

※

We were living in a bach in Paekākāriki, on a hill just back from the beach, with an amazing view of Kāpiti Island and an astonishing number of gaps around the windows and doors. Just outside the house was a power line, and on that power line I began to notice the silhouette of a kingfisher, a kōtare. It would only stay for a few minutes, but it seemed uncanny how well-timed those short visits were. I'd be crying, staring out at the sea, trying to summon the courage for another round, and/or grieving the last, and there it would be, such a distinctive shape against the pale blue of the sky. I had no particular connection to or knowledge of the kōtare — but I loved its stoutness, the oversized beak, the arch of bright teal as its wings took it away.

The kingfisher came to feel like a friend, a kaitiaki or guardian. As if the kōtare was a sign that we would succeed, that we should keep trying, that everything would be all right in the end. I began to look for it rather than just notice it. When we moved house in the middle of the whole trying-to-conceive scenario, I thought we wouldn't see the bird again. But after a couple of weeks a kingfisher arrived at our new place. I saw it in the morning when I was walking back down the drive after a trip to the dairy. That squat shape, brilliant turquoise and long beak, on the new house's weather vane.

I hadn't realised before we started trying to conceive with a donor that there is a very strong belief at large that using a syringe and jar instead of a penis substantially reduces a woman's chances of becoming pregnant. I guess because I have had long-term relationships with men in the past, and spent most of that time trying not to get pregnant, I had a slightly different perspective. Plus I'd done the research.

I knew that if we kept the syringe warm and clean, and the donor did the same thing with the jar, we had a window of about 20–30 minutes with very little loss of sperm life or motility. I knew I didn't have to have an orgasm to get pregnant, and I expect if anyone thinks about it for even a short time, they would realise that the world would be decidedly less populated if this were the case.

I knew also that I didn't have to be 'relaxed' or 'thinking good thoughts' or meditating or doing karakia or lying with my legs up the wall or rotating like a rotisserie chicken every ten minutes for two hours or being positive or any of the other things that were infuriatingly and constantly offered to me as solutions by well-meaning friends, parents and acquaintances. Don't think I didn't try every single one of these things, though. Some more than once.

✳

Our first donor (there were three in all), 'A', was someone who worked with me and had become a friend and my touring sound engineer. A had a very full work schedule that might see him working different shifts from week to week, and having to fly to Auckland or Christchurch or Dunedin at short notice to mix a band or an orchestra, or record some international celebrity. Plus he was leaving in eight months for China and Mongolia, where he planned to bike for a year doing his OE. As well as this, he had just met a new partner and they had decided that when he got back they wanted to try to have a baby of their own. This would preclude any more trying with us. So this was our opportunity: eight cycles with A, right here, right now.

The first time was at his place in Wellington. I was so hopeful. Chris was terrified that I actually would get pregnant. She could hardly be in the room with me while I set up my baby-making nest: multiple pillows, duvet, paper towels and a syringe. A was embarrassed and flustered. He didn't warm the jar. Christine was the courier, collecting from A upstairs and delivering to me downstairs as soon as he had sent the 'OK ready!' text message. Christine is what some would call a 'Gold Card Lesbian' — she hasn't had much to do with men in an intimate capacity, shall we say. She later told me that when A handed her the small jar, with its modest 6–7-millilitre contents, it was all she could do to keep herself from saying, 'Is that all there is?' I think she was expecting a bucket.

My joy when I got pregnant — the month before A left for China — wasn't immediate. It felt surreal. The first test was a clear positive, but I only had one in the house and I wanted to be sure. So my friend Alia gave me one from when she and her girlfriend had been trying. That was positive too, but later we found out the test was expired, and a strange feeling began settling in the shadows of my delight.

I was coming up to my fortieth birthday, and to celebrate it we had booked, along with two very beloved friends we hadn't seen for ages, a canoe trip in Golden Bay. We would kayak around the beaches and camp on the golden sands. I was really looking forward to actually celebrating a milestone that in fertility circles is pretty much thought of as the end of the road. Without thinking I would be pregnant at the time, I had deliberately booked to do something nourishing and fairly adventurous, out in nature because I needed the space, I needed the healing, I needed to be around old friends, not a bunch of people at a party or a dinner who I had to pretend to be happy around if I still wasn't pregnant.

But as it happened, I was. And by the time the trip began I couldn't have been happier. I felt high. I'd never been so full of joy or optimism about my future. I had visited my GP earlier and given her the news, and was kind of shocked when she didn't believe me. She made me do two more pregnancy tests that same day and the results were inconclusive. Not surprising, I thought, I'd already done two that day, I was pretty much out of urine let alone hCG. But again, I could sense that dark feeling making itself a little more comfortable in the wings.

The doctor took some blood, and told me that kayaking would make no difference to me if I was pregnant, and that I should go and enjoy my holiday and come to see her as soon as I returned and she'd give me the results of my blood test.

I didn't have to wait for those test results. I woke up on the second to last day of our kayaking trip knowing it was all over. I howled into the long-drop, I gasped and choked with tears and screaming grief in our tent. The resident penguins of Observation Beach must have thought a banshee had moved in. I know our friends did. They were completely at a loss to help me. Christine was probably more relieved than anything. Miscarrying there on that day, and for the days following while we tried to carry on with our canoe trip, was the most alone I have ever felt.

I was probably pregnant for about 21 days: what fertility specialists and doctors often refer to as a 'chemical pregnancy'. And although I hope to eclipse it someday, at the moment they remain the happiest 21 days of my life.

I don't think I could ever fully express how grateful I am to A, or to anyone who donates to help someone else have a child. It's such a singular act of love and generosity, and in actual reality it is a colossal pain in the arse. It intrudes on all aspects of life, not least your sex life. When A finally left for China, many of our friends generously offered to help us, but because of my already compromised fertility, we were looking for someone with few risk factors themselves. This meant someone whose alcohol and drug intake was minimal, and whose maturity and reliability wasn't. Someone who could understand the pragmatic implications of saying yes.

❊

Our new donor, M, was just as busy as A, but unlike A he was married, and his husband was simultaneously donating to another woman. The practicalities of this new arrangement were much more challenging. At one stage I had to follow M to Auckland and book myself into a motel room down the road from where he was staying for a work trip. We managed to coordinate the inseminations around his busy schedule, sometimes even managing two inseminations a day, and I spent four days on my back looking at the worst plaster ceiling in the entire North Island.

All the while I was excruciatingly conscious that I was getting older. The months had become years and as the number of unsuccessful cycles mounted and my wellbeing plummeted, I knew on a very deep level it was probably my age that was getting in the way. I've seen the line graphs that drop off like a deep-sea reef after 40. But by nature I like achieving things against the odds. I'm the daughter of an All Black — a Māori All Black, to be precise — who survived a horrific childhood in a Catholic orphanage, then tuberculosis at age 19. He did so by defying all medical orders never to play contact sport, drink or exert himself in order to 'maybe make it to 40'.

He represented his country against the Lions in 1972 with one kidney and half a bladder and a scar like a shark bite. I grew up with the subconscious and very powerful expectation that if I wanted something, even if my body wouldn't absolutely cooperate, even if the doctors told me it was impossible, I just needed to work really hard and I could make it happen.

This approach probably works perfectly well for many situations, but trying to conceive is profoundly not one of them. I was faced with a process that defied striving, defied effort, defied planning, control and expectations, and defied the deeply felt well-wishes of my friends and my parents. It defied my own breaking and broken fucking heart. I could not 'effort' this into happening. I could not 'try harder'. Since I'd begun the process of trying to conceive, a number of my close friends and family had gotten pregnant and had children. I stopped counting at 18. Many of them were same-sex couples. One cousin was single when we started. He met his partner, moved in with her, got married, got pregnant, had the baby and separated — all while we were still trying.

During the years this whole trying-to-conceive process took, my 'line in the sand' — the measure of what I was prepared to do to try to get pregnant — changed many times. Initially I thought I would never ask anyone except A — if it didn't work with him, I would just accept it. But it didn't, and I didn't. We moved on to M, but if it didn't work I thought I would never go down the fertility treatment route. It didn't and I did. But it still didn't result in a baby. And I had to realise I had reached that place, that moment. I no longer wanted, and I was no longer able, to move the goalposts.

Still, it took me another couple of months to really articulate it. Even now I find it hard to say: I will never give birth to a child, I will never have a baby, I will never be a parent, and perhaps most painfully for me as a Māori woman, I will never be an ancestor. People leap in with comfort suggestions of adoption or fostering or whāngai or even getting a dog. I can't even consider any of these things. It's not that my desire to be a mother suddenly ceased — quite the opposite. I could simply no longer endure the constant waiting. The relentless handing over of my future and my happiness to someone else, to something else, be it fate or a doctor or a hormone injection or my own ovaries or an adoption or fostering agency. I could no longer tolerate not being the main agent in my own life, being controlled by something that was starting to feel as potentially destructive to me and my loved ones, and as all-consuming, as any addiction. With my depression in full swing, I realised I could no longer live any kind of a healthy life — mentally, physically, spiritually, financially — unless I let this dream go.

※

A few months after we had made the decision to stop trying, we were having afternoon tea on the deck of our home when Christine noticed the body of a bird — quite a large bird — lying in the corner. We drew closer, and saw that it was a kingfisher.

How or why that kingfisher turned up dead on our deck will always be a mystery. Our cat was not a hunter — and although I know most native bird-loving cat-owners want to believe this of their pets, with our cat, I believe it really was true. He'd never brought us kill of any kind. Maybe it was a neighbour's cat or dog. Or the kingfisher could have simply flown into one of the windows.

Whatever had caused its demise, neither Christine nor I had any hesitation in putting two and two together for ourselves. Before the others could notice, we gathered up the bright-feathered body and took it down to the bottom of our garden. We thanked the universe, the god energy, the atua, the tīpuna, Chance herself — whoever — for bringing us such a profound confirmation of our decision. And we are still grateful, more than anything, for having had something, a being, a body, something that brought us love and brightness even if for a short time. Something we could bury.

We dug a hole in the soft peaty soil with our hands. We said a karakia, crying like babies. When I placed the kōtare into the ground, its feathers were still warm from the sun.

Shaping space

GABRIELLE AMODEO

I beckon to you. You lean down. Your ear rests on my forehead. I whisper something to you. Something between us. You smile against my brow. Straighten up. I still feel your ear as a curl of cold on my forehead. It lingers a long while.

The spring chill is still on you, even though we've been walking through City Gallery for some time. We've come to *Imagined in the Context of a Room*, the retrospective of Joanna Margaret Paul's sprawling practice: painting, drawing, poetry, film, photography. It's our nineteenth anniversary.

Earlier, on our walk to the gallery, a helicopter flew over the buildings. The gap between the buildings a bright, jagged passage of blue, and the red dot of the helicopter arcing through it.

'I used to call them high-duggers, when I was a kid,' you say. I smile. I know this, but I like following conversations we've had before, after all these years. 'Catherine used to call them hock-a-la-wahs,' you continue. I know this too, and the path we're taking. In turn, I follow your younger sister's hock-a-la-wahs with my youngest brother.

'Jack used to call them ubba-copts. It must be the best word to hear a kid learn how to pronounce.'

But you move down a new path.

'Worth having a child for, to hear them mispronounce helicopter,' I hear you say. At least, that's what I remember, but maybe you remember it differently.

I glance up at you. It's a path I'm still not sure I can follow you down.

☀

'm trying to work out the shape of things. The contour.

The life-drawing studio is suspended mid-set-up. A handful of easels form a partial circle around the model's platform. Bags left in the middle of the floor, folders leaning akimbo against them. The students perch on stools in front of me. Most are late-teens. I look at them and realise this year I've aged into being comfortably old enough to be their mother.

'I want us to shift our thinking,' I begin. 'When we draw, we want to avoid using outlines. But we do perceive an edge to the body, so how do we think about that? We shift from thinking about outlines, to thinking about contour.'

The words of this lesson rise easily, as if the studio walls still hold their echo from past classes.

'Contour is three-dimensional: you can touch it, follow its path through space. And it changes as the form moves. Take your finger and run it along where you perceive the edge of your arm being.'

I demonstrate on my own arm, feeling the tickle of my finger. The smooth curve of muscles moves into the hard fin of the ulna; jutting knobs of carpals; fleshy palm wrapping around the outside edge of my hand; the rise of the knuckle into my pinkie.

'Now run your finger over your arm to the other side.'

I take my finger over the surface of my upper wrist now, describing its arc from outer to inner forearm.

'This line through your arm is also the contour. Contour is both surface and what we perceive as the edge of a form.'

I'm trying to work out the shape of the space I take up. The negative space presses against me.

'But we can't think about form without thinking about what's around it — the negative space. If we're looking at the model, then the walls, the floor, the model's platform — all of that is our negative space. And it is integral to how you perceive the form that you're drawing.'

I put my hand to my waist and point to the irregular triangle gap between my arm and torso.

'In drawing, this space has value. It has its own shape and tones. It shares a contour with the form you're drawing.'

Contour writes its form on space, and space pushes in to meet contour. Like the boundary where the sand slips beneath the sea, they wash against each other, define each other.

※

I open the photos I took at City Gallery. I stop at Paul's drawings *Untitled, from the Edges of the Room* and their related docent label. There are four drawings in the series, all sparse pencil on a modestly sized piece of paper, and I photographed all of them as a group. One, though, I photographed separately.

Paul lost a baby. Imogen Rose. She died of a heart defect at nine months. I cannot imagine the profoundness of Paul's grief, but it felt tangible in the exhibition, like sensing what the tooth of paper feels like without having to touch it.

In her grief, Paul stopped drawing for a time and turned to poetry. In 1978, two years after Imogen died, she published a now-long-out-of-print collection called *Imogen*. I want to find a poem from *Imogen*. I know its title, but only through echoes on the internet: a single mention in an old exhibition review I downloaded, its URL now defunct. The poem is called 'this is the cup of your heart'. I keep searching for it, but only circle its absence.

The drawing I'm looking at is from 1980. It's a partial glimpse of a room: part of a doorframe intersecting with the deep traditional skirtings of a colonial villa and, obscuring the skirtings, a sofa with a cushion. The perspective is as if we're seated on the floor before it.

A pencil line drops, like a string with a weight on its end, down from the top edge to just below the paper's midline. In its fall it gathers other lines running in parallel to it, forming the contours of the doorframe. A hard line, a soft line, a broken line and then the deep strong fall of a cast shadow. The sofa is partially rendered with a handful of discontinuous lines — it disappears into the wall, the skirting — except for the shadow of the sofa's arm falling across a collapsed cushion. The cushion holds the echo of a weight that's left it. Cupping space.

The economy of the drawing. Its tender rendering of an overlooked space. Surfaces barely described. A few deft lines, careful weight changes of the pencil deepening or fading the contours. The use of shadow to not obscure but to emphasise. Her restraint. An exquisite lesson in negative space and contour that, in ways deeper than I can fathom, at once stops my breath and lets me breathe again.

☀

One recent night I initiated sex with you, because I wasn't sure when I would want it again. I didn't tell you that, of course. It was knowledge I held close. The sex was tender and sweet and I remember feeling the curve of your skull, the prickle of your close-buzzed hair, cupped in my hand.

I spent the following day writing about my experience of childhood sexual abuse. Everything I can remember of it. The first futile disclosure of it at 17. The subsequent near-18 years of again suppressing it, even to you. Writing about it (the words only for me) is another step towards processing it. The processing began so recently, and feels like it has come, in important ways, too late.

I was 34 when I disclosed it to my new therapist. Well, disclosed. More like: I howled it out from the centre of my diaphragm so loud that I worried the people in the next room heard. My body burnt. The skin of my back convulsed.

I was 36 when I told you, my partner and love since I was 20. I read you a letter I had worked out with my therapist. I held over my mouth the massive rolled neck of my woollen jumper, scratchy against my lips, and could only look at you in brief glances through tears.

'I'm sorry,' I said when I finished.

You pulled me to you, swift and strong, exclaiming, 'Don't apologise . . .'

You were the first person to give me physical comfort for that trauma. The first person to hold me. The first physical rejoinder to trauma's enduring touch.

I was 38 when I sat in my therapist's office, writhing. My period was late, and it was engulfing me.

Only two days late . . .

Only three days . . .

Only four days . . .

The slight form of my therapist sat opposite me, legs crossed. Behind her, the warm orb of her rice-paper lamp was fissured by the wild tendrils of a fine branch in silhouette.

'My period is late,' I said.

And with the words ringing in my ears as well as throbbing in my mind,

I was beside myself. Almost literally beside myself: in some way beyond and outside myself. I felt rifted, brain against body, repulsed, rage-filled by my body's betrayal and the threat it had let in.

The therapist asked me about the likelihood I was pregnant and I knew it was negligible: 'I'm on a long-term contraceptive. It's more than 99 per cent effective.'

But I couldn't absorb the logic. My body was rigid.

'I don't want this uninvited thing taking over, taking ownership, control, of my body.'

The word 'pregnant' felt like caught vomit, hot in my mouth. I couldn't say it.

'Were you aware of what you were doing with your arms just now?' she asked. She mirrored stiff forearms swiping up and down her body. 'It was like you were trying to cast something out.'

'I want to get my body away from me.'

'Does what you're feeling remind you of anything else?'

My burning skin heaved and prickled. I felt turned inside out.

'It reminds me of the sexual abuse—'

And then the weight of it hit. The sorrow.

More unfolded to me.

Memories of earlier times when the question of children had even faintly, even only adjacently, risen between you and me. Sometime in our twenties. Sometime in our thirties. Somewhere in Auckland. Somewhere in Wellington. Maybe a small comment. Nothing much meant in it. Maybe just you observing how I might be as a mother someday. And then me sobbing, feeling so trapped I would have gnawed my foot off if it would have helped. Caught between the fear you would leave me if I didn't want children and the horror I couldn't yet articulate to myself: that through trauma I had conflated pregnancy, birth, children with the visceral, physical horror and repulsion of sexual abuse. And you, each time, reassuring me — you wouldn't choose an imaginary child over me.

Back in my therapist's office, the sharp details of the Persian carpet liquified into puddles of crimson, muted emerald, cream, powdery blue.

'Maybe,' I went on, 'without the abuse, I might have been able to want children . . . been OK with Justin wanting children. We still might not have had any, but at least it would have been a choice.'

I plucked out, and carefully folded in half, tissue after tissue to cry into.

The manifold ways trauma has oriented my life, and by dint of that, many parts of yours, drenched me.

By the time I got home, my period had arrived.

☀

I was 39 when I could finally articulate the why to you. Say to you, 'I want us to talk about it. I don't know if I will ever get there. But I want to know your thoughts on children.'

I'm 40 now, and trauma still has a phantom presence in me. As I wrote about it, it rose up as spasms across my back, sharp prickling in my armpits, and a spectral ache in my tailbone. I finished writing. Closed my laptop. And then stood under a hot shower until the water ran cold.

Later, I walked along the south coast in the fierce afternoon sun. At the water's edge I took my shoes and socks off, let my feet spread over the sand, press into its surface as it pressed and rasped against my soles, let cold waves wash over my ankles and calves.

Forty now, and I'm nude before the bathroom mirror, tracing the contours of my torso with my eyes. Red lines drawn with pressure sketch my clothing on my skin. The bite of my bra, leaving imprints of underwire channels and firm seams, enclose the contours of my torso. Baggy underwear bunched beneath tight jeans makes crests and troughs like landforms across my pelvis. The waistband seams meet beside my belly button, and the line of the fly falls towards my pubic hair.

My areolae sprawl huge across my breasts, the larger one three inches in diameter, each an indistinct greenish-brown on the edges of their irregular soft copper pink circle, contracting to the deeper red of slightly raised nipples. When I was younger, I was embarrassed by their size. Now I love their expanse. The luxurious spread of colour across my skin. Like resplendent paint splodges.

Trauma broke me from my body and broke my body from the world. Uninvited, not understood, it was an obliteration of my autonomous self. As I grew up and realised what had happened, I wanted my body to break apart to nothing. Even now, passive suicidal ideations come on a metronome tick of particular words in my head — *dematerialise, disintegrate, disappear* — as unbidden images rise: hurling myself in front of a passing truck, dashing my head against rocks at Ōwhiro Bay.

I went to art school at 17, and sank into my senses. I was awash with form, surface, line. Awash, startlingly, with vivid, intense colour that I had, at some point in the maelstrom of post-traumatic stress disorder, stopped perceiving. Going to art school and being taught to *sense* the world again was a new meeting with myself. The starting place for the slow task of pulling myself back.

Forty now, and I sit at the throwing wheel, a mounded lump of clay on the wheel in front of me, glistening and slick.

In drawing, I search for spaces and edges with marks. I use tone, line and the blank white of paper to shape the empty space of the page into form. Throwing is a different way of finding spaces and contours.

As the wheel spins, I cup the mound with one hand and push the thumb of my other down through the clay to form a well. The mound slips smooth and wet under my hand till it becomes tacky, sticky. I splash it with water, making it slippery again. I replace my thumb with my index finger and draw it against the well's edge, against its bottom and side, compressing the base. Drawing space to form the hollowness of the cup it will be. With the unformed sides pinched between the negative space of my fingers, I draw the clay up from the base to give height to the cup.

In throwing, I am making space from form; in drawing I make form from space. I use the curved edge of a wooden spoon to push the cup's straight cylinder into roundness. To, as the teacher says, 'belly out' the cup.

☀

I could see my abdomen, wrapped in red pressure marks just now in the mirror, as a hollow space waiting to be filled . . . But I don't think that I want it filled.

I love my life, our life, as it is. Our quirks, in-jokes, small routines. The way we mark and shape our time and space as a family of two. The places we intersect, the places we overlap, and the places we hold separate from each other, but nevertheless care for on behalf of each other. The space we've created between us already feels replete. We are enough.

But the lingering concern that if we don't, we'll miss out on something . . . what? Something remarkable? Life-changing? The most fulfilling thing you can do? The greatest love you'll ever know? I already have a great love.

The question hovers between us: a potentiality. An unformed thing that could unform us from the shapes we've created from ourselves, of ourselves and between us.

I've been torn apart by someone else. To lose that autonomy again? To intentionally hand it over, to invite that risk of again being unformed? The thought makes my heart skitter, my breath quicken, my body feel like it's swooping in vertigo.

So I keep toying with the shape of my life, of our lives. Of our life together.

※

Our conversations come erratically, when I blurt out, 'I know this is a bit out of the blue . . .' and I try again to find out what you want, how you imagine our future.

You've told me in the past, many times, you're open to it, but you don't want a child unless I know, absolutely, that I want one. The risk is too big — for me, for us, for the child — if we're not certain it is what we want. If I'm not certain it is what I *want*. You want me to choose. You want to give me space to choose.

The space you offer me is so generous, so expansive, so selfless, I struggle with the corresponding lack of space I feel I offer you. That the space I take up leaves you with no choice but to be generous, expansive, selfless.

You don't want to talk me into something I don't want to do, so you are reluctant to tell me what your wants are. But the choice is so monumental it hangs like a millstone.

And in the negative space of not knowing your wants I worry you stifle a world-building where you imagine, maybe, running alongside your kid on a bike, their first two-wheeler, the one you built up especially for them. Throwing a cricket ball for them. Reading *The Hobbit* to them. You assure me you don't. But still . . .

We talk in scales, using our hands to mark outer edges, and where we might sit along it: I can't remember your exact words, just the contours of them: 'If here is not wanting kids and here is wanting kids, then I'm somewhere in the middle, neutral,' you say.

My scale is different. Its Overton window was set at an extreme that's hard to rationalise because it's formed on the irrationality of PTSD. A fierce repulsion that left space on its opposite side not for an opposite, just a less emphatic no. My world-building has brief flashes of fragile ribs rippling under soft, new skin. Small arms outstretched. Later, maybe, paper scribbled with crayons strewn about. But even in those softer imaginings is a feeling of constriction, of my body not being my own, of being repelled by a child's touch and the damage I could cause in my repulsion.

I try imagining with you what the shape of that world would be. Earlier, on that crisp spring morning, before we left for the gallery, I said, 'We wouldn't have much support in the hellscape that is the first three months.'

Not missing a beat, you replied, 'In those precious first few months.'

A wry smile on your face.

In the two years since that realisation in my therapist's office, I have shifted from visceral, body-shuddering abhorrence, to a soft, sad *I don't think so, but I just don't know*. And my time is running out.

To nudge pregnancy, postpartum against the early, as yet unknown, contours of perimenopause? Do I want to do that to my body? And to nudge the inherent loss of bodily autonomy that comes with pregnancy, postpartum against the echoes of trauma that still reverberate through me? Do I want to do that to a baby?

I think of the times you have led me through my moments of terror. Guiding me off Helicopter Hill, me scooting down on my bum, when vertigo left me unable to do anything but sit with my hands cupped like blinkers around my eyes, so I couldn't see the height I was at. Coaxing me into letting go of the rocks I clung to, petrified, above Pararaha Stream, convinced the 5-foot drop would kill me. Helping me climb a ledge on the Mount Holdsworth Jumbo Circuit, frightened my backpack was going to pull me backwards and pitch me into a mist-obscured drop that would last forever. And after each time, you, there, holding me, telling me that I did it, that I was so brave, that you're so proud of me.

Could you do it again? With something as fundamental as parenthood?

You don't want to talk me into it.

And I don't think I want to be talked into this lifelong decision on the basis of momentary triumphal experiences, tender as they are.

So, in brief, erratic spurts, sometimes with months between them, even as time runs out for us, we try to figure out the two different shapes of our futures. Two different shapes that are irreconcilably different from each other: a shape that contains a child and a shape that doesn't.

A friend levels with me. Straightforward. No nonsense. Sitting across from me over coffee and pastries. A mother herself.

'It's better to regret not having children than to regret having them.'

I cherish this advice: brutal and sensitive. Holding regret as a risk for both options and asking, which regret is better? Whichever shape we choose, we will inevitably grieve the other.

As I look at the photo of Paul's drawing, my focus changes and I see your silhouetted reflection in the frame's glass, hovering in profile over the drawing. Peaked cap. Strong brow ridge curving into straight nose. The moustache of your beard bending into your lips. Lips into chin. The collar of your Swanndri projecting out, and then down to the curve of your chest.

Perhaps that's why I took the photo.

I know you're caught in the reflective surface of the glass as only silhouette, shadow. But, without knowing I'm doing it, I fill your silhouette to full three-dimensionality. I see all the planes and surfaces I know of you. Sense the warmth of your skin, your smell, the space you fill moving through the house, across the kitchen table, in the next room, in our bed. Against me in an embrace, our contours and space pressed into each other.

It was the docent label that drew me to Paul, so I draw you to me, and you press your ear to my forehead. The label ends: 'In the same way that Paul positioned physical objects as signifiers of relationships, places and moments in time, spaces and voids become metaphorical carriers of mourning, empathy, time and silence.'

And that cool echo of your ear.

Selfish

DONELLE MCKINLEY

At first, she wanted six. Her best friend was one of four, and that looked like fun; surely six would be even better. What she wanted most was to name them, and then she would set about discovering their talents and curating their creative lives. Evie, Isabel, Ava, Samuel, Toby and Sebastian. A writer, a painter, a musician, a dancer, an actor and one to spare for good measure. Yes, six would cover it. She read a lot of Noel Streatfeild in primary school.

Later, when she realised that having children was less like a project and more like a life commitment, she thought perhaps four — enough people to cosy up around a large wooden kitchen table and fill an old rambling villa on the edge of town. Mention of four raised fewer eyebrows than six, but it still sounded like a lot to many. Evie, Isabel, Toby and Sebastian. A writer, a painter, a musician, a dancer. Yes, four would be perfect.

Around the time that she might have started having these children, she was curating her own creative life. She was challenging her handspan with the score from *The Piano*, abstracting landscapes on canvas in bold immersive colour and channelling the Beat poets on a clacking Olivetti. Discovering she had left it a little too late to start ballet, she switched to hip hop, and was learning the lines of *A Respectable Wedding* so she could tiptoe kiss Brecht's bridegroom in drama class. She was consuming languages and history in heaped platefuls daily, breathing art and literature like oxygen.

She began to reconsider. How, with four children, would she have time to continue doing all these things? There was so much she wanted to do, to be, and she had only just begun. And if *she* could be all these things, why have children at all? She adjusted: between two and four might be nice, but perhaps one would be sufficient? She supposed she ought to wait and decide with The Other Person, although this approach did not come naturally.

❋

The Other Person, when they revealed themselves in her thirtieth year, was a godsend. Her husband was open-minded, flexible; four sounded rather a lot, but perhaps one or two? As they started down the path of prospective parenthood, they began to pay closer attention to those around them who were already beyond the point of no return. They quietly chalked up the sights and sounds as they socialised with new families, comparing notes and summing up in spurts of horror and fits of laughter on the drive home. Walking through their front door they would pause to bask in the order and calm, the piles of books they had plentiful time to read, the blessed relief of silence.

It didn't take long to dispel her idyllic notion of a home filled with children; within months of focused observation she was struggling to make a case for the benefits of motherhood. At best, it would begin with appalling and completely avoidable sources of misery: sleep deprivation, mind-bending noise, mess, restriction, the epic sacrifice of precious time and talent for brain-deadening tasks. If she was lucky, there might be a period of relative calm before the years of teenage stupidity, slammed doors and shouted disrespect across the generational divide. Perhaps her marriage would be salvageable after the inevitable and irredeemable exchange of passion for domesticity, but this was unlikely. Eventually, the children would leave, only to boomerang back with broken hearts and empty pockets until they were old enough to visit out of duty.

The things other women, her own mother included, championed to counter all this — a different kind of love, unconditional, incomparable, primal, fierce, all-consuming — she saw only as debilitating. Her mostly happy childhood memories of family life could not compete, even for a heartbeat, with the joy and drive and strive of her own rich, unburdened adult life. The thought of spending years teaching someone banal skills, when she could be learning wide and high and deep herself, bored her to tears.

She supposed that many who chose to be mothers were seeking to fill a gap in their being that she did not have. She could relate to the romantic tug of procreation, the hazy desire to create something beautiful and alike out of your love for each other, but even this, she suspected, didn't add up. Why, if you loved someone that much, treasured what you had together so much, would you intentionally commit to a lifestyle that was certain to change you both?

Wrestling with all this, but holding on stubbornly to a strange fascination with pregnancy and the fear of missing out on something she couldn't yet understand, she scanned borrowed books about what to expect until finally she was met, care of a life-saving, no-nonsense author, with the starkest of truths: having a baby is like throwing a grenade into your life. If that's what you want, please proceed to Chapter 2. She read it twice, like a welcome slap across the face. She put the book down and cocked her head to the window, staring out to sea. Is this what she wanted? Hell no.

The next Saturday morning, as the two of them lazed in bed, balancing books, coffee and croissants, gloriously free to go anywhere and nowhere, do anything and nothing much, she proposed a total retreat. Her research was complete, and all evidence pointed to the advantages of the status quo. Remarkably, the conversation was brief and without drama. Her husband was somewhat relieved; he too, saw little sense in swapping contentment for a minefield.

※

The Decision, when others caught wind of it, was met with everything from shrugs to surprise to sadness. Her grandmother labelled her a bluestocking, a badge she accepted with pride. The most irritating response — there's still time to change your mind — she continued to deflect for years. The most outrageous was the rebrand. By choosing to swim against the tide of social expectation, they were no longer a Nice Young Couple — prospective providers of grandchildren, cousins, playmates, consumers and tax-paying citizens — but Selfish. It wasn't always expressly airborne, but she would forever catch it in the slight frowns of mothers, the sentences left hanging, the polite but vague murmurs that acknowledged but disapproved of her contribution. Its sting was harmless, but it bothered her that it didn't add up.

It appeared that the generally approved guidelines to 'follow your dreams' and 'fulfil your potential' were relevant only until the stage of life when you were best placed to enjoy it and achieve anything of note. At that point, you as an individual became less important than your generic capability to produce another person. The prehistoric rationale, to ensure existence of the species, no longer rang true; any child she produced would be environmentally surplus to requirements. Instilling superiority in self-sacrifice for a person you yourself created was a nonsense she associated with tired Christian values. Contributing to the government's economies of scale at the expense of liveable cities made little sense either. She was not obliged to entertain any parent who would be otherwise crushed at the prospect of life without grandchildren — they could find something else to do.

※

She would, mercifully, not be joining The Club, many recent members of which were doubling down on self-sabotage by choosing a child–parent partnership model, so that they never had time to finish a cup of coffee before it was cold or hold an uninterrupted conversation with an adult. Constructive discipline was a dying art. Children once instructed to be 'seen and not heard' were now the fickle sun around which adults revolved, encouraged to 'speak their words' regardless of who else was already speaking. Their parents — otherwise competent employees, business owners, highly trained specialists — were now so hobbled by being responsive at knee height that they struggled to achieve low-level goals like getting out the door on time.

She would not grieve the loss of membership, but her friendships with mothers would long suffer a disconnect; she could not relate to their tales of bringing up, bedding down and fielding crises in miniature. In turn, their eyes would glaze over at the question of what they were reading, what films they had seen lately, what their career plans were for the year ahead — as if she were speaking in a language they once knew but had forgotten.

She would resent the disruptions in the workplace, when parenting colleagues arrived late and exhausted, or dropped everything early to run little people between school and sports. When annoyance got the better of her she would question them about the benefits of parenthood, about whether they ever wished they had chosen the other path. Almost without exception, they swerved the questions defensively, as if avoiding a pile up on the motorway, and toed the line: they couldn't imagine life without their children now. It was against Club rules to answer any other way.

After decades of being without, she would still be unable to summon a single example of how her life would be better with children. It would amaze her that despite so many questionable life decisions, she had got this one so absolutely right. By then, she and her husband had sadly but amicably gone their separate ways, uncoupling without complication to pursue lives in different hemispheres. By then, she had learnt the word for how she experienced emotions, and suspected that motherhood would have made it even harder to balance on a tightrope between two poles, the falls more damaging.

She lived in an old house on the edge of town, where she hosted dinner parties for her friends at a large wooden kitchen table. She started weekdays at her writing desk, contentedly following her dream and fulfilling her potential. On rainy weekend mornings she played piano before hanging her coat on the back of the garden shed door to paint at her easel in joyful bursts. She had cultivated a passion for gardening — a new way of painting on a grand scale — and spent fair-weather days in a state of timeless, blissful industry.

When she wasn't being captivated in the dress circle of a theatre at night, she feasted on history and literature from the bookshelves in every room as if her life depended on it, which it did. At the age of 46 she had bought the house from an elderly woman she didn't know, who insisted there was still time to change her mind; surely she didn't want to spend the rest of her life here alone without children? Actually, yes, she replied, that sounds nice and quiet — that would suit her just fine.

Why are there so many songs about rainbows?

KATE CAMP

The Peeled Banana Dance Company ran twice a week, Tuesdays and Thursdays after work, in the surf club at Island Bay. I would drive there with a friend, and we would be staggered for a moment at how lovely it was down at the coast: the sky changing colour behind the island, the fishing boats *Marco Polo* and *Gemini*, the grey-brown sand and the single line of curling surf making a sound like the tearing of an envelope.

And then we'd go in and start the class, doing grapevines and box steps and our favourite, a swirling hand motion like witches whipping up the steam off a cauldron, or Kate Bush with long, flowing sleeves. And after we'd practised the steps we'd put it all together as a class and perform the whole dance to a song and, as a room of middle-aged women of moderate fitness doing a synchronised dance with many mistakes, we were, we felt, transcendent: beautiful, graceful, joyous.

I explained to my doctor that I might have pulled a muscle at Peeled Banana. The words 'groin strain' were in my mind, probably from watching rugby. But when I told him where the pain was he said it was probably related to the ovary, and he poked around my stomach and said yes, it was definitely pain in the left ovary, and it could be a number of things, but one of the things it could be was ovarian cancer, and that was unlikely but very serious. If I could afford to go privately to get it looked at then I should, because otherwise I'd have to wait six weeks and that was not an amount of time he would recommend.

At some point he said that I was very calm, and I remember thinking, *I don't really see what the alternative is.* Were there patients who would burst into tears or shriek 'No no no', or say, 'Well that's just fucking brilliant isn't it'? I said something like, 'Well there's not much point in getting upset at this stage.' I had a therapist at the time — she was a Scandinavian of some kind — and I remember her saying to me once, in her northern European accent, 'I find it interesting that you say there is "no point" in feeling a certain way. Do you believe that emotions should serve a utilitarian purpose?' It was the kind of annoying question you pay good money for.

When I got home from the doctor I googled ovarian cancer and found out that once you get symptoms it's usually already at stage four, and it has a high death rate, and they end up removing all your reproductive organs, just scooping you out like a fruit was how I thought of it. I was single, 36, and had always imagined, in an abstract, unfocused way, that I'd have kids someday. Now I was thinking I might be dead before I was 40.

I drove out to Bowen Hospital for a consultation about the surgery; I was on my own, never thought to take anyone with me. The surgeon explained that the biopsy might involve taking quite a bit of the ovary out, or removing the whole thing, depending on how it looked when they got in there. I would need to give consent for them to grab as much as they needed. If he removed the ovary, he said, I needed to be aware that it would be removing half the eggs that were in my body. When you do that, the other ovary runs out quicker, so it would have a major impact on my fertility.

It would be like becoming five years older overnight, he said. Any woman in her thirties knows how huge that five-year difference would be. But of course there was no option: I needed to know if I had cancer, and if I did then having kids would be, if not the least of my worries, then certainly something down the other end of the telescope.

When I came to after the surgery, the surgeon said he'd taken about half the ovary, and, while they didn't have the lab results yet, it didn't look like cancer. It was this other non-life-threatening thing called endometriosis, which causes pain and blah blah blah. I'd stopped listening. A couple of weeks later I was back at the hospital, and he explained what endometriosis is, how it gets stuck all over everything like chewing gum and keeps growing and shedding and has nowhere to go, which is what makes it so painful, because your body has no way of getting rid of it.

He said mine was pretty bad, around a seven out of ten. If I wanted to have kids I'd better get onto it right away, because the endometriosis was going to make it hard if not impossible. He could put me on a drug called Danazol to stop the pain, but it would also stop my periods, so maybe I could buy myself six pain-free months by taking it, and in that time I could work out how the hell I was going to try to get pregnant.

✻

I wasn't sure I wanted kids, but I certainly wasn't sure I *didn't* want them. I felt like I had to try; that if I didn't there was a door that would be closed to me, and not because I'd chosen it. And I felt on some level, not fully consciously, that it would be a failure not to have children, that it would be something that other people had done and I hadn't, an experience everyone had had except me, and they would always be able to lord it over me — I would always be *less than*. It tapped into a sense I'd had of myself since childhood, of being unattractive, rejected, a 'wallflower', to use a word from the Wildfire Romance books my sister and I had — a word that she had once, cuttingly, called me as we were walking to school.

And having kids, the idea of having kids, was a kind of default setting, too. Growing up we had The Game of Life, with its colourful wheel instead of a dice, and there were the little blue or pink pegs that you put in the back seats of the car that was your playing piece. No one ever didn't have little pegs in the back. As teenagers we'd worked out how old we'd be at *the year two thousand*. I would be 28, I figured out, and I felt quite daring predicting that, while I would of course be married, I might not have kids by then. I felt I would be the kind of progressive person who would have kids later in life, which in my teenage mind meant my early thirties. Without saying it out loud, everyone just assumed that everyone would have kids. I guess that's the definition of a social norm.

For whatever mix of reasons, I decided I wanted to try, and as a single woman of means I entered into the world of private fertility treatment. Getting approved for donor sperm from a stranger takes time, something to do with

HIV testing that I can't remember the details of, but if you BYO donor you can go right away. Time was something I didn't have, so I needed to find my own sperm. The mental list of possible people was pretty short. This would have to be someone who would do me that kind of favour, who I could cope with always having in my life, and who would be happy to be the donor, not the father. I settled on my ex, Jonathan.

Jonathan and I had met when he came back to New Zealand for his brother's funeral. He had been out of touch with his family for years, in a yoga cult, and then he came back for the funeral and eventually he and I had got together, and I'd been on and off my pot addiction at that time, and I'd once got so out of it I'd pissed the bed, and I wasn't sure if he was gay, straight or bi, and maybe he didn't know either, and eventually we broke up but stayed close.

All of that seemed to make him a good choice, because we'd already had some intense emotional experiences together, and he was someone who would always be in my life, who was tied to my family, and he was also someone who could deal with things by being dry and humorous and detached, which was how I like to be when confronted with emotional trauma. He said yes, and he went and masturbated into a cup in a room at Fertility Associates — they had both gay and straight porn to look at, he told me, and we laughed about that. It is hard to think of a truer act of friendship.

Jonathan's sperm was approved so I went off the Danazol and on to fertility treatment. That meant injecting myself, in the fat of my stomach, twice a day, at 7 a.m. and 7 p.m. The device they give you is like a pen that you put a syringe inside. First you get the syringe, and you take it out of its sterile pack, and take the cap off the needle, and they teach you how to draw the right amount of hormones out of the vial, and how not to get any air bubbles in it, and then you put the syringe in the pen, and there's things you have to click and twist, and then you hold it against a roll of fat, and press the button at the end of the pen, and the needle, finer than a hair, fires out into your flesh and retracts back. It really doesn't hurt at all. If you weren't looking you wouldn't even know the needle was going in. But your body has a natural resistance towards stabbing itself, so even though you know it's not going to hurt, and you're doing it all the time, there's always an adrenaline surge of fear, a gritting of the teeth to overcome it and a relief once it's done.

They give you a little yellow sharps disposal thing to put your used syringes into. And the whole process, having the vials of hormone in the fridge, and remembering to do the injections at the right time, and handling the syringes, the unfamiliar technology, the fear of hurting yourself or doing it wrong, and the high stakes, and the secrecy, because you don't tell people you're doing fertility treatment because they say the stupidest and most hurtful things, and the doing it sitting on the toilet, because you want to be in a locked room, the whole thing is incredibly stressful. You're existing in a constant state of suspended anxiety, which you realise later is called *hope*. It's your first insight into just how toxic that emotion can be.

✺

A round the time I started my first three-week bout of hormone injections, I met Paul on FindSomeone. On our first date we went to an amateur production of *The Darling Buds of May*. Our second was an open home for the house he ended up buying. Our third was to an underground disco night to mark the death of Michael Jackson. A couple of times he'd been over at my place when I'd needed to do my 7 p.m. injection. My small house didn't allow much room for privacy, but after years of handling illicit substances I was naturally quite sneaky, so I'd managed to smuggle my vial out of the fridge and go into the bathroom and inject myself without him noticing. We hadn't even slept together, but as it came close to the day my eggs would be collected and fertilised I decided I needed to tell him what was going on.

I practised in my head what I was going to say. I knew it needed to be really clear, no acronyms or jargon, and I needed to remember that men generally know fuck all about the reproductive system. There shouldn't be a big preamble either. If I started with 'There's something I need to tell you that I think you have a right to know . . .' he'd probably die of fright before I got to the real information. I said something like, 'Hey I think I should tell you that because of some medical issues I'm trying to get pregnant tomorrow by having a doctor inject me with a friend's sperm.' I can't remember what he said right away — he probably asked some questions — but what I do remember him saying was, 'Well, if you do it again, I hope you'd think about doing it with me.' Yes, Paul comes out of this story very well.

It turned out I couldn't have the procedure that time round anyway, the hormones hadn't worked and my eggs hadn't matured, or done whatever they're supposed to do. The fertility doctor had been asking me if I'd been feeling any side effects from the hormones, any breast tenderness, night sweats, strange emotions, and I'd been happy to report that I hadn't felt a thing. Now I was coming to realise that my body's stoic insensibility was a bad thing. I was under-reacting, just like I always did. They said they'd change the hormones and I could try again.

For Paul and me to do IVF as a couple, we needed to have couples counselling. We explained we'd only been together a few months, and the counsellor said that could be a good thing; doing IVF placed a lot of strain on relationships, but being in the first *in love* phase might help with that, keep us connected. And it did help, I think. We were still at that stage where you've never been truly horrible to each other. You're still, to some extent, on your best behaviour. I also think doing IVF so early was good for our relationship. It forced us to have conversations in those first months that would usually take years. We saw each other cry. By the time we'd moved in together it didn't seem like a big commitment, given that we'd been trying to make a baby for the past year.

The results of the next round of injections weren't spectacular, but they were good enough for me to go in and have an egg collection. Paul came with me to Fertility Associates. The process is done with a large needle, which they put through the wall of the vagina, through to the ovary to collect the eggs, guided by an ultrasound. I was sitting up on a table with stirrups I think, awake — they sedate you with one of those date-rape drugs so you can feel the pain but you don't really care, and you don't remember it very well afterwards. I just remember seeing a lot of blood on the pads on the table once I got down.

I was feeling OK, or I thought I was, or I said I was. We drove to Pranah in Newtown to get some food, and I don't remember if we ate in or took away, or how the logistics played out, but Paul had parked miles away and I had to get upset at him, to make him realise that, actually, after having a huge needle stuck through me I was not really in a state to walk to the car. And then I was crying, and it probably wasn't anything to do with walking to the car, I probably would and should have been crying anyway, because the whole process had been quite frightening, and there was so much at stake, and it was something I couldn't control, and something I was not good at, in fact my body was proving to be very bad at it, and I wasn't used to that, wasn't used to not being able to do the things I wanted if I really wanted them and really tried. And I was exhausted, because although I don't remember it, I know I would have been so damn charming on that blood-soaked table, I would have been remarkably calm and no doubt would have commented that it was not as bad as I thought it might be, that it really wasn't that bad at all. And you have to invest a lot of energy to maintain that unaffected air.

I have always observed but am still surprised by the fact that, when you pretend to be OK, most people think you are. You're expecting at least some of them to see through you, but they almost never do.

I have a recurring dream that I am being held hostage, or in some dangerous situation; some threatening men are there who I know mean me harm. Whatever the situation, I know instinctively that the only way to survive is to pretend I don't realise they are a threat. I need to behave as if everything is fine, while calculating my escape. In one version of the dream, I am lying in bed with an intruder next to me, crouched by my face; I pretend I think he's a family member and tell him, groggily, that I'm asleep. In another I'm being held in a compound, but I walk around with my captors, politely commenting on the landscaping, while secretly looking for a way out.

The dreams never resolve one way or another, but the sense on waking is of the enormous pressure of knowing your safety depends on cheerfulness, on your ability to convince others that you are blithely unaware of danger. I know my sister has the same dream sometimes.

As well as battling my under-reaction to the hormones, we had been struggling to get Paul's sperm in the system. He dutifully went into the masturbation room, with its lockable door and varieties of porn, and did what was required. Thanks for that, they said, but there doesn't seem to be any sperm in it. They recommended trying at home. The pottle of sperm could be kept against the skin, down your pants to keep it at the right temperature, and then brought in to the clinic. Again and again, Paul did the job. Again and again, nothing useful.

How he felt about this process — the pressure, anxiety, humiliation — I can only imagine. I just remember the feeling of being so dependent on him, and simultaneously trying to apply zero pressure. The experience of every couple doing IVF must be different, but this part must be the same: the desire to take the pressure off each other, which becomes a kind of super pressure in itself, as each of you withholds your feelings lest you put the other one off their stride.

They weren't sure exactly what the issue was with extracting sperm from Paul's ejaculate. I must admit, I was thinking *I thought there were billions of the fuckers; we only need half a dozen!* They offered the ominous-sounding *surgical retrieval*, and Paul said yes, so the next procedure was his. I was there holding his hand while they cut open his scrotum and fossicked around in there. He couldn't see what they were doing but I could — it was like peeling the skin off a chicken leg. They took what they got into another room to look at it under a microscope and came back in shaking their heads — nothing there. They ended up deciding that Paul's sperm has this kind of condition, something you have from birth, where it never fully matures. Sperm that never grows up. I imagine it as a teenager, for some reason English, like the students at Grange Hill.

It seems horrible to say this now, but I can't even remember whose sperm we used to fertilise my eggs in the end. Was it one of the few mature ones of Paul's? Or was Jonathan's donation back in the picture? And I can't remember how many fertilised embryos we got — actually, they're not even called that: it's the stage before. They tell you how many of the eggs have been fertilised, and then they watch them, and keep you posted, as they divide from one cell into two, and then four, and then eight, and once they reach 32 cells they get called something else.

And you're right deep in the world of it, so you know all the names for things, and the odds of things surviving, so that when you ring up for the news you know exactly what it all means. They hadn't got a great number of viable eggs from me, maybe four, and maybe they fertilised three and implanted a couple, and then it was the weekend and we were waiting to see. I had a good feeling about it. But then, I usually have a good feeling about everything and a lot of bad shit happens anyway.

☀

All these years later I can't remember how we got the news, just that it had failed, that those microscopic specks of hope were just . . . nothing. You can't even call them biowaste — they're just cells that go nowhere, like your body is doing all day long, creating cells and then letting them die and sloughing them off.

Just a note: never say to someone who is struggling to get pregnant, 'Have you thought about adoption?' Yes, they fucking have. It's really not that easy. Not surprisingly, most babies given up for adoption have young parents, and they want their baby to go to a young couple who live on a farm and have horses and a trampoline, not a couple of sad old people living in the city. I knew people who'd done international adoption: a guy I worked with had twin girls from China, a friend's sister had adopted a Romanian orphan. I knew I wouldn't adopt.

And I knew why. It was because I didn't want it badly enough. I didn't want to run down every option, to travel overseas, get a surrogate, find a foster child. I didn't want to keep doing this. I just wanted to stop.

There are two scenes in my mind of when the process ended. I can't remember what order they came in. Paul and I are sitting at our kitchen table. It's round, and it's made of heavy parquet wood with a heavy pedestal base. I always hated that table. And I say to Paul something like, 'I think I want to stop trying.' And he says he thinks the same. We're both crying. And I say, or I think, *I just can't live with the hope anymore.* Because hope has become such a burden by now. It's crushing me.

The other scene is at Fertility Associates. When I was having a smear test one time at the GP, I told the nurse that I was doing fertility treatment there. 'Oh,' she said, 'the doctor there is so handsome, how can you handle it?' The doctor is handsome, and he's kind, and he's a good communicator, he gives you lots of information, and he doesn't talk down to you, he doesn't sugar-coat things. At the last meeting he's having with us, he's going to be giving us bad news — maybe it's about not being able to get any viable sperm from Paul, or maybe it's about our fertilised eggs crapping out, one by one, like soap bubbles popping.

I'm in the waiting room reading a home magazine — it's probably *HOME*, which is hipper than *NZ House & Garden*, and in it there's an artwork of cut-out felt letters sewn onto a white linen cloth, all different colours of letters, and it says WHY ARE THERE SO MANY SONGS ABOUT RAINBOWS. And, in what I can only describe as a small breakdown of the social contract, I tear out that page from the magazine, because I decide I want to buy an artwork like that. We used to sing 'The Rainbow Connection' at school, and Kermit sang it on *The Muppet Show* of course, and I loved the persona of Kermit when he sang, the pathos, and those skinny arms on sticks.

I order the artwork from Australia, even though it's expensive, and I have it expensively framed, and every time I walk past it, for years, I get that song stuck in my head and I find myself mentally singing, at some random point of the day, 'What's so amazing that keeps us star gazing', and I realise it's been running round and round in my head since the morning. That doesn't happen anymore, but for years it did. Anyway, the day I see that artwork is the day of our last visit to Fertility Associates.

No one knows we've *stopped trying*. Well, people know of course, my mum and my sister know, and my dad, and my friend and my grandparents. They all feel sorry for us. 'Enjoy life', my grandma got into the habit of saying to me in the last decade of her life, as an imperative, whenever I would say goodbye to her. I can still hear her saying, *Enjoy life*.

Most people who do IVF don't get pregnant, but you don't hear about that much. Every story you hear is about how awful it was, how difficult, how the embryos died and the sperm wasn't viable and the relationship was strained and then — and then — it happened, and here they are, with their miracle baby, their miracle family. *I never understood the true meaning of love until I had children*. It's something people say all the time. And I always think, *Yeah, fuck you too*. I mean, I'm sure it's true, but it always makes me feel bitter. I think it's because it strikes at the real heart of my fear, my grief about not having children, that there will always be some part of life — the most important, most meaningful part — that I can never experience.

✳

For a long time, I don't like being around babies, except for the ones I know well. I hear about people getting pregnant and it's upsetting, and I hate the fact that people know that — they know that I won't want to hear it, they are protecting me, hiding the news from me, because they know I'm damaged, because I tried and failed. People mention the school holidays, and I feel stupid, because I never know when the school holidays are, am never thinking about them.

I don't like going to places where there are too many parents, because it's a world that I'm not part of and never will be. But when my nephew starts at a new school I go to his assembly, and I sit with the mothers and the fathers and the grandmas, and at one point I move to get a better view. I'm standing at the back, and he is anxiously looking for me in the crowd, and when he sees me he beams out a huge smile. Then they start, the little kids, and they're singing 'If you ever find yourself stuck in the middle of the sea, I'll sail the world to find you', and I'm trying so hard not to cry, because how pathetic would that be, to be not a parent crying, not a mother, but a childless aunt, like something out of a Victorian novel, crying as a class of other people's children sing 'You can count on me like one two three I'll be there'.

People assume I have kids. It happens fairly often, and when I say I don't they go into a whole routine of how strange it is, that they would never just assume that, but there was something that gave them the impression that I did, maybe it's something I've said, or they've seen a kid's drawing at my desk or 'Oh how weird, I don't know why I thought that . . .' And if I like them, I rescue them. I'll say something like, 'Maybe you've seen me with my niece and nephew.' But most of the time I just let them flounder. They've assumed I've got kids because they do, because most people do. Or perhaps they assume that I've got kids because I seem like someone who understands the true meaning of love, and they're flustered to discover I don't.

Hey, I think I've earned the right to make that joke.

People who have kids think they know what it's like not to have kids, because they were childless once. But they don't know. It's different, once you know for sure, once you know you'll never be anyone's mother, anyone's grandmother, anyone's ancestor. At the most basic level, reproducing the species is the purpose of life. After my emotional grief and the sense of failure had faded, I began to experience not having children as a philosophical question. I was already an atheist, and this was like another void, another absence that threatened to suck the meaning out of life. What is the point of me, if I am not part of this primal human chain?

There isn't an answer to that of course. Or there is an answer, which is that there's no point to anything, no point to anyone. Our whole existence as a planet is just a highly improbable, unexpectable accident. It doesn't mean anything. It just is.

Years go by, friends struggle, relationships and families get damaged and break up. *Hey, people with kids are unhappy too*, I realise. So many of them are grieving for something. They have children, but there are still things missing in their lives, holes they can't fill, failures that only they know about. And I start to notice the things I do have, especially the silences, the long, solid silences that can last for hours; the spaciousness of the days as I live them, from the orange light coming in through the pines at dawn to the nights as we lie in our dark grey room, listening to moreporks and the tinny voice of podcasts under our pillows. *I can hear your one.* Those are the things we have. Instead of children, we have space and time. And I try not to take them for granted.

And now, when I see a baby, it doesn't hurt my feelings, and I'm older now so no one says 'cluck cluck' or anything else like that, and I'm not thinking, how pathetic, a childless woman who wants to hold a baby. I just pick it up and smell it, or wave at it, or squeeze its fat little arm. And then I walk away, without it.

Gender rebellion: An Iranian birthright

GOLRIZ GHAHRAMAN

When I was 15 years old I wrote myself a letter. It was to be opened when I turned 30. I forgot all about this, and found it by chance when I was 36. I felt guilty opening the handwritten envelope so late. This 15-year-old woman-to-be had extended her friendship, had made an effort to be remembered by me, to preserve a sense of her in a future she didn't yet know. But reading the letter, I realised she was asserting accountability. It was all about recording her values and expectations, which I better not have violated or failed.

She wanted to be a journalist, like Lois Lane (the TV show *Lois & Clark: The New Adventures of Superman* was big at the time). An international journalist, travelling the world bringing down evil corporations and uncovering injustice. This was all termed in hopeful language: 'I hope by now you are winning awards as a journalist.' Then the tone changes sharply. 'You had better not be married or have any children!'

I was relieved to not be answerable to the uniquely brutal judgement of my 15-year-old self. I wasn't winning awards as a Lois Lane-esque investigative journalist, but I was, and remain, childfree.

The next paragraph before closing was a hilarious and uncomfortable aesthetic description of the boyfriend I was allowed to have. Feminist subversion of gender objectification norms or superficial 15-year-old? We will never know.

✳

But this glimpse into 1997 Golriz does raise questions for me about how my decisions have been shaped over time. Have I been immaculately true to a value system I always had, or have I been wildly overinfluenced by rigid adolescent ideas of what makes a strong, independent woman?

That reflection requires a deep dive into parts of my identity as a woman of colour, an Iranian woman, a child asylum seeker and, most recently, a disabled woman — the intersections of me shape my decisions. The idea of bearing or raising children begins firmly in the place and time of my birth, as well as the fact of my family's displacement as refugees.

I know that when Western society perceives someone like me, a first-generation woman of colour, they do so in terms of the cultural or religious influences of my birthplace. And so there is a strong presumption that I will want or be pressured into the traditional roles of wife and mother. If I choose not to, that is a rebellion. My cultural context, as a child refugee from the so-called 'Muslim World' — though not in fact Muslim — falls squarely within that presumed identity. But while my identity as a heterosexual woman has been fundamentally formed by that background, the influences have pushed in the exact opposite direction to the typecast.

For me, the timeline of impact goes: deep and all-encompassing gender-based persecution and resistance in Iran; refuge, but with it a new sense of othering or alienation in Western white hegemony; seeping of generational trauma and, with that, a sort of survivor's guilt. From that has come a militant rejection of traditional gender roles in response to oppressive patriarchy, rejection of 'normalcy' in response to perceptions of real exclusion from the dominant culture of this adopted Western homeland, and the drive into particularly demanding career pathways to 'earn' the salvation and freedom that so many others did not get. None of this is conducive to parenthood or domesticity.

✳

Being an Iranian woman is a heavy birthright. The war on us began in earnest the year I came into the world — 1981. That year, in very freshly post-revolutionary Iran, women's bodies became a true battleground. Islamic dress codes were imposed by theocratic decree, with a particularly oppressive interpretation of Shari'a law. The Islamic Republic has since proven itself one of the most violent in the modern world, targeting minorities and dissidents with torture, public execution and mass disappearance. But women were always targeted most zealously. Iranian women have taken to the streets by the hundreds of thousands to protest the law, in the face of armed violence, from the beginning. The war on Iranian women waged by the regime rages so furiously even today that it has necessitated several special meetings of the United Nations this year.

I was raised by a generation of Iranian women who saw regime-sponsored, gender-based violence, and resisted it. This was such a deliberate aspect of their lives and identity as women and they openly drilled it into us, the children of the post-revolutionary era. Our homes were filled with absolute shock and anxiety about the sudden repression outside, but also with open discourse about how best to resist. They wanted that resistance known to us. I was brought up not to value marriage over education, travel or financial autonomy. I was raised to speak even where my voice is unfamiliar, unexpected or even unwanted. Because if we submit to gender norms when we have been given the gift of escape, are we wasting it?

Escape came when things became too dangerous for my parents, and we fled to Aotearoa. That anxious journey eventually ended happily when we were recognised as refugees — we were granted asylum and began the work of building new lives. Like any of the more known pressures of migrant children — to excel at school, help with the family business, be proper — as a child of political asylum seekers from a place of gender atrocity, I have always known gender rebellion is my responsibility. This has always been a culture with feminism as fierce as the force facing it.

But the terror of the regime was itself a very palpable part of being a woman during my childhood in Iran, and not easily forgotten. I remember it in the ritual of dressing to leave the house. Checking and rechecking the length and colour of an overcoat, wondering if it was dark enough, long enough, loose enough. Then, defiantly, my mother would paint her lips red.

The patriarchy wanted us to be shapeless, colourless, desexualised. So, feminism over the decades of the Islamic Republic has meant women show as much of their form as they can, and assert their joy and desire as calculated acts of rebellion in the face of death and torture. It is all a rejection of an imposed version of women as pure and virginal, or as servile mothers. While Western women reject sexualisation as part of feminism, we use it to fight the patriarchy. In a world with so little control, every minute act is political.

That defiance was asserted in the face of death, or torture. Only last year, a young Kurdish woman, Mahsa Amini, was beaten to death for wearing her hijab 'improperly'. Mass protests erupted across the nation. A generation of Iranians who have never experienced freedom were willing to die for it. That is what Middle Eastern feminism looks like.

The fact that my worth would never come from 'landing a husband' or having children hasn't been just liberally affirmed. It was an expectation of my upbringing that I would resolutely prefer to forge career paths, become overeducated, travel the world and commit to activism over marriage and motherhood. It's almost comical to think of the disappointment I would have caused if I'd chosen a secure marital match, a big white wedding and children in my mid- to late twenties.

※

As I hit my mid-thirties, and age created a finite point of decision-making for the question of children, I asked myself if I was deliberately childfree. Was it the pressure of escaping gender oppression, or the sense of otherness since? I don't want the brutal misogyny of the Islamic Republic, or any degree of Western white supremacy, to define my life. As much as I hold love and affection for that 15-year-old Golriz of 1997, I also know that her declaration of independence and power was formed as a teen grappling with the trauma of those contexts.

So, I looked into it more carefully. I did the fertility tests, just like many women of my generation. The doctor presented me with my results accompanied by the full chart of fertility gradings, and mine were represented brightly with a little yellow dot of fertility in the 'good' section. After that affirmation, I felt like I could put this over-intellectualised question on the back burner.

Then, life suddenly brought it into sharp focus. Due to stabs of unending pain in what I thought was my gut, I learnt I had a massive fibroid tumour on my uterus. It had gone undetected for so long that it was threatening my other organs and causing infection. I needed urgent surgery. My surgeon, thankfully a woman with great empathy, was committed to doing this by keyhole and didn't force any intrusive questions about babies. Except that due to the size of the tumour there was a chance that things wouldn't go as planned. So the question came: Would I rather she perform a hysterectomy if things got complicated, or should she sew me back up so I could make the decision later? To my own absolute shock, I said I would rather keep my uterus.

I think that as women we're often treated like a machine with parts. Our cycle constantly reminds us of it, as does the persistent question of when we will do our job of creating children. I was shocked that I wasn't immediately just glad to be rid of that dehumanising function. I felt I would miss her, my wee uterus and, with her, that part of myself that may still find meaning in the biological opportunity of motherhood. But I didn't think about doing it for real until years later.

I don't think that I've ever consciously deprioritised parenting for my career or other priorities, as I know others have done. I just never felt the pull. I have been lucky that other meaningful paths have had desperately urgent pulls upon my focus, and my heart. I've never found the demands of my work, moving across the globe, or being an MP to be a burden in this regard (on mental and physical health, yes, but not as delays to reproduction).

When I finally decided to have a serious conversation with my partner about whether we might have children, that conversation happened in the context of us living and working across two cities. Life isn't conventional in terms of domestic partnership. It means that I live with friends I think of as family in one place, including my daughter-cat, June. My life doesn't need to be measured against other relationships, human priorities or ways of creating good. So, when we did talk about it, it was from a vantage point of what we might like to share between us, if we were to bring a new person into the world. How we would manage intergenerational trauma — and my disability. We are both from backgrounds with race, migration and poverty in our childhoods. In my case, add to that war and a displacement. Familial relations can be fraught in those contexts.

The question isn't just 'Do I want to have a kid?', but also 'Should I actually have a whole lot more therapy and sit this one out?' What child wants a parent who just wrote an essay about something as intimate as motherhood by talking about the history of the Iranian Revolution? Is it OK to carry that level of, let's face it, trauma, into another generation without a lived experience of what caused it? This poor kid would be visibly and in name Iranian (because if I have to live with unproducible Farsi soundscapes every time someone says my name, they'll have to).

And they'd be raised by me, a mother who won't be able to read Farsi stories or cook Iranian food (devastating). It isn't about that, but it is about being Iranian enough for those of us born elsewhere or who moved as children. I get that there are self-loving answers to all of these questions. But asking the questions is important, and so is having the safe space to talk them out without the easy answers, without judgement.

This was a conversation my partner and I could have because we both felt it. I don't feel like I need to share our responses to those intimate questions, but I do want to acknowledge that the questions and conversations are different to what others may expect. For me it really hasn't been the one that is in dominant culture — not 'whether women can have it all', or 'career vs motherhood' — at all.

❋

I realised after six years in public life that my job is not just as a legislator, but as a representative. That includes every bit of me, from my refugee background to my gender — that is what people see when I step onto a stage or give a debate speech.

When I speak at gatherings where voices like mine have clearly not been platformed, there often comes a 'well-meaning' question: 'How do we help other migrants assimilate as well as you have?' I would always respond with a question: 'What makes you think I've assimilated at all?' The responses are generally a list of compliments about being a Westernised woman. 'You're a feminist, you're independent, you're educated . . . you wear modern dress.' I explain that I learnt feminism from feminists who were willing to face tanks for equality. Nothing gives you the undying urge to burn oppressive gender norms to the ground like knowing people were tortured for it.

But teaching people the strength of non-Western culture isn't the central benefit of this platform. Representation matters to our own communities, who are internally diverse. Being a brown, unwed woman, with uncertainty over whether motherhood is or will ever be my thing, is also representation. I know there are others with the insecurities and pressures, internalised and overt, that I have faced. They are very different to those of status quo groups, and we should probably talk about them.

Of wire and cloth
GRÁINNE PATTERSON

I find out the real reason I can't have children through a podcast.[1] I'm driving at the time, and when it hits me I hold my breath, become very aware I'm supposed to be in control of a vehicle, and squint through blurry, tear-filled eyes to find a safe place to pull over. I find a ramp that drops off the road and into a parking area right on the edge of the ocean. Mine is the only car here, my body is free to fall apart. I pull up the hand break, push back my seat, fold myself as far forward as I can, and sob.

When I come back up for air, hiccuping and decorated with the salt tracks of my tears, I notice my car is facing waves crashing against a sea wall. I realise I'm a few miles from Paekākāriki. I'm on my way to visit a friend, a brand-new mother, ecstatic and exhausted. She has named her baby, born between the spring equinox and the summer solstice, Jasper. Beside me, sitting in the passenger seat, are two lasagnes, one to freeze, one to eat, some tiny clothes wrapped in paper. I message her to say traffic is bad and I'll be a bit late.

The podcast that rendered me unable to drive explored and explained the initial experiments that taught us the basis of everything we currently know

---

1   Blindboy Boatclub [David Chambers], 'Attachment Theory', The Blindboy Podcast, 14 July 2021.

about attachment theory. I had somewhat smugly put it on — attachment was a safe subject for me, having 'done the work', investigated, prodded within myself, found my aching wounds, healing what I could and monitoring what I couldn't. A podcast on attachment was theoretically a break for me, a victory lap for all the work I had done. But I hadn't ever heard about the experiments before.

❋

Before attachment theory, scientists used to believe that whoever fed a baby would become a mother in the baby's eyes. But in 1958 they conducted The Wire Monkey Experiment. They took newborn monkeys and put them in cages without their mothers. Instead, they fed them with mechanical monkey-like wire structures with bottles attached. They wanted to know if the babies would attach to an inanimate object like they do to their mothers if this object was their source of food.

I imagined the baby, being fed by this hard thing, gripping their tiny fingers around bald metal, mechanical elbows, rigid angles made for rejecting, searching for fur to cling to. Their fingers evolutionarily primed to grip the moment they begin falling, with nothing to hold on to. Left to climb the empty scaffolding where the warm heartbeat of their mother should be. Feeding, looking up and searching for eyes to look back at them.

In their cages was another fake monkey, which had no food source but was covered in soft cushioning and cloth materials that the baby could snuggle into. Surprising the scientists, the babies would feed just enough from the wire monkey but then spend entire days clinging to the cloth mother. In further experiments, they removed the cloth mother altogether, to see how the babies of the wire mother would turn out.

They learnt that when those babies grew up to have their own children, the ones who had been raised by the cloth mother were able to be parents themselves. The ones raised by the wire one weren't. Mating was a struggle, and those who did mate and manage to birth a baby were utterly incapable of being a mother. The worst cases report the mother smashing her baby's skull into the concrete floor of her cage.

❋

was a daughter to my mother before I was a mother to her, but not for long. When I was four years old, she became unable to care for me. I have a few memories of her before this time, holding me, releasing myself completely into her warmth. We're always cast in sunlight, which can't have been possible given that it was Ireland, but it feels true in my memory. Then things got harder, and every day she became less and less able to be the mother that I needed her to be. And while other kids were out getting temporary tattoos, friends and personalities, I spent days at the pub with her, made sure she got home, sat up all night, holding the eggshells of her together. I cared for her, was a planet drawn entirely into her orbit, until I was put into foster care when I was 11.

A friend once told me that she felt she needed to have a child because people who don't never live through the experience of giving themselves entirely to another human. I thought she was right until I realised, in caring for my mother from a young age, I had done that. She had been the centre of my universe. I breathed for her, edited every single instinct I had for her, protected her, cleaned up her bodily spills. I had lived for her, I had mothered her. This is something I've known in the background of myself for a long time. But I don't pull all the pieces together until the podcast does it for me.

※

remember a story I wrote when I was seven called 'When I am 21'. I boldly gave myself four children with my devoted husband, a thriving career as a vet, two large dogs, and a house by the beach that I own. That version of me, that young me with absolute disregard for realistic timeframes, believed that she could be a mother, a good mother, so good that she could have more and more children, that her capacity and love and energy would never end.

She believed she had everything she needed to love and raise another human being in this life. But as an older child, teenager, adult, I would scoff at the idea of ever having a child, shielding myself behind remarks about kids being a burden, of wanting to travel, to save money, a snobbish look down on those who chose to procreate on an already heaving planet.

I would resent having a period each month — why should I have to keep dealing with my womb if I'm never planning to use it? I considered a hysterectomy, I considered being a surrogate. I felt like one of those people who doesn't know how to use their oven so they store jumpers in it instead. The core of me, the essential, life-giving cocoon of my body, utterly redundant, embarrassing, like bringing a hiking bag to buy bread at the dairy.

But reasons to not have children were all softeners to the truth the podcast revealed to me, to that I, due to have four kids by the age of 21, with my responsible management job and all the people who look to me for answers, who is trusted to look after the offspring of my closest friends: the deeply held, terrifying, secret belief that if I was a mother, I would smash my baby's skull into the concrete floor of my cage.

I wondered if it was part of my design, like a finger pressing down, pushing a jigsaw piece into a shaped hole that fits just right. Is it the sort of thing that happens on purpose, for purpose?

Are we supposed to judge the monkey who kills her baby? Are we supposed to be surprised that she has anything in her other than exhaustion and rage? If the neurons of your brain are formed by constant rejection, when a little one comes to love you, surely all you have left in you is the ability to reject them too?

※

When I take care of my friends' children, I don't explicitly share the image with them, the fear that I am a traumatised monkey, ready to brutally kill my offspring. It's different with their children. I can hand them back, remember that the buck for them ends nowhere near me. I can be present and play, hold them while they cry, let them sleep on me. And then take a nap to compensate for how much energy it took for me to be with them.

Sometimes I take my friend's baby on walks; they sleep in a front pack, face nuzzled against my chest. People pass, nod at me; in their eyes a mum, holding my beautiful, nurtured, safe baby. I nod back and, for a moment, allow the feeling of it to sit inside me.

Yes, I am that person you're imagining
Yes, I'm a mum and have always wanted to be
Yes, I can handle the late nights and the feeding and just how much this
little one needs me
Yes, I know they cannot distinguish my body from their own
Yes, I grew them inside of me
Yes, they will always be a part of me
I am their mother,
a person who knew enough about what being mothered felt like
that she was able to try it herself.

And then they pass, the moment passes, I am not that person. And I bring the baby home, back to their mother's soft arms.

I've recently discovered 'mother energy' as a concept. It was first described to me by my therapist as a salve for those who walk around this world without a present, caring, capable mother. He said it lives in nature, in gushing rivers full of life, in the grass that holds me up and the tree that allows me to lean my back against it, in the kindness of strangers, a barista or clerk who is much nicer to me than their job demands. At first, I called it bullshit. I told him that I didn't want some shitty patchwork of a mother crudely glued together from the scraps of the universe's abundant and withholding table, that I wanted a real mum, a proper mum like everyone else had, one that was just for me.

But in time, I softened to it, realised he's right — this mother energy, it lives in many places, and most of all it lives in me. So when I found myself desperate to feel the love of a mother, I would take myself out for hot chocolate, go to an op shop and let the little wound in me wander the toy section, buy finger paints and big crayons and other things that can be used to express what life feels like before words can be formed. I'd build sandcastles, ask my partner to hold me, plant flowers and watch films made for children. I'd hold the unmothered parts of me and whisper different secrets in their ears.

I'm glad you were born.
I have all the time in the world for you.
You can rest in me.

❈

On one particularly hard day, as the insides of me were crawling, desperate for some relief from the pain I was feeling, I found myself, somehow, standing in a baby store.

One of the staff members approached to ask if I needed help. I told her I was fine — just browsing — for a friend — she's just had a baby — two weeks ago — the birth went well — I kept adding even though she was walking away from me. I went straight to the bottle section, deciding simultaneously that I'd never come back here and that I'd come too far to leave empty-handed. There were so many to choose from: just teats, just bottles, sets of three, newborn, toddler, temperature-controlled, slow-flow, anti-colic (pro-colic?), plastic, glass, plain, sparkles, lions, birds, polka dots. I grabbed the one closest to my outstretched hand and brought it to the counter.

'You know, this bottle isn't one you'd buy for newborns, do you want me to show you the—'

'No, no thanks, this is for a different baby, they sent me the link, not the baby, the mum, this is the right one, thanks.'

❋

At bedtime I went downstairs to heat up some milk from the fridge. My housemates were around, cleaning up after their dinner, my partner away on a hike. I am just an adult heating up some milk before bed. A little childish, maybe, but not weird. If it was a hot chocolate or a cup of tea no one would bat an eyelid. This is fine, this is fine, this is fine.

I obviously didn't bring the bottle into the kitchen. I carried an adult cup of warm milk up to my room, shouting goodnight to my housemates as I went. I pulled the bottle out from its sordid hiding place between a pack of watercolours and a colouring-in book, and while there I pulled out my pink Care Bear teddy, too. I triple checked the door was locked, and then poured the warm milk into the bottle.

What am I trying to achieve? I asked myself. But questions like that are made of words and words aren't really a part of what I'm doing. If I had words when what happened to me happened to me, I wouldn't be 32 and looking at a baby's bottle that I'm about to drink. No, the pain happened before I could use words and when the pain returns, it renders them useless. Sometimes it happens when my partner is with me; the pain rises up my spine, into my brain, stealing my words, my thoughts. 'Just talk to me,' he says, exasperated and betrayed. I stare out at him, gagged and desperate, wishing I could.

I got into bed; I'd saved my nicest, softest pyjamas for this moment. I pulled the blankets over me, pulled the teddy close. The milk was hot, and I squirted some onto the underside of my wrist to check the temperature. I paused, mid-ritual, reminding myself no one will see me, reminding myself I never need to tell a soul I'm doing this.

And then I do it, I snuggle into the blankets, lie back like I don't need to hold the weight of my own head, and I drink. My hand lifts the bottle up for me and I pretend it's not mine. It feels how I expect it to feel. It's everything. I feel a rush of being young, being held. I feel a rush of holding something that I love more than anything else in the world.

It's love, it's entirely made of love.

When I'm finished, I put the bottle back into its hiding place in case my partner arrives home or a housemate drops by unexpectedly. Then I lie back down, belly full, heart full. Warm, not even remembering to feel silly about it.

And all at once, I am full of the feeling of finally having a mother, finally having a baby of my own, all at the same time. It's not the same, it'll never be the same, but it's something.

✳

J asper is almost two years old now, and I am 34. Recently we all moved in together, a group of friends, eight adults to circle and enwrap this little soul.

I get home from work and run up the stairs to find my little friend. They're already waiting at the top to greet me, their face smushed hard against the bars of their baby gate.

They reach up to be held with a smile and a 'Ganya uppy'. When I lift them, they wrap their tiny legs around my arm so I can't put them down. We walk out onto the deck; 'moana', they whisper, and brush their soft cheek against mine.

✳

T here are those who want to be parents and can't, who don't want to be but can. There are those who are parents whether they want to be or not. And there are those of us who never got the choice because the role was given to us at an age too young for choice or consent to happen. I've grieved the feeling: not the grief of not being a mother, but the grief of not having the option to be. Sometimes it's easy and sometimes it's not. But for now, with this beautiful toddler in my arms, the sunset in their eyes, pointing out manu and producing a soggy cracker from I don't know where and placing it gently into my mouth, for now, it's all I could possibly want, I can't imagine ever wanting more.

The feminist shelf

HAZEL PHILLIPS

The nightmares began the day my mother told me God had spoken to her and, according to his will, I would marry Robbie Andrew.

Robbie was a beige-coloured man with plentiful flesh around his middle, pants held up by an extra-long belt and chins that wobbled when he laughed. He was the sidekick of Harry, our youth pastor, who food-shamed me if I ate anything at church functions — although if people in glass houses shouldn't throw stones, Harry must've had shares in Novus.

'Figures, ladies, figures,' Harry would crow, leaning over me, the coconut flakes from the lamingtons he shoved into his face flying like bark off a logging truck.

I was fat too, I knew, and 'beggars can't be choosers', or so my mother's finger-wagging friends reminded me. I learnt it was safer not to eat in public. Fat men could eat; fat girls could not.

'I've had a word from the Lord,' my mother informed me one day, her face beaming. 'You are going to marry . . . (she paused here for maximum emphasis) . . . Robbie Andrew!'

The triumph in her voice I can only denote here via an exclamation mark, but it was much more than that. It was the joy of a mother whose fat, plain daughter hadn't caught the attention of any of the young men in the church youth group and, at the old age of 18, was a spinster left on the shelf. *Finally*, I could see her thinking, *I can join the other mothers in reading bridal magazines and planning a wedding.* I could see her envisioning herself sitting in a pew with me and my good Christian husband Robbie to her left, babies slowly being added next to us as the years went by.

That night I woke up in a cold sweat, with Robbie Andrew naked on top of me, crushing me so that I was unable to breathe or cry out. I had no agency, no choice. Robbie had all the control.

Nightmares tend to disappear quickly, like tendrils of fog on an early morning lake. This one persisted even as I lay there in bed, calming my panic. Finally I had to get up and turn on the light to fully convince myself that Robbie *wasn't actually there* and I was safe.

☀

In Bible study we discussed the story of Jesus' conception. The angel Gabriel visited Mary, a young virgin girl — they reckon she was as young as 13, as that's when Jewish maidens were considered marriageable — and told her she'd be having his baby.

'You will become pregnant, give birth to a son and name him Jesus,' Gabriel said to Mary. 'He will be a great man and will be called the Son of the Most High.'

Mary told Gabriel that was impossible. 'I'm a virgin,' she said. 'Fuck off.' (I made up that second bit.)

Gabriel told her how it would happen — the Holy Spirit would 'come' to her and 'overshadow' her, and then a holy child would develop inside her.

Mary had no control over her marriage, her life or her impending pregnancy. Her father had handed her legal rights to Joseph, her husband-to-be. The Bible's narrative is that Mary submitted obediently to this — because she said 'let it be' — but conveniently ignores the power imbalance and Mary's utter lack of autonomy. At 13 years old, being informed of her fate by an authority figure means she couldn't have consented.

And all that makes Christianity not a very nice concept.

My nightmares started to take on another dimension, one where sweaty Robbie had somehow magically impregnated me. I was forced to carry the baby unwed, going to church with my mother sitting in another pew, her lips tightly closed and her gaze resolutely not meeting mine, my bulging belly a tangible marker of shame.

In another nightmare, an alien baby punched its way out through my stomach and I lay on the pulpit bleeding to death while Harry the pastor stood over me, a vein in his forehead pulsing while he screamed 'SATAN, BE GONE!'

※

T he model of the good biblical nuclear heteronormative family had been drilled into my brain, but when I got to university in Dunedin in 1997 I found that nobody was particularly interested in me romantically, even if I was interested in them. So the idea of having to get married or accidentally getting pregnant was moot anyway.

But it stuck in my head, those first few years at university: *You're going to have to get married and have babies at some stage. You don't have a choice, even if you do manage to avoid getting hitched to Robbie Andrew.*

One day, on a mission to find a reference for an essay, I inadvertently discovered the feminist shelf within the Dewey system at the main university library: 305.42, a small and modest collection.

The book that beckoned me was purple with a shiny dust jacket. I ran my finger down the spine and reached up to pull it away from its friends. GLORIA STEINEM, it announced in cream-coloured all-caps across the top of the front cover. And below it, *OUTRAGEOUS ACTS AND EVERYDAY REBELLIONS*. Gloria's face beamed at me with pleasing symmetry, her blonde hair parted exactly in the middle and her aviator-shaped, thin-rimmed glasses giving her just the right dose of intelligent lady chic. The arms of the glasses were tucked into the hair — I would come to realise this was Gloria's trademark look — so that some hair was trapped in between the arms and her face. She looked neither rebellious nor outrageous, but shiny and perhaps Californian. I flipped through the pages. 'I was a Playboy Bunny', one chapter sang.

In 1963 Gloria went undercover as a 'bunny' at one of Hugh Hefner's nightclubs. The get-up was uncomfortable, the sexism rife. She held the gig for three weeks, including undergoing an internal vaginal examination (ostensibly to check for venereal disease), compulsory for her employment. The resulting piece launched her as a journalist and leading feminist thinker.

I took Gloria with me that day. Touching Gloria's purple dust jacket was a tipping point, an intersection in life that sent me down a sudden and unexpected path, like a car swerving left without indicating. Gloria was an angel, a signpost.

After Gloria I discovered Betty Friedan and Germaine Greer, who my mother said was thrown in jail for saying 'fuck' (she didn't — she said 'bullshit' and was arrested). Naomi Wolf's *The Beauty Myth* relieved my angst over not looking pretty enough to attract boys, and Gloria made me understand why I didn't find them that interesting, anyway. Most of all, Gloria flipped the switch on the idea that I didn't actually have to get married, or have babies.

And so I didn't.

❋

Whenever I said I didn't want children, I'd be subjected to condescending platitudes: 'Oh, you'll want kids one day.' 'Oh, I used to say the same and then I had this massive surge of hormones and I changed my mind — the same thing will happen to you too, just you wait.' 'You'll want kids when you meet the right man.' The compulsory heteronormativity blows my mind.

I was warned my body would scream for impregnation before my fertility began to decline before menopause. It never happened. I never wanted children, and I also never feared that I might change my mind. I knew I didn't want them. I knew my own mind.

The first person who ever took me entirely seriously when I said I didn't want to have kids was my gynaecologist, who I saw when I was 43 after suffering heavy periods with pain that didn't ease even with up to 30 painkillers per day in a cocktail of ibuprofen, naproxen, codeine, tramadol and gabapentin. And yes, I was off my chops with all of that, but still the pain persisted. I spent days each month lying in bed with a heat pack, gripped by waves of stabbing in my uterus.

My GP said it was all in my head and recommended 'mindfulness techniques', and I said, 'Fuck you'. (Yeah, I made that last bit up too.) I demanded a referral to a gynaecologist. 'You tell a good story,' the gynaecologist said at my first consultation, referring to his suspicion that I had endometriosis. I felt that the word 'story' was loaded with another meaning: that I was making shit up, that it might not be true.

I didn't think I had endometriosis, but I knew something wasn't right. I was suffering from persistent pain, a feeling of things pulling on each other, of something inside me that was constantly pushing on something else.

I reassured him that if it came to it, I'd happily have a hysterectomy and not to worry, I didn't want kids. He laughed. Like, he actually laughed.

'Hazel, you're 43, it's never going to happen.' His laughter tinkled down the corridor.

That was the first time someone had taken me seriously when I expressed that I didn't want to have children.

On performing surgery, he didn't find much to show for my 'story' of suspected endometriosis — but he did pull out a fibroid and an assortment of other weird tissue, and detached my organs from one another. The fibroid looked like a garlic bulb, and its absence was an immediate relief. The next month I took four naproxen for my period pain and continued on with normal life. But of course, those mindfulness techniques would've been just as effective.

❋

Women who have babies take on the risk of getting done over by their partners. I'd witnessed enough horror stories from women who had to do all the childcare, cooking, cleaning and emotional labour as well as holding down a demanding job. I saw how risky it is for women if the husband is violent, or he leaves, or just opts out of being a father altogether.

A coworker got pregnant and decided to have the baby when the father swore he'd stand by her, only for him to turn around later — when it was much too late for her to have a termination — and decide he couldn't really be faffed with that, after all.

I also didn't want some*thing* taking over my body. The idea of my body not being *mine* for nine months — not to mention the ongoing breastfeeding and demands and being 'touched out' — was unbearable. I already suffered period issues, headaches, migraine and iron deficiency, and all of that was enough for me in terms of my body doing things I didn't want it to do.

❋

There was a brief foray into step-parenting after I met a bloke who had three kids to two women and I walked right past all the red flags and into a relationship, finding myself very quickly in the position of an overloaded stepmum to two out of the three kids. I was terrified I'd turn into my mother but those fears were unfounded, as I loved them in my own way.

Their mother, though, sharpened her knives for me, unable to cope with happy reports from her kids on a Monday morning about what we'd done on the weekend. Letters to lawyers were littered with false accusations. I began to wonder where this toxic vortex of drama ended and reality began. The relationship ended, to my relief, and my mental and emotional health were mine again, my life back under my own control. I had no one wanting things from me constantly and I was freed from the parental tug-of-war. There was quiet, mental peace and space where there had been none for so long. Contrary to what people had always told me — 'You'll want kids when you meet the right man' — the stepmum experience validated my decision not to.

'You're selfish,' people tell you, but they forget that the world we live in isn't really fit for bringing more people into, and the world's population is bursting at the seams.

'Who will look after you when you're older?' they ask. I eventually became estranged from my own mother, and it felt like the mother–daughter dynamic was no guarantee of ongoing security, anyway.

I've played around with words to try to find a label that fits. They'll call you childless, which sounds like you wanted them and failed. Or childfree, which sounds like 'carefree' and implies you're a lifestyler with bags of cash and a stone-cold heart. I came across 'unchilded' but that too connotes desire without production. You might be sterile, infertile, barren, unfruitful, infecund or impotent, the thesaurus will inform you, all the way to dull, vain, pointless, uninspiring, dry, uninteresting, vapid, aimless and commonplace. But somehow we can't wrap our heads around the idea of someone being childfree by choice. *You don't know your own mind.*

At some point people stopped asking me about kids, probably realising that I was too old for it before I realised, though my gynaecologist certainly did. I continue to go about my life happily childfree, never doubting my decision, never doubting my lack of doubt, knowing myself even if others don't know me, or want to doubt me.

※

I never married Robbie Andrew. I did look up some of the people I went to church with way back, flicking through Facebook photos of smiling babies, Christian memes, Bible verses and selfies from the anti-vaccination 'Freedom' protests. They've all adhered to expectations — all neatly coupled off with 2.5 kids, a white picket fence and plush leather covers for their Bibles.

I still have the nightmares, though Robbie Andrew is more faceless now. Sometimes in my nightmares I see not myself but a young girl. She's surrounded by church people, trapped and silent, but she's holding a slim purple book to guard herself against other people's fixed ideas. If I look carefully, before the edge of waking grips me, I can make out the title: *Outrageous Acts and Everyday Rebellions.*

We're your mother now

HELEN RICKERBY

We have a daughter. She is always between the ages of about four and seven — I am not very good at judging people's ages and children are no exception. She has his hair, but my hair colour, and so looks basically like Shirley Temple at the height of her fame. She is sweet and, while precocious, is the kind of child who can entertain herself. Like us, she learnt to read early, without much effort. She is not fussy, she is never annoying and she never impinges on my life. This is because she is not real. I would not say I love my hypothetical child, but I am a bit curious about her.

※

We were aged about 15. We were in Z's room. She was lying on her bed and I was sitting on the edge. Not long before this, the American missionary lady had visited town, the one who was beautiful, fat, single (divorced) and everyone was a bit in love with her. She had dyed black hair, wore clothes made of shiny fabrics in bright colours and always had that young Indonesian man with her (I assumed it was platonic). I think she probably had something to do with what I was saying to Z, which was that I thought I was going to be a missionary in Africa. That I would never marry, never have children, and most probably would be martyred for my faith. Z is crying. She doesn't want me to die. I don't especially want to die, not usually (though it's true I do sometimes look at rafters, pills, sharp objects with a sort of longing), but there are going to have to be sacrifices. I don't know then that in only a few short years I will lose my faith entirely. But I will have decided to live.

✻

I never actually disliked children — well not all of them, not all the time — but I sometimes joked that I did. That is probably why S felt he needed to have that talk with me so soon after we'd gotten together. I hadn't been looking for a relationship of a serious sort, but it had become very serious very quickly after that first almost-accidental kiss at a post-wedding party. It dawned on me with a clinical clarity that he fitted me in a way no one else ever had; and I realised I was in love when, after a trans-Tasman phone call (I was in Melbourne on holiday), I had an image in my head of two goldfish swimming in water: we were the goldfish and the water was love. We both knew this was probably 'it'. We were sitting in my large bedroom in my small flat: 'I'd like to be a dad one day,' he said. Or was it a question? I felt neutral enough that I was willing to consider it, found I was open to it, seeing as it was what he wanted, and perhaps I wanted it, too? One day?

✻

Most days I message with M and L. We tell each other what's been going on, what's bothering us, what's making us happy. We sympathise. We listen. We advise. M's mother had already died more than a year ago. L's mother had died only an hour or so before I got the call. I immediately put on my shoes and ordered an Uber. I took some chocolate, because that was all I could find. She cried, I held her. L's almost-grown-up child made us cups of tea. We drank them. We ate some chocolate. Recounting it, it sounds very strange even to me, even cruel, but what I said to her was: 'We're your mother now,' meaning M and me. L knew what I meant, that I meant a continuation of a voluntary process that had begun years ago, when we started opening up to each other and caring for each other, and would continue probably until we are all dead.

✻

I have heard how the biological desire for children can come on like a fever —
like a kick in the stomach. Other women have told me their stories; women
who had children and women who didn't. Women who had been convinced
they would never want a child, until suddenly that was a hunger they couldn't
sate any other way. Women who had always known they wanted a child, and
now cried every time they got their period. Also women who, in their hearts,
knew they did not really want a child, even though their body was trying to
trick them into thinking that they did. I kept half an eye out for this hunger,
this ache, but it never came.

※

In my teens, when I was first allowed to catch the train all the way to
Wellington with my best friend, K, we'd wander through the city, have lunch
at McDonalds, and shop for clothes at Shanton. We would stand in for each
other's mother as we emerged from the changing rooms: 'It looks nice, but
are you *sure* you want it?' And it was K who, when I got my first period on her
birthday, stood in the bathroom doorway waving the sanitary pad her mother
had given her, which, for reasons I didn't and still don't understand, I was
reluctant to take.

※

I am not good at making decisions — I feel, rather, that decisions make me. I
could make lists of pros and cons, like you're supposed to do, but if I already
know what I want, I would ignore the list, and if I didn't know what I wanted,
I would not just choose the option with the most pros or least cons. In the
same way as I do everything else, I make decisions in an intuitive way. What
sits right with me? What do I feel sad about losing if I think about choosing
the other option? When we came to select our first tenant for the little flat
below our beloved house, after the tenant we inherited left, S, who is a policy
analyst, suggested we create a framework of decision-making criteria. 'But I
already know who I want,' I said, and he said, 'Well, we'll write the criteria to
fit that.'

※

It was always five years in the future. It was always an intention rather than a
plan. It was something for later, for when it was time. But then it was time that
if we were going to do it we had better get on with it, and we found, without

very much soul-searching — on my part at least — that we didn't actually want to do it after all. But, writing about it now, I wonder if that is really how it went? When did I stop taking the birth control pills — was that before or after we decided? It had been a long time since the 'scare', when we thought I might be. When we talked about what we would do, how we would go with it, make it our life, how it would be OK. But no. I wasn't. And I was relieved.

※

I have gotten off lightly, I know. In many aspects of my life. My dad tried to get me to do statistics in seventh form, but I didn't. I recall no fallout. (Though I did know to not even try to take practical maths — 'cabbage' maths — instead of 'proper' maths.) I was not expected to do law or medicine. I was not presented with a blueprint. When my teacher threatened me with failing sixth-form biology because I had stopped paying attention, my mum told me that she failed something once, in a calming sort of way, so I wouldn't feel my life would be over. (I did not fail.) I also remember her saying to me, about children: 'It's different when they're your own.' And once or twice asking me if I was quite sure I didn't want any. But otherwise, silence.

※

When we first saw this house, I fell in love with it. I fell in love, specifically, with the view over the city and harbour. Cloud height, birds' flight, the light. It was something I wanted, no pros and cons, but not something I could just have, no matter how much I wanted it. You can pray to gods, you can try spells, you can wish, bargain with entities that may or may not exist. Despite what reality TV contestants seem to believe, you can't win something just by wanting it the most. But we did get this house, in a tender, probably because we were the least afraid of the slip at the front of the property, and the most willing to put up with the weirdness of the rooms. Buying a house is like buying a future, buying a space for a future, the ghosts of your future selves wandering through it. We were still thinking that we might, five years away perhaps. That we might be needing a space for a smaller person or people, who would then grow and need more space.

※

Novelist Sheila Heti and her interviewer are talking about motherhood. And *Motherhood*. The concept, and the book (by Heti, which I have not yet read).

Heti says she feels guilty for not wanting to be a mother, and the interviewer says she feels guilty that she wanted it so much. I do not recognise myself in either of these women, but I am feeling angry. I blame society, I blame capitalism, I blame the patriarchy for always wanting women to feel guilty. There are a lot of things to feel guilty about, but for me this is not one of them.

※

I hope I don't appear to others as a selfish person, but I have arranged my life so I can be. So I can mostly do what I like, mostly when I like, with who I like. That is not to say that I don't consider other people and their feelings and needs — I do, or try to. People have said to me that I would be a good mother, and I know what they mean. That I seem to be fairly patient, even-tempered, gentle. I am often someone who swoops in with a hug, listening ears, advice — well-meant, but maybe sometimes too much. But then I get to go home. Then I close the door.

※

The closest thing to a biological kick in the guts was perhaps after G married her girlfriend and they planned to have children. With her talk of sperm donors, S wondered aloud to me if he might want to do that, be a sperm donor. And, being a picture-thinking kind of person, I had an image of some child, perhaps the Shirley Temple girl, who was part S and not mine, who did not belong to me, and I felt a strong, maybe biological, reaction inside myself that I did not understand, did not approve of, which did not match with my values and the way S and I run our relationship, and which screamed *No! No! No!*

※

When I was about seven, most afternoons on TV they would show at least one ad for Baby Alive, a baby doll that had eyes that closed when you laid it down, opened when you picked it up, that would eat mush of some kind, and then would transport it through its torso, somehow, before excreting it like a real baby. It's hard to imagine — I mean, it sounds only creepy and messy — but those ads clearly worked on me because I desired one with an all-consuming passion. I can feel that white-hot want even now as I remember how I would sneak over to the kitchen where my mother was making dinner: 'Please can I have a Baby Alive? Please, please, please?' I went so far as to write her a little begging note, saying how much I wanted one of those marvels, and possibly how completely and eternally happy it would make me. My mother did not give in. And I did not save up all my pocket money to buy one — probably they were several times the cost of a Strawberry Shortcake doll. Far, far out of reach, like a Cabbage Patch Kid.

*

There may not seem to be much conflict in this story, but the more I write, the more I feel it just under the surface. And not only because it has been simpler for me than for S, though that is his story, not mine. I have rarely had doubts, and I think I am realistic. I know how we like to live, how we both say every now and then, with great gratitude and relief, 'Thank God we don't have children!' But is there a parallel universe in which we have a real child or children, not hypothetical ones. Is our life richer? Are we happier? Are we better people? Or are we just more tired?

*

My friend F is telling me how not being able to conceive another child destroyed her confidence; not being able to do something that she felt she should be able to do, something that was natural. I start to understand things I didn't before. And I realise that it is probably just as well I didn't want to, because it has become increasingly clear to me that we probably couldn't have, even if we had wanted to. I have saved myself some heartbreak. I know the ache of wanting something that you cannot have. I understand how it can twist inside of you, slicing you up.

*

Because I am not anyone's mother, my mothering relationships are rarely one way. If it's too unbalanced, and I find I'm the looker-after-er, the listener, the unpaid counsellor, then it's not a relationship that is going to last. Like when I suddenly became the confidante of a girl at school who suspected she was pregnant. Why it was me and not her better friend I'm not sure, but I went to the doctor with her, to get the test to confirm what she already knew, to tell the doctor what she'd already decided, and to make the plans for the abortion. Having been brought up in the way I was, I thought abortion was basically murder, but even then I knew — as I told my mum in the car after she'd picked me up — that it was the right thing for her to do.

*

Some of my best friends are parents. They talk to me about their children, and their problems with their children. I am always sympathetic, but I often find I put myself in the place of their child. Having not been a parent, that place is more familiar. M (who has three) once said that I was useful at giving a child's perspective, which I chose to take as a compliment, even though it was a little backhanded. Recently I have noticed a flurry of articles by and about women who are childfree or childless, and some of the childless find other people talking about their children a sharp pain to their hearts. And I realised how hard it would be to stay close with my dearest friends if every time they talked about their children it caused me pain, grief and envy, rather than the mild relief that their lives, as much as they suit them, are not mine.

※

When I got there I realised what they hadn't told me. That she was not in quite the same reality. This had not happened before, not as far as I knew. She was fairly calm when I found her, lying across the chairs in the corridor that doubled as the special waiting area, and she was sort of trying to sleep — something she hadn't been able to do for a few days now. I was already tired and had been on my way to bed when the call came. I didn't want to, but I knew I should, so I did. My tiredness, and knowing I couldn't leave and was now in charge, led to a rising panic inside me. I was not sure I could handle this. I was not sure I could breathe. I had a horror of the uncanny. But I could pretend to be calm, pretend I was an adult, though I did text S that I was feeling a bit overwhelmed. She wasn't sleeping, she was chatting like a hyperactive but quite bossy child. I resisted a strong urge to just leave, to run away. I stayed. After a few hours someone came to take us to get a blood test. She had a phobia of needles, but she was also scared of what was happening to her, so she wanted help. The nurse was gentle and kind, explaining what she was doing at each step. The other nurse held her arm so she couldn't jerk it away. I stood in front of her, holding her small body with my large body, hugging her like I was a human cushion. I knew I needed to be safe, I needed to be steady. She was crying, but trying to be brave, but terrified, and just as they were about to start I had a brainwave — I remembered something I had wanted to tell her about a poet we both loved, and this distraction pulled her up out of her fear for just long enough, and we were both so pleased and relieved and elated, and afterwards I was so full of adrenaline that when S called me, having seen my somewhat desperate text when he woke up in the early hours, I turned down his offer of swapping out. I said I thought I could manage, and I could manage. I could manage sitting up through the long night, when nothing happened and no one slept, where I fed her the bananas I had stuffed in my bag on my hurried way out, where I tried to find other edible foods in the snack machine, where I kept her calm and feeling safe, where I took notes about the thoughts she was having at an increasing rate, where I was able to reassure her that the *tap tap tapping* was not an aural hallucination of her own but just rain on the skylight above us, where I stayed until morning until a kind soul, who I will love forever, messaged that she was on her way to swap out with me. As I caught an Uber home, I had been awake for 24 hours. I climbed up the stairs to our house and let myself in. S was just waking up. I slipped into our bed (bed!) with such gratitude and slept for most of the day. It may have been the hardest thing I have ever done. It was only one night.

❄

It was some kind of public holiday. We were out driving around the coast because it was unexpectedly sunny. I had been writing this, thinking about this, and it was bothering me. I knew it wasn't so clean, so simple. I said to S that I was sorry I had taken away his chance at being a father, while also feeling that I had always thought it was a decision we'd come to together ('It was,' he said, but . . .), and also feeling that I was pleased, relieved, it had gone this way, and that he was too, that the idea of having a child could only have been what he wanted hypothetically, and that in actuality he wouldn't like it, while also knowing that if it had happened he would have loved it, or at least the child, because it would have been our life, and layered on top of all of this was something I had started to think about in the shower in the morning — about how he, the kindest, least violent person, had pushed his brother off the back of a couch when they were children, breaking his arm, and how this close but somewhat dysfunctional relationship had continued for their whole lives — that all family relationships are somewhat dysfunctional, that all families are fucked up, even the good ones, the happy ones, but 10 minutes later I arrive to have lunch with my own family in a garden in the sun on a warm, still, beautiful autumn day and my brothers make mean jokes about things that matter to me in a way that no one else would, and it's very ordinary and I know they don't mean to hurt me but they do, and even though I stomp off to the bathroom we don't speak of it, and this dynamic is familiar, though I feel I have just recognised it, though I thought I'd grown out of it, and I start remembering things I had never forgotten and think about the way I am, how I am, and why that is and I can't quite tell if this feeling is grief, sadness or fury, or all of the above, or something else entirely.

✸

When we still thought we might have children, we were joking about how we would live in a castle, and I would have nothing to do with raising them. S said they would see me wandering around the hallways wearing a flowing dress, possibly with attendants, and they would say, 'Daddy, who is that lady?' And he would say, 'That's your mother,' and they would say, 'Ohhh,' with hushed awe.

✸

I don't usually like to share my writing before it is finished, but I do love to talk about it — about the ideas I am turning over in my head and scribbling down — and I love to listen to what other people think about those same things. (And sometimes, I confess, I steal what they say.) While I've been writing this, I've had conversations I would not otherwise have had. People with children have told me they weren't sure they wanted them and are still not sure it was the right choice. Others admit they always did but aren't sure why. There are those who are happy without, never wanted that life, and people who didn't and then, suddenly, did. I am at a party when a woman I have met several times over several decades asks me about my writing. I tell her that I have been trying to write something about not having children and not wanting to have children, but how I have started reflecting on everything and wondering why, and it has come to seem so much more fraught than I expected for something that hadn't seemed fraught before. I tell her I don't think I can finish it. She says, while we are still on the dancefloor, that I must write it, I must finish it. She says that women must know that there is a choice. She was once told she couldn't but then, unexpectedly, she did, and now she has three sons with a man I went to school with, all already tall enough to tower over me. She does not regret her life, her choices, where they have led, but later, in the dark cocktail bar, early in the morning, she insists again: 'Women need to know that there are other ways to live a life.' I assumed that this was something women knew by now, in this day and age, though we are always going backwards as well as forwards, but I wouldn't presume to tell them, when I'm not even sure how to tell my own life, because everything is always too complicated to be set down with complete veracity, in its entirety, with all its contradictions.

Stranded on a shore I never wanted to visit

IONA WINTER

A s tamariki in 1970s West Auckland, we often witnessed death — or the life, death, rebirth cycle, if we were talking about plants or insects. We'd investigate dead things on our explorations in the ngahere at the back of our whare, including the possums that hung grotesquely (apparently humanely) outside my bedroom window in an apple tree. But then, during adolescence, friends and acquaintances began dying, including my best friend aged 17 on the motorbike I was forbidden to ride. With these deaths, there were things I was prevented from seeing or knowing — presumably for my own good.

Being a suicide-bereaved mother goes against the natural order of things.

※

M y first diagnosis of cervical cancer, early stages and treatable, was at 18. Was it selfish to want a child, when I was told that it was unlikely, and knowing that someday I would die? Multiple surgeries later, at 25, I gave birth to Reuben. The labour was an arduous 48 hours, and I'm certain that if it had been the old days, we both would've died.

When he was five months old and I was a single parent, I started to worry about my death and leaving him alone. I made a will, just in case. But I also worried, perhaps obsessively and forebodingly at times, about his death because his birth had been so perilous. The doctors should've done a caesarean. My tama came out grey and floppy, and it seemed an age before he cried. When they sewed up my bleeding and torn perineum, I felt nothing but joy for this precious wee soul I'd been entrusted with. My diary entries from the month after Reuben took his life, however, speak of something entirely at odds with that notion of joy.

3/10/2020, Green Bay

It will come as no surprise to you that the rage in me at times is phenomenal, but I doubt that it's all about you. You'd promised me you wouldn't take your life, so many times, and you'd said, 'I couldn't do that to you Mum.'

Sometimes I wonder what it is that stops me from screaming — ever the polite and understanding woman, rage now seethes inside me like an ancient tuna.

Mā has said, several times since Reuben died, that I'm a strong woman. Friends have said the same. And I'd forgotten that out of everyone in our whānau, it was me who held our 20-year-old cat Dusky while the vet euthanised him. I don't know about strength; it doesn't fit the 'me' who is enduring this experience of my only child's death.

As a kid, my maternal grandfather was my singular safe male. I worried constantly that he would die, whenever I lay listening to his sleep apnoea in the middle of the night, way down the other end of the hallway. I'd wait, my own breath held, for him to snort-snore his way back to us. He was 14 years older than my grandmother and had heart issues, so death was a grey spectral thing that lingered in the doorways.

Grandad died when Reuben was four. When Gran called to say he'd gone, I remember she sounded very calm. But perhaps that's my memory all jumbled up, which grief tends to do. I went to the funeral home alone, knowing I needed to do a ritual for Grandad that would enable him to return safely to his tupuna. I can't remember exactly what I did, but I was into Celtic rituals at the time, and I sat with him for ages, because the idea of him being companionless felt inherently wrong to me.

6/10/2020, Green Bay, in your garden

Today, I felt your pulse when I laid myself alongside this rākau with its exposed and weathered roots, kissed and battered by the elements, and my whare tangata detected the drag of you — stretched between Papatūānuku and me.

The only choice is to allow this painful severing to continue.

How am I meant to find you? Is it in the wind in the trees, or the manu who visit (and I try to interpret their messages to find some relief)?

And how the fuck was I meant to prepare myself for the coldness of your skin? You hate the cold. I never dreamed the words 'Reuben, coroner and morgue' might fit into the same sentence.

I've perfected a watery scream in the shower, where nobody can hear — but it's only momentary relief.

At the funeral home I was allocated two minutes alone with my beautiful 26-year-old son, after he was finally released from the morgue to the undertakers, thanks to Covid restrictions. While I have the patience of a saint, those three days I was forced to wait to see him created another trauma alongside his suicide, and a chasm of bitterness.

We were under obligation to choose who could come through the whare to grieve, and for no more than 30 minutes. The decision on how long our tangihanga would be was made for us, because everything was shrouded in rules and regulations: like setting up bloody hand sanitiser and sign-in sheets at the front door. As if that would've protected Reuben. I'm sure he'd have laughed, shaking his head and smiling that gorgeous smile in a way that always relieved my frustration.

In groups of 10: one waiting on the driveway, another in the whare with Reuben, and another on the lawn smoking ciggies and having a kai afterwards, we watched loved ones arrive and depart. Clock watchers, all of us, during a time when the clocks had stopped. Nobody was allowed to stay. Innumerous people missed out on being able to say goodbye to Reuben, in his waka at home. Some were excluded, not through malice, but because of rules that had absolutely nothing to do with a 'normal' grief process.

And while his beautiful mates did their absolute best to give him a magnificently loud and raucous send off, we weren't allowed more time at the chapel. We were rushed out the door, the haka from his cousins cut short, the hearse sitting idling, belching fumes in our faces, and the keening was silenced too.

Reuben's dad and I did what we could to hold the space, but there was no poroporoaki or wake afterwards — no kaputī to make things noa. But, those of us in the same 'bubble' stomped the bejesus out of the whare when we came home from the service — a small, semi-cathartic consolation.

It was nothing like how it should have been, culturally, emotionally or physically.

9/10/2020, Green Bay

I visualise you alone, getting cold, your body free of pain, and leaving us behind, with me stranded on a shore I never wanted to visit.

It's fucking exhausting helping everyone else along. Yes, I know that you're sorry, ka aroha bub. Unfortunately it doesn't soothe me at all.

Without shame, I am envious of those who have living children, when you are not, of those with partners who support, love and hold them close, and of those who got to see you, when I did not.

I don't know why you thought I'd be better off without you. This is the worst rejection of my life; the biggest fuck you, and the most painful rupture. It can never be repaired.

Pandemic restrictions created a death-process experience that was robotic, inhumane and devastating. At the time of writing this essay, we still haven't been able to scatter or inter Reuben's ashes, as decision-making was rushed due to the C-word (Covid). Three years on, we've been unable to gather as whānau and friends to farewell my tama because of ongoing restrictions.

Those of us bereaved by suicide in Aotearoa already wait upwards of five years for coronial results, and now that appears to be stretching towards eight. We know things other people do not. Being prevented from gathering in grief heightened our loss of what might be considered 'normal' grief rights — in my words, basic human rights, for both my tama and those of us still here.

10/10/2020, Green Bay

I cry in my sleep and wake with salted tracks beneath my eyes. I'm wearing your clothes and wishing I could channel you somehow, hear your voice, see your smile, feel your hugs.

I stood in your kitchen for an hour while roofers banged and their children ran in circles. I had to wait until they were gone in order to sob.

Fuck suicide. Fuck you. Fuck this. I will miss you for the rest of my life.

Why did they have Reuben in a nappy at the undertakers?

I didn't know that I would see my dead tama in a nappy, his chest crisscrossed with autopsy tape and his ankle broken. Nothing prepared me for that. When I saw him, at the funeral home, he wasn't intact. I sensed that many things had been taken from him, so where did they go? Into some offal pile at the morgue?

I didn't wail or make a scene, simply took care of the process in my practical Capricorn way because we had such limited time with him. After my two allocated minutes alone with my only child, I sang him a waiata so he could return to his tūpuna safely.

Two fucking minutes.

I regret not demanding more time. I've since learned that the coroner/morgue/hospital should've and could've waited for me to arrive in Tāmaki before they autopsied my son.

Nobody asked my permission to mutilate his tinana.

☀

The other day, I tried not to see, couldn't help but see, a discarded baby walker chucked on the side of the road, and I wondered if that meant they'd lost a baby, too. It's impossible for me to ignore the always-asked question 'Do you have kids?', and while my replies are always honest and clear — 'Yeah, but he died' — I watch people's faces drop.

What bloody tenses am I supposed to use?

Westernised people have become adept at avoiding grief, funerals are whizzed through on the hour, we receive a booklet with a nice photo and some pleasant words, and get three days leave from work if it's a close relative or partner. We tend not to experience death up close, and bereavement is disassociated from the everyday rhythms of life. More so during a pandemic.

We are expected to 'get over' grief, not wallow in it, and on all accounts not show your teary-eyed, sleep-deprived face to anyone. Except if you're me — these days I say bugger that. As Naja Marie Aidt states, with a resonance that hits home, 'Grief is like a fucking prison.'[1]

26/10/2020, Koputai Port Chalmers

Two dead ducklings set me off this afternoon, and the mention of your guitar that none of us can play because you were the maestro.

I lay down on the spare bed at your Nan's whare tonight after a bottle of beer and felt depressed. Then she came in and we lay there together in tears, anger and laughter — like some kind of weird fucked-up collab in your honour.

Reuben is the third mokopuna of our whānau in two years to take their life, the fourth in three years, if you include extended whānau. I was firm, from the outset, that I would call Reuben's death what it is — suicide.

And I've copped some flak for that decision, but as Carl Jung wisely said, making the darkness conscious is disagreeable and therefore not popular. I don't need to win any popularity contests, and thankfully I'm one of the least competitive people I know.

It is vital to speak about suicide because, even on 'a good day', meaning one where I haven't lost my shit or sat sobbing on the floor, all it takes is a venture into my mother's garage for a random object, and then the crushing mourning blackness becomes ever-present. It's in the dinosaur jumper I can see through a plastic storage box, or the remnants of my last flat where Reuben visited me before lockdowns.

March 2020 was the last time I saw my tama alive, on and off for three days, while he shared himself around his Nan and good friends. Then cranked-up restrictions in Tāmaki meant Jetstar cancelled my flight to see Reuben in early September 2020, and I couldn't afford to rebook on Air New Zealand. We shared our mutual upset in a phone call, because the distance was urging us to be together. My only other regret is that I didn't find the money.

The week after I was meant to be with Reuben, he took his life. The one

---

1   Naja Marie Aidt, *When Death Takes Something From You Give It Back* (London: Quercus Editions, 2020), 35.

thing I feared for years happened.

There is no grief like this.

I kōrero with Reuben daily, and sometimes he cops an earful if I'm in a foul mood. Because he promised me he wouldn't kill himself, after my niece and nephew took their lives. He promised me, after his best friend suicided. He promised me that he would pick up the phone and call if he was ever on that godawful ledge again.

Reuben said that he wanted to die that day. And he did.

A counter of moons

Sometimes the smell of Reuben comes upon me unbidden, and the longing catches in the back of my throat. He smells like fresh washing, incense, mānuka smoke and the damp earth — a signature hello.

My tama: loved to be thrown high in the air, beat me at chess at seven, and his first word was 'star'.

My tama: loved to laugh, make his guitar wail, and he gave the best hugs.

My tama: talked before he walked, opened the Big Day Out at 16 — 16 years after being in my womb at the 1994 Big Day Out.

Sometimes I can see all his faces, like a film spanning 26 years, before sleep.

10/11/2020, Seacliff

Everything has become about your death. Each sentence begins with, 'My son is dead'.

I can't finish teaching you to drive.

It was my worst nightmare — that you would kill yourself. Did I somehow manifest this?

Counting has become a tad obsessive. The boxes of his childhood things, the months circled in my diary, beautifully made woollens from his nan and great-gran, collections of vinyl, comics, photographs and ephemera, they all lie spectral in Mā's garage. Each time I venture inside I find a fucking Pandora's box and am forced again to face facts — Reuben is dead, and I'm not. There'll be no grandchildren, he won't return in this lifetime, and I live with a gaping hole in my chest. Whenever I hold a bag on my lap/belly/breast it reminds me of how I used to carry him everywhere when he was little; a wee limpet who never liked to be separated. My goddess, how deeply we loved one another.

21/11/2020, Seacliff

I sit down on the floor to weep. Week 9. This is the week of weeping.

Last week was the week of the brave face.

I care for very little now. I just want you back.

When you come in my dreams, it's all at once this overwhelming sense of your physical death and spiritual continuity. I mourn you, and all the walks we never got to take.

I unpack his things knowing he'll never be back to collect them. Mā washes his baby clothes to give to people who need them; there'll be no descendants on our side of the whānau and I cannot see them go to waste. I'm inextricably drawn to touch them, in fact I must do it, to inhale Reuben's absence.

What does he get to do, I ask myself, other than be dead? I have to endure this pain every day, and find reasons to stay alive when I feel flayed apart. Like a desiccated moth in a spider web, the best bits are gone.

Naturally, other people's lives move on, weathered by different storms; but I remain in this place of grief, withered.

In my mind I see my boy's body on the floor, curled as if in sleep, with no one to hold him, and tremendous waves of sadness well up in me. I feel dragged along the sand as they pull effortlessly backwards and up to begin their ascent, him, me, others, love, death. It's over, this life, for him, but how can that be true, when he feels so very alive to me?

29/11/2020, Tāmaki

Last time I made this trip you were dead. Nothing's changed there. No more excitement at me flying to see you, or you me.

Fuck COVID restrictions for cancelling my flight the week before you died.

For the last few weeks I've woken with mourning sickness. Now I have to wear a mask, and all I can think of is how you stopped your breath, destroyed yourself, and flew away — it's triggering as fuck.

I stand at Mā's kitchen window, watching the manu in all seasons. Sometimes we talk about Reuben's absence, and usually I cry.

A friend asked me how I felt about looking in the mirror, as an exercise, after I'd commented on not knowing who I am anymore. And I realised that I don't look much because I see Reuben in my reflection. It's such a visceral reminder.

As linear time passes, you're left with a weird sense of life moving on, yet part of you remains at the very moment you knew your loved one was dead. There's nothing easy about living without the person you loved more than yourself. The person who you'd do anything for, without question. The person you worked so hard to love, support and nourish.

2/12/2020, Piha

I dreamt I was with you last night. I knew you were dead but we were someplace else.

Friends often say positive things like, 'You're doing so well. I don't know how you're doing it. You're amazing.' But I wonder if they feel pressure to validate my process because they think I need it, or if their kupu reflect their fears about how they might manage this, if the roles were reversed.

I'd have laid myself down and taken your place, without a second thought, just so the world might know more of your beauty.

It kills me that I will never have you back in my life, that we won't share laughter, kōrero or tears, and you've left me to bear the weight of what you could not.

And today, I swear if another person asks me how I am I might just scream.

I remember the first time Reuben attempted suicide. I was furious. How much of that attempt was about my relationship with him, as his mother? And how much was about him? I remember other times Reuben tried to take his life, always the same method, and always it failed. Not the last time, nothing saved him then.

Perhaps, like a cat with its nine lives, he'd used up all his chances and there was no backing out. There was no note. No explanation. Just did it, probably because he'd had enough of living in pain. I wasn't there. All I could do was call his dad and say, 'Go over. Now. He's been found unconscious.' Even then I knew that he was dead, because I'm his mother and I felt it deep within my whare tangata.

Sometimes, writing about Reuben's death and my grief (I can't call it loss because he's not lost to me) I find that words fall short of conveying how it feels.

I read poems about what this mother-grief looks like. There's a component of our own madness responding to what's occurred, when our babies take their lives, and it is something that is mostly unexpressed.

On bad days, I think about everything difficult I've endured: violence, sexual assaults, grief, cancer, medical misadventure, isolation, shame, chronic pain, multiple gynaecological surgeries over 36 years — the list goes on, but none of it comes close to the death of my beloved son. None of it.

As his mum, I must take responsibility for some of it, because we're all shaped by our early experiences in childhood. I'm attempting to be real about what the process is like, and it feels important to name this.

6/12/2020, Seacliff

Nobody knows this grief; well that's what I tell myself. No one can understand. They're just trying to carry out the impossible task of making it better.

You shut me out those last few months, led me to believe you were pai (despite living with fibromyalgia and chronic pain), that you were doing things that brought you joy — working on your puoro, growing your māra. And you were in therapy.

I've been left to flounder in that enormous wake.

8/12/2022, Goodwood, Otago

I HATE THAT YOU ARE DEAD.

Your absence in every breath is unbearable.

Your voice in my head tells me things I cannot believe, like 'I'm sorry Mum, I'm here.'

If I had regrets I think it would be easy to follow you.

11/12/2020, Seacliff

Why do I have to be strong enough to bear the pain of your death?

Am I supposed to get rid of your drawings, stories, and your first pair of boots? How can I reconcile the fact that you are dead, when in some ways you feel so very alive? What a headfuck.

The reduction of you can't be limited to a set number of boxes.

I wish I could've made it better for you, taken away some of your mamae, soothed your last year of hurts.

Three months, or is it 13 weeks? I don't understand how counting any of this shit makes it better.

20/12/2020, Seacliff

Last night I dreamt your father, aunts and I were searching for you and your cousins in an underground labyrinth. You three, who took your lives in the space of two years.

FUCK SUICIDE.

Nothing frightens me anymore.

I won't hear again your sounds of domesticity, your voice calling from the kitchen, 'Need anything, Mā?', or in the garden showing me the massive variety of chillies you were growing and then discussing what else to grow, preparing complicated and delicious kai together (me the kitchen hand), listening to your latest music before you release it, or the potential of mokos bouncing a ball.

I saw a woman driving in her car with a human-sized bear strapped into the passenger seat. Maybe I should get myself one to take the edge off this unbearable absence of you.

Kupu I avoid when playing scrabble: suicide, death, mother, son.

The first time I returned to stay with whānau, in the city where Reuben was born and took his life, I was struck by how intense the noise was, and how deafening the silences were. I wore a Radiohead shirt, thinking it might channel him somehow. I hadn't worn band tees since I was hapū with him.

There's an old photo of me standing side on, puku extending way beyond my knees, with an unlined face, wearing striped tights and a Living Colour shirt, purchased from the gig we attended with my protruding belly. I went to a lot of gigs — no wonder my tama became a muso.

Reuben arrived two weeks late, after a two-day labour, cord around his neck and barely breathing, but surrounded by people who loved him. My GP told me, six months after childbirth, 'You don't need to eat for two anymore, Iona.' Make of that what you will.

The night I remembered this was at one of the parties to celebrate the posthumous release of Reuben's album *Milk III* in 2021. The GP turned up because he'd seen the ātaahua mural of my tama on the side of the Rockshop on Karangahape Road. Another person with living children, who handed me their condolences like a Band-Aid. He didn't know that since 17 September 2020, I'd returned to eating for two.

Can I still call myself a mother?

*

Random memories surface, particularly when visiting places Reuben and I lived, and often they border on being intolerable. If I'm with loving friends I'm struck by their carefulness, and beautiful as that is, I'm also aware that this experience of bereavement, as a mother, is uniquely mine. I've become acutely attuned to other people's awkwardness, and their quick gear shifts away from my tears to another distraction, including laughter.

I play Scrabble on my phone as a means of escape.

I'm reading books, intermittently, by other people with dead kids. There's not a huge selection, but I guess that speaks to an inability to put any of this dreadful shit into words. It takes a massive effort, to find kupu that connect with the lived experience of suicide bereavement.

Linear time is irrelevant, because the spiky, painful, gut-wrenching nature of suicide has the capacity to take me to ground-zero in an instant.

What's it like where he is now? Not the son I knew, but his beautiful, shiny wairua. I'm looking forward to seeing him again, when that day arrives.

Once more I ask, can I still call myself a mother?

While I don't want to live in a space with a NO TRESPASSING sign, the reality is that sometimes I do, because there resides a dead part inside of me, that nobody else can touch.

The mamae descends
along with the call
karanga mai

        do you see me there   alongside you
      can you feel my skin   where yours used to be

keening   *longing*   *waiting*

I hear your voice
above and below
the gulls

you there   me here

lost   *found*   *scattered*   *regrouped*

      where my hands end . . . yours began
                hearts joined
          souls intertwined

Possible names for myself

HENRIETTA BOLLINGER

Helen has decided the collective noun for our family members is a babble. A babble of Bollingers and a ferocity of Pharazyns, my cousin has aptly named us — the branches of our loud clan who gather in Mārahau Beach every five years for a family reunion. These descriptors fit well with the family motto someone else has already painted onto an improvised family crest. Under a painting of two walruses locked in heated debate are the words: 'Why not?'

There are kids everywhere. There seems to be an endless stream of them running in and out, stopping to find someone who looks old enough to help them put on shoes, teach them a card game or a song. They pull on the hands of adults who look like they'll be willingly dragged down to the beach. The adults are usually immersed in a conversation, which they pause to attend to these requests. We do this because we remember being the kids here.

But it is the adults who ask my dad to read a bedtime story aloud. When he had done this for us kids 10 years ago, an adult had called out from another room for him to speak up. The cousins of all ages had pricked up their ears. Dad willingly revives the tradition.

One small cousin has stopped talking to me, but every time I catch her eye she growls at me.

'I'm a tiger!' she explains. She giggles when I growl back and hold up my claws. I am reading a good book and I'm tired and sore so I like this little interaction. It doesn't demand full sentences from me.

The newest member of the family is only in her first week of life. I look up from my book to see her sleeping in my aunt Thomasin's arms. I shut my book and push myself closer.

'You want a baby. I can see it in your eyes,' she says. Her own eyes remind me of my grandmother's, her mother's. They are sparkling a bit.

She has voiced something I was half thinking. I am surprised and grateful that she can read me like this. But I try to shrug it off. It is a thought that wells up sometimes — it always has. But lately, when it feels impossible, I retreat into the comforting thought that I'll write books instead. I'll have time. The uninterrupted expanse of it.

'You could do it. You'd just need good support,' says Thomasin.

There will be good things about getting back to the city. I am looking forward to smooth concrete paths and my own bed. But here — just like the kids, I have a babble of loving people who will help me put on shoes and get down to the beach. And there's always someone holding a baby. I could do it here, I think. I indulge the thought. Maybe this cocoon of a world could last longer than a week in the summer. Back in Wellington, I wonder what it would take.

❊

2   The health professional — not my usual doctor — wants to know: 'Can you have babies? Carry them, I mean?'

I was sure. I'd watched documentaries, read up online, once or twice met disabled parents and, still, her uncertainty makes me waiver.

'I think so,' I say.

I imagine how uncomfortable it would be to sit over my own pregnant belly in a wheelchair. I consider making a joke that I might have another womb in the picture anyway. My unsuspecting future wife has been signed up for the task before we have even met, the poor love.

If this professional doesn't know what's possible for me, then the fantasy of my future isn't something I want to invite her to look at. She writes down my 'think so' and I forget about it until the next time someone like her asks me.

3 The couple are both in wheelchairs. The dad leans down and lifts their baby out of the carrier somehow attached to the front of the mum's light-frame wheelchair, positioned so the baby can see its parents. The baby looks up at him, smiling. I have been stared at, so I try not to stare.

※

4 I learn about the Adoption Act through disability rights work. My boss, Esther, is on the phone patiently explaining to a journalist the need to take a rights-based view.

'The support was already in place,' she says into the phone.

'What was that about?' I ask afterwards.

She explains that a woman with a learning disability is about to have her baby uplifted — taken from her. There had been a plan in place to support her and then somewhere along the line something happened.

'They can do that?' I am incredulous.

'Yeah. They can.'

It turns out that our Adoption Act is a relic of the 1950s. Children are treated as the chattels of their parents and in some cases, doctors can determine who has the physical and mental capacity to parent.

I'm thinking about the disabled people I know who have been called selfish for becoming parents, or questioned about whether they really wanted their pregnancies, if their partners did. I have heard of people asked to confirm the kids are really theirs. This situation is all that, honed to its sharpest point.

※

5 I'm going for a walk, but the kids have questions. The five of them stand in a row pressed up against the kindergarten fence.

'What's that?'

'My wheelchair.'

'Why do you have that?'

'To get around.'

'Why?'

'The messages from my brain don't get to my legs.'

'Is it fast?'

'Yes, look!' I give a demo and regret it when a small hand shoots through the fence.

'No, I'll drive it myself, thanks.'

'Why can't I?'

'Because it's like my body. You tell your legs where to go. I drive my wheelchair.'

'Where do you live?'

'Next to your kindy. See that white fence?'

'Where's your mum?'

'My mum lives in a different house.'

'Why?'

'Because I'm a grown-up. I live in my own house.'

'Are you a boy or a girl?'

'A girl, I guess . . .'

'Do you have a baby?'

'No, not yet.'

'Why?'

'Because I don't have anyone to have a baby with.'

'Why?'

'I haven't found them yet.'

'Oh. Do you like my shoes?' Now a foot comes through the fence for my approval.

'Yes — very sparkly.'

And someone else's foot. 'What about mine?'

'Yours, too.'

'You know, you dress like my dad.'

'Oh, do I?'

'Why do you wear that?' Pointing at my shirt.

'Because I like it.'

'But you look like a boy.'

'Girls can look like this, too.'

'Where are you going?'

'To get food.'

'Why?'

'I'm hungry.'

'Why?'

※

6 I tell my support worker, Whiro, to start using they/them pronouns for me.

'Sure,' they say. 'Did always think it was weird you used she/her but didn't want to say anything in case it was important to you.'

Another morning, they help me into a binder and give me the space to grin and laugh at myself in the mirror. It makes strange sense that they knew before me. I like my body just as it is, almost defiantly so, but I like this, too. I really like this. My flat chest.

'Shall I come back a bit earlier today? Like 2 p.m.? Help you out of it?'

'Why?'

'I dunno — to make sure you can breathe!'

☀

7 At the arrivals gate my old friend Harriet greets me — her teenaged visitor — with a one-armed hug and hands over her baby.

'Here. You take him, and I'll push. Do you have many bags?'

'Just one. We can hang it off the wheelchair.'

'Thank God.'

The baby, Baxter, is quiet and wide-eyed. I put my arms tight around him so he won't slip off my lap. I'm trying to reassure him, and myself, through my grip. That I'm adult enough to be responsible for such precious cargo.

'Hello, I've got you.' I nuzzle the top of his head. Right now, I'm feeling particularly young and acutely aware of my unreliable limbs. 'We've actually met before but last time you fell asleep on me,' I tell Baxter.

'Harriet, you're going quite fast,' I tell his mother.

'Just getting us out of here.'

I, too, want to get our weekend started as quickly as possible but instead I find myself pointing out that people are staring.

'I bet,' says Harriet, 'I wonder what they think.'

'Aw cute baby!' someone calls out.

That's a new one and I like it. Baxter kicks. I smile and hold on to him tighter.

At departures a few days later I am talking fast and drinking coffee slowly, willing the holiday not to end. I have a question that I keep losing the words for, but she understands anyway.

'You'll get there,' she says.

'Get where?'

'One day, you'll find someone who thinks: *Gosh, I want to push Etta around everywhere for the rest of my life.* Literally, I mean.'

'OK.' I nod. She generously stokes this hope by always remembering to ask about my love life.

☀

8 Chrissy works quite close to her due date.

'Work as long as you like, but just don't have the baby here,' I joke one morning. I mean in my wet-area bathroom where she is helping me get ready for the day. She promises she won't. She gives me as much time as she can before the baby comes. Showering me, dressing me and taking me to the swimming pool that is heated to bath temperature. I love the way my muscles relax in there. Chrissy loves being off her feet. Our bodies have the same needs from water. To be relieved of gravity for a bit.

One Monday she texts: 'I think I'll take maternity leave now it's getting close.' On Wednesday there is a baby.

When she later becomes a midwife, she tells me she's attended births where the parent was disabled. She reassures me: 'Bodies know what to do.'

☀

9 The people at the SPCA are kind and practical. They are happy to work with my request for a confident cat who won't be scared of a wheelchair. My flatmate and I had been looking for an older cat.

'Yeah,' we had agreed, 'no little babies.'

We choose three-month-old Magnus. Mostly because the tuxedo kitten scales the side of my wheelchair for a cuddle. He adopts me instantly as his human cat tree. The SPCA workers want to reassure us that his unusually short, tufty tail is nothing but a genetic quirk. He was just born that way. He might be a little bit unbalanced but otherwise it won't affect his quality of life.

My flatmate and I lean on our respective mobility aides and reassure them back: 'He'll fit right in.'

☀

10 'Is "Auntie" the right name for you, my genderqueer love?'

My friend Jess and I met as young writers in Auckland at a time when we were growing into our voices. We were learning to know ourselves. We were stuttering Pākehā embraced by Pasifika wordsmiths in South

Auckland. We were both queer, too.

I think I was out as gay first, but Jess was older, and they impressed me. They knew what to do on stage. They taught me it was a feminist statement to not wear a bra. They wrote into uncertainty, into an in-between.

This ongoing conversation about our identities we are having is a recent reignition of our long friendship. Now that I'm in Wellington, this long-distance digital mode of connection fits into our lives. It is possible to message while feeding a baby, as in her case, or lying in bed with back pain, as in mine.

I don't know. 'Auntie' feels fine, and I can't think of anything else. But I love the generous question and it is accompanied by a picture of their baby. I reply with something about the great-great aunts I admire in my family history, who spoke all number of languages and were staunchly themselves. Elsie, Alice and Madge were part of a generation whose men had been sacrificed to the First World War. These women lived together and managed to get along while being of three different — and possibly conflicting — religious persuasions.

I think of the aunties I grew up with too: Thomasin, Aly, Cathy, Jo. Their love has looked like everything from letting me stay with them to stepping in to help me get up in the mornings, reminding me to let my body wake up, to surface and stretch. Teaching me to make things like jewellery, and budgets and apple crumble. Always applauding the juvenile rap songs I wrote with my cousins and showing me secure ways to hold a baby.

For the moment it is enough to align myself with them without knowing exactly where I fit — to borrow their name: 'Auntie'. *If nothing else*, I think, *I'll wear it in for when my sisters have children.*

With Jess and me the trade is this: I send a collection of exclamations, examinations and expletives about my adventures into sexuality and gender and dating. Jess sends pictures of their baby, along with reflections on their newfound non-binary parenthood. We have a gentle disagreement about who is getting the most out of our exchange. I'd say I'm getting the cuter end of the deal, that's for sure. But Jess insists that my contributions are just as good — just a different pace perhaps from having a newborn sleeping on you.

Jess is finding their way between being someone's momo — their genderqueer moniker — and settling into what they call the 'comfortable armchair' of being someone's mama.

'I like "Momo" for you,' I say. *For me?* I wonder.

One night, I finally share this quiet question with Jess: 'For me?'

The systems around me that make my disabled life possible: physical support, income support and wheelchair repairs, among other things, are feeling restrictive just then. They are not feeling functional and freeing the way they do on the best days. When my sense of independence is challenged it can feel like not only this moment but possible futures, too, are slipping out of my reach.

The sharp edges of ableism feel close. With a pang I know I'd want to protect my theoretical child from all of it. That I already do. But would there be any way to soften the staring, the assumptions, the questions? I admit to Jess: 'I would hate to bring a child into that world.'

'But what a gift,' replies my friend. 'They would have you.'

Atmosphere

LUCY O'CONNOR

The morning is overcast and muggy. My partner is next to me, driving. We're on our way to pick up a takeaway coffee. I needed to get out of the house and distract myself from failing to write this essay.

'I can't find the thread. It's too complex!' I groan and lean my head against the car window.

He puts his hand on my knee.

'What exactly are you trying to say?'

I look out the window and ponder. I have the choice to have children, or not. I can choose not to have children. What else *is* there to say?

☀

I am seven and obsessed with *Xena: Warrior Princess*.

My teacher sets up a writing exercise for class one morning, asking, 'What do you want to be when you grow up?'

I write 'stunt person'. I'll have a house and a million dollars by the time I'm 20. 'What about having children?' my teacher asks over my shoulder. I write 'have children' because everyone else does, but really I just want to be Xena.

☀

After my partner and I arrive home with our coffees, I trudge back up to the study to work on this essay. I open my laptop, then click into Instagram. A quick scroll won't hurt.

Twenty minutes later I'm still scrolling. The sponsored posts stand out more than usual. They're full of baby strollers and rompers.

I exit Instagram and an uncomfortable thought occurs: Am I finding it difficult to write this essay because I try to avoid this topic? As a teenager I used to say 'I may not want kids' as an act of rebellion; those five words always garnered a response. These days it remains true, but I try my best not to bring it up. It's often interpreted as if I'm challenging the choices of others or declaring superiority rather than preference. It leads to questions that I still can't provide neat, satisfactory answers to.

※

'Why don't you want kids?'

I'm having dinner with friends. A few have children already, and most aspire to in the future.

'Not sure. More pasta, anyone?'

'But, like, *why* don't you want kids?' The same person asks, persistent.

All eyes are on me. My cheeks start to flare. 'Why *should* I want kids?'

People are quick to fill the space.

'You'll be lonely when you're old.'

'You never know love until you have children!'

'My sister didn't have kids and she regrets it!'

I sit, mute and amiable. Most of their reasonings induce anxiety, but scratch the surface and not one is particularly convincing.

※

My computer screen goes black with inactivity. Perhaps I need to try a new angle; one that isn't steeped in resistance, but possibility.

I try to imagine what it might be like to have a child. A montage starts to play. There's a ribbed midi-dress stretched over a pregnant belly. Hair in a messy bun, clenched eyes and short, sharp breaths. A baby wearing a onesie lying on a mat looking just past the camera with big, curious eyes. Then my partner's there, holding a baby awkwardly but endearingly. He's crying, always crying, in such awe of the baby he fathered. There are flowers and books and ladybirds and playgrounds. There are tears and pain, but somehow it's all beautiful.

As the montage plays, what's missing from it is me. I'm not behind the camera, either. I'm stepping along the fringes of the frame as deftly as I can, tip-toeing somewhere beyond expectation and traditional ideas of what women should be. I'm striving to know myself. I am old and elusive. I wear black turtlenecks and tortoise-shell sunglasses. I observe and I write. I drink black coffee and I write. No pastel-hued film plays for this.

✻

'm in my early teens and having dinner at my friend's house with her parents and brothers. Her dad is at the head of the table.

'Women who don't have children are selfish.'

The boys snigger. I take a bite of my cottage pie to test the possibility of staying silent.

'What if someone can't have children? Or they don't want children?' I fail. My friend's dad looks at me, chews and swallows.

'There's something unnatural about women who don't have children. Girls are born to be mothers.'

Steam rises from my plate.

'Shut up, Dad!' my friend says.

'Yes, be quiet, you!' I'm grateful for the voice of my friend's mum. 'Times have changed. What'd you get up to today, girls?'

My friend talks about the cliff we climbed and how cold the ocean was. The conversation falls back into a familiar cadence. We finish dinner and the boys keep chatting while the women collect the plates to be washed.

✻

he day is vaporising. I can't afford to let time pass without making progress on this essay. I tell myself to just keep writing. Instead, I stare at the calendar above my desk. My birthday is next month. How old will I be this year? If I minus that number from 40, how many years do I have left to decide?

✻

'm catching up with a friend who works as an independent contractor. He's talking about the challenges of working for yourself, and mentions that his friends have started to have children. He tells me that he doesn't want them anytime soon because he doesn't want to be distracted. His reputation and his career are too important to him. He says there's no rush; he could have children when he's 50.

'Lucky for some!'

He looks at me, surprised. It's as if he's noticing I'm a person who can give birth for the first time.

✳

Daylight is dimming. I need some fresh air. So I don't feel unproductive, I put on my running shoes and download a podcast on the topic of parenthood. My partner is germinating seeds in the garden. 'See you soon!' I open the gate and start running.

The podcast features someone who specialises in helping people work out whether they want to have children. She says that we live in a 'pro-natalist' society — one that encourages and values child-rearing. This resonates; but as the podcast goes on, it irks me that the decision-making process she advocates is meant to apply to all, when the conditions and stakes are so vastly different.

✳

I'm in my early twenties, working for a company that manufactures underwear for people who live with bladder leakage. My job is to research and write articles that destigmatise incontinence. Each day I learn something new about the short- and long-term risks associated with pregnancy and childbirth; incontinence, yes, but also depression, prolapsed bladders, postpartum post-traumatic stress disorder, perineal tears, uterine ruptures, death. Growing and birthing children is dangerous work.

I mention I'm shocked at how little I know about these serious health risks. My colleague is the mother of two young kids and she looks at me, knowingly.

'All things to look forward to when you get pregnant!'

I ignore her use of 'when' rather than 'if'.

'Can I ask, did you know about the risks before you became pregnant?'

She gazes at the ceiling. 'Vaguely, but not really. You sort of just strap in for the ride.'

✳

After my run I take a shower and stare down at my belly. What would it be like for a child to grow beneath my flesh, to share this body with another? How would my muscles, bones, organs and hormones change to nurture new life?

✳

'We gave birth!'

I'm on the phone to a friend.

'Congratulations!'

I ask how his wife's doing.

'Amazing! She's like superwoman.'

'Aw, glad to hear it. And how are you feeling?'

He lets out a trumpeting laugh. 'Yeah, pretty good! Except . . .'

I imagine he's about to complain about a lack of sleep.

'My bloody son. He ruined my playground on the way out!'

I suck in my breath. 'Sorry?'

His laughter tapers off. He sighs and I feel the air rush into my eardrum.

'My son ruined my playground on the way out! You know? That comedian said it.'

I don't know which comedian said it. He asks me about my job and I ask him about his, but I can't focus. My voice starts wavering as I build myself up.

'I have to go back to what you said earlier. About how when your wife gave birth, it ruined your playground.'

He groans the universal groan of a man who's about to be called out. I struggle to articulate anything vaguely intelligent. I say the word 'vagina' out loud and feel my face go red.

'I get it, I get it,' he reassures me. 'She doesn't mind, though. She thinks it's funny!'

I cringe and don't believe him, but who am I to say what his wife thinks is or isn't funny? It's her experience, her sense of humour, her body. He asks about my parents. I ask about his. I congratulate him again and ask him to give his wife and son a hug from me. We say goodbye, and I slide off my bed onto the hard wooden floor.

✳

When I come downstairs after my shower, my partner is setting the table. He's taking on lots of the cooking these days. He's trying to make it easier for me to write this essay. I feel grateful, but also guilty. I aspire to feel as entitled to my writing as so many men do towards weekends playing golf.

I go to the fridge and get a beer. I lift back the tab and the can hisses open. 'Want one?'

My partner shakes his head. 'No, thanks. Anything you want to chat about?'

Suspicion surfaces. Is he hopeful that writing this essay will make me open to having kids?

'No, thanks.'

I put the can on the bench and clock the familiar image of a pregnant woman holding a glass. There's a big red circle around her and a line that cleaves her in two. *Pregnant? Fuck off!*

☀

I'm nearly 30, and at a work lunch.

'I'd never hire a woman in her thirties. I'd take one look at her and think *baby*!'

I look around the table of clients and colleagues. The men wear suits and the women wear strapless dresses. They're all nodding, even the ones who are mothers. I take a gulp of wine.

'I think that's illegal.'

The man, my boss, looks at me with contempt.

'You'd never *say* that was the reason.'

The waiter places a bowl of hot chips on the table.

'Besides, it's a woman's choice to get pregnant. I have a business to run.'

☀

That night I dream I have a child. It appears to me in various genders, at different ages. Suddenly I'm in a large body of water, paddling on a bodyboard.

I bump into my best friend. 'Where's the baby?' she asks.

'Oh shit,' I respond.

The water laps around us.

'Should we go back?'

I hesitate before saying yes.

I wake up and grab my phone so I can record my dream. It seems important somehow, as if it might hold clues about whether I truly want children or not. I laugh as I realise I'm at the point where I'm considering dreams as a source of possible enlightenment. But impartial conversations in real life can be rare.

※

I'm visiting the doctor for my first cervical smear. I'm trying to think of anything other than the procedure while waiting in the reception area. I pick up a magazine. *Hot or not?!* The bikini-clad women seem oblivious to the cameras. *Did she bounce back?* I toss it back on the reception table when the doctor calls my name.

She reiterates what the pamphlets say.

'Cervical cancer can affect your fertility, you know.'

I start to untie my shoelaces.

'I don't know if I want kids.'

Sometimes, I catch myself thinking infertility would be a relief. I lie on the examination table. The doctor walks to the base of it.

'Lots of women your age say that.'

She fossicks on a trolley adorned with medical instruments.

'You'll probably change your mind.'

She picks up the speculum.

'And what if your husband wants children? Just drop your knees to the side.'

I do as I'm told.

※

It's Monday morning and I'm looking forward to going to work. I want nothing more than to be distracted from this essay.

We have a team meeting first thing. A presentation is being given about the new financial year. One of my more progressive colleagues is pontificating about strategic aspirations. He explains where additional support is needed, then laments that a colleague is about to go on maternity leave. He refers to this as her 'holiday'. There's a scattering of awkward laughter that dies off quickly. 'Obviously, I'm joking,' he adds.

※

'm at the birthday party of a one-year-old. The father is addressing the child's mother, his wife, in front of the attendees.

'Thank you so much for everything you do. You look after our home so well. And you're raising such a beautiful child.'

The crowd coos and claps.

'Best of all, you hardly ever force me to babysit!'

Later, I go over to the one-year-old. People watch me surreptitiously to see how 'good' I'll be with this baby. To see if I'm 'a natural'. I say 'Happy birthday!' and pick the baby up. I hope this demonstrates how much I don't hate children.

※

Over my lunch break I browse articles that tell me why I don't want children. I'm fortunate to live in a place where women's rights have progressed, but apparently I've been given too many options: education, jobs, money, independence. Women like me are making the wrong choice by straying from our destiny of motherhood.

Julia Gillard comes to mind. In her time as the Australian prime minister, she was labelled 'deliberately barren'. Jacinda Ardern didn't 'stray' from motherhood, but yet, when she announced her pregnancy there were lashings of fury and outrage. 'She can't do this and be a mother!' people screeched. But, of course she did it while being a mother. Mothers are always so many additional things.

'Got five to chat?'

A Teams message from my colleague snaps me back into work mode.

'Sure!'

It's always nice to feel valued.

※

'm in my late twenties and have fulfilled my childhood dream. I'm employed as a professional stunt double. My day job involves fighting monsters and climbing underneath planes. The strength and skill of my body is currency.

Just before lunchtime, a colleague pulls me towards the wall of the warehouse.

'You shouldn't become a mum. It'll ruin your career.'

I'm caught off guard and become self-conscious. I grasp at some line of defence.

'Don't you have a son?'

'Yeah, and I'm not the one who had to push him out! That shit will ruin your body.'

He chortles. I wonder if this is harassment. I look around the film set and see only men. I go back to practising for the fight.

※

I arrive home from work and feel dread. The deadline for this essay is tomorrow. I heave my bag onto the bench and fall face-first onto the couch.

'Honestly, this is the most difficult thing I've ever tried to write.'

I hear myself and hate her. My partner is sitting in the cane chair watching basketball. He closes his laptop and gives me his attention.

'Anything I can do to help?'

I roll onto my back and gaze at the ceiling.

'Could you help me describe the atmosphere?'

'What do you mean "the atmosphere"?'

'You know,' I respond, 'the persistent pressures around having kids.'

※

It's 2019 and I'm talking to my partner's friend at a gig. I've met him three times. He's sitting, I'm standing, and the index finger of his left hand is suddenly touching the base of my left breast. His palm rests comfortably on my stomach. I suck it in instinctively.

'Don't you think you should give him some kids?' My partner and I have been together for barely a year.

'He'd be such a good dad.'

I look for him in the haze of the underground bar. He clocks me, smiles and waves. I look back at my partner's friend.

'Get out of my womb!'

To my relief he laughs and takes his hand off me.

'OK, but imagine your daughter — she'd be a force!'

So? I think. *I already exist. I'm a force.*

※

My partner comes over to the couch, crouches down, and gently squeezes my arms.

'Just know that I want to be with *you*, regardless of whether we have kids.'

I sit up, rest my chin on his shoulder and let out a big sigh. 'Did you feel pressured to have children growing up?'

He cocks his head. 'Not really.'

I'm amazed, but not all that shocked.

'Did you get the sense people assumed you'd just become a dad?'

My partner nods. My brow knits together as I shoulder the weight of that; I am the barrier to those assumptions. I remind myself that external pressures and projections are not mine to carry.

Get out of my womb. Get out of our wombs.

My partner resumes watching basketball. I go upstairs to write.

Auntie in charge

JACKIE CLARK, AS TOLD TO KATHRYN VAN BEEK

I never wanted to be a mother.

I come from a family of nine children. My father was an industrialist who was a driving force in the development of the family company Crown Lynn. He was born in 1916 and he and his first wife, Joan, had four children, one of whom died. After divorcing Joan he married Josie, a chemist at Crown Lynn, and had three more children. My mother came to work for them as a nanny. Josie died, and a few months later my father called my mother and asked for a date. When my father married my mother, she was 23 and already pregnant. They had me and my two younger brothers.

My father appeared to be quite macho and manly — full of piss and vinegar, he'd say. He was a very big and imposing figure who drank whisky and smoked a pipe. He was a force of nature — I get that from him. He was a yachtsman and he raced sports cars, but he was also amazingly emotionally open for a man of that era. My father was raised with the razor strop. He was raised on Victorian violence. He boxed my ears once, and I called him a cunt.

I remember feeling that my mother and father were very equal in their power, though in society's eyes they obviously weren't. She gave as good as she got. Once he came home late from a sailing race, and my mother hit him on the head with a rake. Another time Dad crashed drunk into the toll-booth barriers on the Auckland harbour bridge and the traffic cop just drove him home. My mother opened the fridge and swept the beers out so they smashed onto the floor — and then told him to clean it up.

My mother called herself a domestic executive, and she had 'domestic goddess' listed on her passport. She raised me to be a feminist. She said, 'When you get married, don't have joint bank accounts.' I remember vividly we were on the ferry once when I was about 14, and I heard the captain say, 'Old Clark's got a young bint.' And I said, 'Listen mate, my mother's not my father's fucking young bint.'

The youngest six of us kids were brought up together, so I grew up in a loud house as my father's youngest daughter but my mother's oldest child. I never felt as if I belonged to my family. My mother was very critical of me because I was so different from her. I was like an alien dropped on her doorstep. I've always been aware of injustice, and of course when I was younger it pertained to me — I was always wondering why people were so critical of me.

My father was the kisser and hugger in our family — Mum wasn't. My dad loved babies. They were a bit frightened of him initially, but he always won them around. Mum was raising six children before she was 30, so she was a yeller. She yelled a lot. When I was a child, I could see other people's lovely families where the mothers were 'mummies', and I used to ask other people's mothers if they could adopt me.

※

Getting to go to boarding school in Wellington was fabulous, because nobody was at me all the time, but when I was 16, I had an argument with my friends about whether public or private schools were better. I went home and said, 'I want to go to a public school.' And so, I started at Rangitoto College in Auckland.

I was on the school bus and this tiny person with long red hair got on. She sat beside me and started talking to me, and we didn't stop talking for 32 years. Carol was the first and only person in my life who I was ever good enough for — who I was ever enough for. She loved me and she loved all of me. She gave me what my mother wasn't able to give me — that's the truth of that.

Don't get me wrong, I had a great childhood in terms of the experiences my father's wealth offered us. And as an adult, I can understand that not all people who have children are naturally lovey dovey. But I had to fight really hard to be me. And then I got married and it was still hard to be me.

I was sitting in a pub. A guy came over and got talking, and I quite enjoyed his company. People warned me about him and said he was a drinker, but I didn't listen. I was a stroppy, independent woman and I was sick of being stroppy — I wanted someone to look after me. I made that old mistake. I thought he was like my father — strong and protective. But emotionally, he was completely broken. He was a redhaired boy from a Māori town, and he was very badly bullied . . . until he became the bully.

We got engaged after three months of dating. On the morning of my wedding my mother said, 'Oh well, it's not quite how I expected my daughter to look.' Carol was the maid of honour, and in the very early days of my marriage she said, 'If you ever leave him, just come and live with me, darling.' She was always my escape route. In abusive relationships you need someone you love and trust to say, 'Hey, I can be your exit plan.'

When I was 39, Carol had a cardiac arrest at home. Luckily her cleaning lady was there and gave her CPR. Carol died when she got to hospital, but they brought her back. I wrote her a letter that said, 'If anything had happened to you, I would have been destroyed.'

※

Early in my marriage, I started feeling sick in the mornings. I put my hand on my belly and wondered what it would be like to be pregnant. I did a pregnancy test, but it turned out it was just rhinitis. I thought, *Thank fuck for that*. I understood in the depths of me who my husband was, and I didn't want that for a child.

There were comments from other people — 'Oh when are you having kids?' — but possibly people recognised that my husband was a cunt. And perhaps I give off non-motherly vibes. I was afraid I'd be like my own mother — screaming and yelling. I convinced myself of that and internalised it. It fit my narrative, because I didn't want to be a parent, anyway.

I was a kindergarten teacher for 20 years. Parents used to ask all the time, 'Why don't you have any children'? I used to say, 'I don't give birth to them, but I teach them.' I had 16 nieces and nephews, and I was very involved in the early life of one of my nieces. I've always been good with kids, but I didn't want to have them myself.

※

I n 2013 I came back to work at the kindergarten in Māngere after the Christmas holidays, and there were all these clothes that had been left behind at the end of the previous term. I rang the local women's refuge and asked if they wanted to collect them. When the refuge manager came, I asked what else she needed, and this list came out of her mouth. I said to her, 'Look, I've got Twitter, I've got Facebook and I'm quite well connected.' And that's how I started getting stuff for the women.

One of the first things they needed was a microwave. I took it to them on my lunch break, and one of the women in residence looked at me and said, 'Thank you for being our friend.' The relationship deepened, and they started to call me JackStar. They very cleverly figured out that the deeper the relationship I had with the women, the better shit I'd get for them. I'd put requests on social media, things would get delivered to the kindergarten, and I'd take them to the safe house.

※

T hat year Carol's tummy did this weird thing where it became a bulge. She was asleep when I arrived at the hospital to see her, and I watched her sleeping. She was in so much pain, even in her sleep. I knew it was something big and serious.

Carol was diagnosed with uterine and endometrial cancer, and she was moved into hospice. I sat and held her hand as she was dying, acknowledging that she and I had the purest form of love — a real understanding and embracing of each other's totality. We'd had that since we were 17, and I wasn't going to have that anymore.

She had been my platonic wife. When the person you love most in the world dies, you feel as though you're going to have a heart attack at any time. It feels as though your heart's about to leap out of your chest. I went to the doctor and said, 'What is this fucking thing?' She said, 'It's broken-heart syndrome. It's literally grief.' I read that your grief is commensurate with the amount of love you have for that person. Carol was my person, my everything. I just miss her so much.

When Carol died, I had two weeks of bereavement leave — two weeks to think. And I thought to myself, *I have to step this refuge shit up.* So, I threw myself at this Aunties thing. That's the kind of thing you do when the person you love most in the world has died.

※

couldn't have done The Aunties if I'd had kids, but The Aunties was just an accidental thing anyway. I was already going to the safe house once a week, and we'd started doing supermarket shopping for them. Then we did Christmas on Twitter and it was manic and mad, with people sending presents for the kids. They're The Aunties — the people who donate money and goods to the women.

Since then, the relationship with the safe house has morphed into a whānau of 27 indigenous women who I provide pastoral care for. I also facilitate donations to community organisations and their clients, and I see people about domestic violence — whether they're in it, or their friends are in it. I have a very niche and particular skillset. I don't know that I could articulate what it is, but people seek it out. It's not motherhood, but it's building relationships with people. I'm pretty good at that.

The 27 women that I work with intensely are all survivors of extreme sexual, physical and emotional abuse. They drive the relationship, and they call me what they want to call me — Jackie, Auntie Jackie, Mumma J. I've never been a parent in a traditional sense, I'm more of a cheerleader.

In 10 years I've probably talked to 8000 people, and I've probably seen or provided sustenance to 2500 people face-to-face. And some of the survivors have this particular quality; I call them 'shiny motherfuckers'. One of the women rings every Friday morning, and we always have good chats. And she says, 'Tell me again why I'm special.' And I say, 'Well, I feel like when that ugly shit was happening to you when you were a child, some part of you wasn't buying it.' She's a shiny motherfucker — they have a rare sense of themselves.

Sometimes the women want to know why their own mothers can't support them and look after them. All of their mothers have been through what the women have been through, and they either tapped out or became bitter old cunts. They didn't survive with their sense of self intact.

The problem with having me in the women's lives is that it can make the contrast between what I offer them and what some of their mothers offer them very stark. And I've been at pains to say, 'They're struggling emotionally and financially themselves; they don't have the capacity to support you.'

Most of the women are survivors of childhood sexual abuse, and for some of them, their mothers actively encouraged it. Sometimes the damage is sustained in such a bone-deep way. One of them still carries her abuser's ashes around; the trauma bond for her is just so strong.

For these women, there was never any doubt that they were having children, because a child will love you when no one else will. The children become their self-worth. As a result of the trauma they've been through, there's a lot of guilt parenting, like buying their kids treats even when they can't afford it.

Every woman I've worked with face-to-face says, 'I do my kids first.' I try to encourage them to change that narrative for themselves, to 'do yourself first'. Everyone knows that thing about putting on your own oxygen mask — but for anybody who had trauma as a child, looking after other people is the way we divert caring for ourselves.

The women are extraordinary mothers. How do they know to love the way they love, when no one showed that love to them? It's important to understand how extreme the violence in their lives has been. They parent successfully with empathy and compassion — not always, there's a bit of shouting — in a way that's a thousand times better than how they were parented. They have parented incredibly consciously considering the situations they've been parenting in. That's miraculous to me.

※

I think about parenthood all the time, because it's what shapes us. The people who raise us shape us. They're the people who nurture you and care about you the most — or you might be raised and abused in addiction and chaos and violence.

I have a lot to do with Oranga Tamariki. It's the most awful fucking place. It's the state saying, 'We're better parents than you are,' and always to Māori parents because that's the way you retain control — you take their babies away.

I know lots of neglected children from houses in Remuera and the likes — homes where there's really extreme physical and sexual violence — and those kids aren't being uplifted. There are very few Pākehā kids in care — 75 per cent of kids in Oranga Tamariki care are Māori.

When you take a child away from their home, it doesn't matter how much trauma they're experiencing there — it's more trauma to remove them. Because what a child needs is attachment. One of the women had her daughter taken off her and put in an abusive foster home. If you're going to take these kids away from their families, you'd better make sure they're going to a safe space.

When a child is removed from a parent and uplifted by the state, the primary attachment — usually the mother — also spirals downwards.

Because without their children, they see themselves as having no worth at all in this world.

Parenting is fucking hard. You're dealing with societal expectations and your own expectations — it's a lot. It's reason one-million-and-seventy-trillion why I haven't had children. The women are also really aware of society's judgement as single Māori mothers. They're very aware of being seen as statistics. But there's no one way of parenting, and to expect some sort of stereotypical ideal is crazy. Is your child fed? Is there a roof over their head? Do they have consistent routines? Do you love them? Then they're fine.

✳

I tell the women I love them often, because that's what they need to hear. I never see myself as their mother, but the mother thing comes in quite strongly. When I did an interview for a magazine, one of the women was talking to the journalist. She said, 'I have a mother, but Jackie's my mum.' This woman is 63 — older than me. It made me feel really sad. She was the product of her mother's affair, and she was thrashed to within an inch of her life because she was a reminder that her mother had been unfaithful.

I'm not their mother, but I'm paid to be available for them. They know that someone in the world has their back and is always thinking about them — so in that way, I play a similar role to that of a mother in their lives. One of the women said, 'Darling, I had a lovely mother. But she didn't protect me. You're the mother that protects me.'

Society has taught us that children need their fathers, but abusers don't really care about the children. They use the children to get to the victim of their abuse, because that's the person they have power over — and they're not letting go of their power. And the children feel that in their bones. I know, because I was married to a person like this.

✳

My husband died four and a half years ago. He drank himself to death. From the beginning it was obvious to others that it was an abusive relationship — but not to me, because it never is. I lived through really extreme psychological stuff, but I only came to understand that with the women at the refuge. They asked me about my story, so I told them. We were sitting and smoking on the steps of this little state house in Māngere East, which has the worst domestic violence stats in the country, and they were gasping.

I never left him. He had leukaemia. He had treatment for a year, then he went into remission and came out of remission. The effects of chemo lasted the rest of his life. He was never the same as he was before. He had chronic pain syndrome, and he was always a heavy drinker. He fucked his liver. He would occasionally broach the abuse, but he wouldn't get very deep into it. On the last day he was lucid when he was actively dying, he said, 'I hope I wasn't too mean to you.'

When he died, I had the opportunity to understand what my boundaries should be. Not having boundaries comes from people trying to fill their emotional needs. I came to realise that the love I'd had for him wasn't healthy — it came from that emotional need.

The police will say 55 per cent of women live or have lived in abusive relationships. It's a miracle to me that *anyone* knows how to be in a healthy relationship.

People assume that I'm really kind and loving. *Fuck off, no.* I work with power, everything I do is about power. My work's all about recovery and healing, and reminding people how powerful they are.

※

When I think about the word 'mother', I think about my wish that everyone can be who they are in the fullness of their being, whatever that means for them. As Auntie in Charge, that's what I'm about. The Aunties' byline is, 'Find your light, stand in your power.' I fought really hard for myself to do that.

※

One of the women has been nursing these monarch caterpillars. She's been talking about coming out of her own cocoon, turning into a butterfly. We looked at that metaphor and went back and forth. And I said to her, 'As I see it, you're not turning into anything — what you're doing is just stepping back into yourself.'

When I see someone who has stepped into their light, it's like finding a flower in the fucking desert.

The Addington house

LILY DUVAL

I was 22 when my friend Alice gave birth in the living room of our pokey Addington flat. She laboured in the blow-up pool for hours. Garish fish swam along the inflated plastic sides as she breathed and pushed, breathed and pushed. We (her partner, our other housemate, Clara, and I) wrung out hot towels to put on her lower back. We took photos and stoked the fire. I was wowed by how contained she was, her pain threshold honed from years of kidney stones. She made birth look powerful and strong.

Still, it was a lot. A beautiful, mind-bending, life-altering lot.

❋

Homebirth and child-rearing were the unexpected backdrop to the first half of my twenties. While other people I knew were experimenting with whatever substance was on hand or starting serious careers, I was bouncing babies or building block towers. This wasn't by design. I needed somewhere to live after my flat dissolved and a friend of a friend knew two women who needed a flatmate. One of them, Clara, had a one-year-old baby.

Alice and Clara were already friends, but I slipped easily into their world in the way you do when you're young. We bonded over books, crafts and a collective belief that the nuclear family was nuclear. Our partners lived elsewhere — including the father of the child. We wanted to create a women's space.

Living with a baby turned out to be fun. I also discovered I was quite good with them. I could hold them confidently, sling them from hip to hip as I popped the kettle on or checked the mail. I could calm them down or entertain them with nonsense noises. This was a mutually beneficial arrangement. When I was on the floor drawing with crayons or reading stories, I forgot myself. The depression and anxiety that had dogged me since childhood dimmed. Compared to the hot mess of university parties, life with a child felt wholesome and meaningful.

As much as I enjoyed this new life, having my own babies was not on my mind. Children seemed like something for later — something that was situationally dependent. Children, I thought, were to be considered if the right person came along. I was good at considering things — I'd racked up four years of student debt doing it.

I was still young enough to find new and unusual things exciting. And living with children in my early twenties fit the bill. In our society, you don't usually live with babies unless they're related to you in some way. The house was a unique opportunity to experience life with children without the weight of a lifelong commitment.

⁕

I t wasn't only the baby that made our house different. Nothing we did was subtle or coincidental. Everything from the décor to the food we ate was carefully planned. We idolised women's communes from the 1970s and radical activists like those who occupied Greenham Common Women's Peace Camp. We plastered the living room walls with feminist icons and our shelves were stacked with books by Anaïs Nin, bell hooks and Virginia Woolf. One day, at a secondhand store, I found a book called *Lesbian Nuns Tell Their Story*, and proudly sat it alongside *The Enchanted Broccoli Forest* and *Cunt: A Declaration of Independence*. Our house was a cauldron of religious-flavoured idol worship and raging wannabe-lesbian separatism. Even our letterbox wanted to 'Smash the Patriarchy'.

The house was our collective creative womb. We sewed, crocheted, knitted, painted, scrapbooked and cooked. We blended the aesthetics and skills of storybook grandmothers with radical feminist ideology. We were militantly vegan. We hosted 'Food not Bombs'-style community meals in the park, where we foisted baking made from chickpea flour and tofu on unsuspecting neighbours.

Each of us, at different times, shaved our heads. Even though I'd sported a short and shaggy style since high school, the experience of buzzing my hair to a thin layer of fuzz was more intense than I was willing to admit. I felt a sense of loss, as if my hair had sheltered me from the hard realities of the world. With my hair went my grandma's floral dresses and unwanted attention from men. I started a lifelong love affair with overalls and checked shirts.

Bit by bit, we turned the back lawn into a riotous vege garden. We lined the kitchen window sills with used soy milk cartons made into seedling trays. That first summer, sunflowers arched overhead and sweetpeas, borage and nasturtium tumbled from curving brick-bordered beds. We planted the 'three sisters' — corn, beans and pumpkin — and saw ourselves in them: the corn tall, straight and supportive to give the beans something to climb, while the pumpkins provided shade for the roots. Out back, a ring of stones marked a pagan circle where our women's group concocted a pastiche of rituals celebrating female goddesses and the seasons.

All this wild creative energy manifested in other ways. By the second summer, Alice was pregnant. I remember taking her picture in the third trimester of her pregnancy; she held her belly while the garden rampaged around her, swollen pumpkins at her feet.

This seemed like a natural trajectory. What was more organic and women-centric than giving birth and nurturing a child? I wasn't about to get pregnant, but I found ways to contribute my thoughts, writing an honours essay about Margaret Atwood's *Oryx and Crake* and male jealousy of the power of birth.

In our house, birth was more than a remarkable physical triumph of the female body, it was deeply symbolic. Clara had taken the high she experienced giving birth at home and channelled it into studying midwifery. We spent many evenings discussing how homebirth could give women power over their own bodies. Clara had her birth picture up on the lounge wall. In the photo, she cradled her first child, her henna-ed hair flaming against the redness of labour. Anyone who came over for a cup of tea could see the bloody naked triumph of her motherhood.

Life was electrically ideological. It was also hypocritical.

After Alice's baby was born in the living room, the energy in the house changed. Rather than three women to one child, there were two children to contend with. And from my vantage point, newborns seemed impossibly hard. Baby cries percolated in the night, occasionally bubbling over into long screams. Morning brought little reprieve. As well as the breastfeeding, there were buckets of soiled nappies to scrub and washing to hang out. Mothering looked beautiful but also chaotic and stifling. I had no idea how Clara and Alice were coping. I think often they weren't.

Tensions had always simmered beneath the sisterhood, but with two babies in the house, they started to escalate. From Clara, I endured comment after comment about my childfree privilege — jealousy over my ability to pick up or put down a baby depending on my mood. I was given the silent treatment one day and then asked to babysit the next. I was always both inside and outside family life. For all the help I tried to offer, I couldn't make milk flow from my breasts.

At times, I thought about bowing out. But if I felt as if I wasn't ready for this life, how did Alice and Clara feel? I felt compelled to stay and help, and I watched as motherhood swallowed them.

There was the mundanity of rent, food and bills, and external pressures, too. As hard as we tried to fortify the world we'd built, the outside world insisted on ignoring the letterbox. There were the frowns of disapproval from my housemate's parents at the way the children were dressed (boys in dresses!) or the strange separate living arrangements with the fathers. And there were the men themselves.

On paper, there was never much space for men in our world, but the children of the house told a different story. Men had always lurked on the periphery. I think we were ashamed of them. Mine snuck in my sash window at night. They were the quiet click of the front door at bedtime, the odour change in the 'if it's yellow let it mellow' toilet. They were like good Victorian children or obedient ghosts.

By the time Alice's baby was born I'd ditched cis men for queer partners, but parenthood tied Alice and Clara to the fathers of their children. The difficulty of ferrying small babies between households eventually wore down any separatist fantasies we'd nurtured. Men started to come through the doors, in the daylight.

Clara gave birth to her second child in her bedroom, behind a closed door. Only her partner and the midwife were in the room with her. Before the baby arrived, I'd shifted into the garden shed, where bamboo forced its way through the floorboards and strange moulds crept along the walls. It was a high price to pay for a sense of independence. I wasn't the only one not coping. Soon, overwhelmed by expectation and the relentlessness of living up to our own self-imposed doctrine, Alice moved out to live with her partner and some other friends. When the earthquakes shook the feminist icons off the living room wall, I decided I'd had enough, too.

※

Our vision lasted no more than a few years, but I still find tendrils of that experience curled around my adult self. The years I spent in that flat were formative — I became a feminist, learnt to cook and garden and craft, and I learnt a lot about children. But they were also damaging to my self-esteem.

It took me a while to embrace my freedom. Eventually, I began to think that if it was a privilege to be childfree, then the opposite must also be true. Privately, I started to feel that if everyone could spend some of their early twenties living with children — and especially with babies — then far fewer people would decide to have them later on.

For the remainder of my twenties, being queer proved to be its own form of birth control. Still, my childfree state was never a conscious decision. I've never felt that certainty about not having children I've heard expressed by other women. For me, it was mostly down to circumstance. At 21, I'd wandered into a situation that proved to be more effective than a long-lasting IUD. And though my opinions might have softened by the time I hit 30, my chaotic romantic life made children look like a laughable fantasy. I felt the tentacles of my family's depression and anxiety questing for the next generation. I didn't want to create anything it could sucker onto.

When I started dating cis men again in my thirties, I realised I might need to firm up my position. And when I met my partner of the past five years, the topic came up pretty quickly. He's older than me and has never wanted kids, so it was not up for debate. Although it felt like another situation I'd simply wandered into, I was happy to have some certainty.

Now that I know I won't have children, I've fortified my childfree narrative. If I ever feel a pang for my future old-biddy self, I focus on all the time I have to go tramping, lie in bed in the mornings, and write a book.

※

was 26 when I held my sister's hand as she brought my niece into the world. She was at home in a birthing pool. Unlike Alice's, this birth felt more like how mine might go if I was to have a baby — a frenzy of uncontained agony and joy.

It was another successful homebirth. My sister was powerful and strong and my niece emerged in the tumbledown living room of my sister's Woolston house in the early hours of the morning. I held her as my sister showered, and she did her first poo on me. It was the perfect benediction for a new auntie.

Being present for the birth of a child is a real honour. I can see why people want to become midwives — how they become addicted to the electricity of birth. There's something so good and hopeful about bearing witness to the beginning of new life.

But, however powerful birth is, I've come to put more stock in the next part. Because despite the madness of that Addington house there were some things we were right about. It's important there are more people in a child's life than their parent or parents, so with my free time I take my five nieces and nephews on adventures — foraging for fungi, playing dinosaurs or simply reading books before bed.

My childfree privilege is the privilege to be in their lives — not as a mum or a dad, but as an auntie.

Blinded

ANNA BORRIE

A nthony, you mean well. I say this because you have shown more interest in my case than the last two, but you still can't stop forgetting that you are not a gynaecologist. I'm sitting in a chair opposite you, my notebook of questions in my hands. I have learnt more about parts of the body in the past six years than I ever did in any biology class. Today we are talking about my feet, yet within a minute you bring up my uterus — asking me if I want to have children.

This speech reflects many previous ones, yet for some reason this conversation feels like the last drop that threatens to break the dam. I am practised at keeping my reactions neutral while within specialists' offices — something that I cannot say about the hallways and footpaths outside them.

I ignore your comments and focus on the questions that I want answered. The lines on the pages do not blur this time. I leave the hospital numb, but sometimes numbness feels worse than feeling angry or upset — the constant disconnection between mind and body.

But Anthony, you were not the only one, nor were you the worst.

☀

My uterus often gets in the way of diagnosis, as though doctors are blinded by my female reproductive organs. Medical appointments reflect the inappropriate job interview I had straight after graduating, where my age, marital status and desire to reproduce were of the highest importance.

Sometimes it's comical — isn't that right, Xavier? I laughed in your face when you asked me if I wanted to have children. You stopped with your nasal camera apparatus in hand, and did not seem amused. You did not see the humorous side while you cleaned my snot from the implement.

Other times, the question is downright disrespectful and deserves a verbal slap in the face. I won't apologise for that, Carlos, and if I left that review on Google you so desperately wanted it would sound like we had gone on a bad date. Compliments on how I look for my age, on what I'm wearing, and advice on when I should start having children were not the services I was seeking from a podologist.

There is more understanding from those who also have uteruses, but the topic still slips into conversation. While I was lying on a massage table and you were manipulating my shoulder you couldn't help yourself, could you Diana? You professed surprise that I had chosen my own health over reproducing. The conversation wheezed to a stop as I closed my eyes and focused on my breathing.

As I lay covered in needles, about to be pricked with more, it seemed like the right time to bring up the question about having kids, or so you thought, Melina. As tears filled my eyes, I said nothing but gestured my hands at my body, communicating that the last thing it needs is extra physical strain.

※

The one time I am prepared to talk about it is when I go to see a gynae-cologist. It is a long overdue eight years between visits — previous trauma has made me not want to open my legs for a white coat. I waited extra months to avoid seeing a man, the last one having left a very painful impression.

You're not what I'm expecting, Marta. You don't ask me about when I want to use my bits, but you do ask why it's been so long between visits. I give you the short answer as I place my legs in the stirrups.

Your hand pauses on my thigh and I recall that last time I was in this position, someone who had never had abnormal cells burnt from their cervix told me that it wouldn't hurt a bit.

Marta, you seem shocked, wanting to know where this malpractice happened, as I received no pain relief or sedation — just a man in a white coat telling me not to overreact.

※

I t's a hot spring afternoon, the terrace is full of friends and one baby. It's been seven months since I was released from the hospital, and I'm still recovering from the summer when I nearly didn't make it out of the ICU. This is seared into my brain, but apparently not yours, Jamie. I have never had my partner jump to my defence as quickly as when you bat the 'do you want to have a baby' questions towards me. He physically puts a hand between us, telling you to leave me alone, that I've been through enough.

When I'm asked if I'm joining the pregnancy 'club', I can't stop the words tumbling out of my mouth, can I, Sara? You hear about my sleepless nights, the constant abdominal pain, the tiredness and need to lie down. My symptoms match yours rather well, and I rhetorically ask if you'd like more of this. You have the decency to stop talking.

Then there was the scare that had the tiny gossipy medical clinic in a spin. They saw my nausea symptoms almost as a positive test. The words of my specialist, Paula, were like a glowing neon sign in my head: pregnancy would be detrimental to my recovery. She was right, I could feel the unbalance and wobbliness in my body. It had only been 16 months since leaving the hospital. I talked to you, Leah, a childhood friend, while I waited for the results. My reasons were not sufficient enough, in your eyes, to not want a child — but then again, you are not living what I am.

It is in these moments that I am relieved that the younger version of myself never idealised reproduction. I remember looking at a billboard and thinking, *Of course population equals pollution.* I never really thought about the future me, which makes the deconstruction of my body a purely current pain, not an ongoing sadness for the life that I had hoped to live.

※

N ew health problems appear like weeds along a pavement, to distract me from the possibilities of my uterus. I have no energy to discuss the topic with the able-bodied. For some of us, the option is off the table for whatever reason — being childless has not been a choice, or it has been a hard choice to make.

The medical world has made it clear that my uterus is impossible not to pass comment on. So far it is the healthiest part of me, and yet it would be unhealthy to put it to use.

This has been written with the aid of a text-to-speech application, because I am unable to effectively type with two hands. Which was something that I brought to your attention, Rosa, as we sat opposite each other last week going over the pros and cons of hand surgery. You didn't ask about my bits. Thanks for getting it — not many doctors do.

I am not on a beach

KATHRYN VAN BEEK

nfertility essays typically conclude with a final paragraph in which the author reveals that they had a baby.

This is not one of those essays. In this essay, all the babies are dead.

Wilhelmina (Willa) Elizabeth

Wilhelmina is not seven years old. She is not named after her maternal grandparents. She will never inherit her great-nana's engagement ring, or her Dutch great-grandparents' walnut-veneer clock with a smiling picture of the moon. She doesn't have freckles and sun-streaked hair. She doesn't love kittens, and drawing, and jumping on the trampoline. She doesn't make moss gardens with tinfoil rivers and rice shores. She doesn't sneak into my study when I'm writing, perching up beside me to write stories of her own.

Wilhelmina seemed like a sure thing. But just as I was making the switch from regular to maternity clothes, after we'd put up the curtain in her nursery, after we'd seen her flicker on an ultrasound screen . . . something changed. Her heart stopped beating. It was a missed miscarriage, and I had to have an operation to remove her.

Wilhelmina (Willa) Elizabeth lies buried in our garden, beneath a white iceberg rose.

Beginnings

But does this story begin with Wilhelmina?

Or does it begin with our first IVF cycle — the injections that left a metal taste in my mouth, the doctors with their BMWs, the way a little white spark flashed on the monitor each time an embryo was implanted?

Perhaps it begins earlier, with the charming anecdote about how my husband and I raised the day-old kitten I found on a footpath?

Maybe it starts before I was born, when Grandad was deployed to Japan in the aftermath of atomic blasts. When there's no obvious narrative, you search for the beginning anywhere you can.

How to cure infertility

- Just relax!
- Eat pineapple.
- Lie with your legs up in the air after sex.
- Lose weight, stop smoking, stop drinking.
- Avoid caffeine.
- Buy some expensive powders from a naturopath.
- Have some operations!
- Harness the vibrations of the universe to manifest what you want.

It is important to do all these things because it is a proven fact that no overweight, stressed-out, coffee-drinking, pineapple-avoiding smokers who failed to lie with their legs up in the air after sex have ever become pregnant.

Of course, there are also clinical options:

- Do IVF.[1]
- Do IVF but with a donor egg.
- Do IVF but with a donor egg and donor sperm.
- Do IVF but with a donor egg and donor sperm and a surrogate.

At what point does a baby become a commodity?

Does it matter?

---

1   If you qualify for publicly funded treatment or can afford to go private.

I am holding a pencil

I'm sitting at my desk with a pencil in my hand. I should be drawing an illustration for the children's book I wrote about that cat I found. In this version of the story, it's a little girl who finds the day-old kitten on a footpath. I should be colouring the golden pigtails of the girl. I should be colouring the lavender dress of her mother. Instead I cry at my desk, coloured pencil in hand, for two days.

Do you have kids?

Sometimes people ask if you have kids. What a great question. Here are some answers I prepared earlier:

- 'Ha ha ha, I have cats! Do you have pets?' (Used frequently. The other person starts talking about their pets, and social crisis is averted.)
- 'Oh, it didn't work out for us. How about you?' (Used infrequently. The other person looks briefly mortified, but then talks about their own kids.)

Untested answers:

- 'Despite trying for many years, having a healthy lifestyle, undergoing several operations and interventions, doing IVF, becoming pregnant three times, doing the Oranga Tamariki adoption and fostering course and eating pineapple, no, I do not have kids.'
- 'Did you know that one in four pregnancies ends in miscarriage?'
- 'Fuck off.'

A baby is better than a book

Writing a book is nothing compared to having ~~sex~~ a baby.
Face the facts:

- You can't have a gender reveal for a book.
- Babies don't have any challenging ideas.
- A baby will grow up to contribute to the economy. Will a book?
- Everyone understands babies.
- It takes *so long* to read a book, whereas you can admire a baby in 30 seconds.
- You can't buy a onesie for a book.
- A baby will grow up and make more babies. Will a book?

Some life events are so big and important that the grinding gears of capitalism can be stilled to allow them to be celebrated at work. These events are:

- Leaving your job.
- Having a baby.
- ~~Writing a book~~.

Everyone loves participating in baby showers at work. What a great part of the workday for everyone. Ask the person who wrote the book to organise the baby shower!

Wolfgang (Wolfie) Peter

Wolfie is not six years old. He doesn't have flat feet and a blonde rooster comb of hair like his father. He doesn't love going up Flagstaff Hill and looking down at the cranes and trains in the port below. He doesn't dress up in Wilhelmina's butterfly costume and spin around the lounge with his wings outstretched. He's not scared of windy days and the neighbour's gentle Labrador. He doesn't tell me I'm the bestest mummy in the world.

Wolfgang (Wolfie) Peter gushed into my jeans while I was doing the dishes. The rest of the 'pregnancy tissue' was removed in hospital. His tiny life is remembered with a yellow rose.

More great questions

Q: 'Why don't you just adopt?'

A: 'Why don't you?'

Q: 'Because I had my own baby. Is passing on your own genes really so important that you wouldn't adopt?'

A: 'Well, it didn't seem to occur to *you* to adopt. But frankly, it's not really an option in New Zealand.'

Q: 'Why don't you adopt from overseas?'

A: 'It's really expensive — and kind of an ethical minefield.'

Q: 'Why don't you foster a kid?'

A: 'Why don't you?'

Q: 'I'm asking you . . .?'

A: 'OK, we actually went and did the Oranga Tamariki adoption and fostering training course. But fostering didn't appeal for a wide range of reasons.'

Q: 'But what about the Home for Life programme? Isn't that basically the same as adoption?'

A: 'I spoke to an acquaintance who'd looked after a little girl who was on the Home for Life pathway. But ultimately, her birth parents got her back. That was probably a great thing for that little girl. But I couldn't set myself up for a loss like that.'

Q: 'Why don't you use a surrogate?'

Thank heavens for the 'pro-life' brigade

No one cares when you have a miscarriage because a miscarriage is a dead baby and everyone knows you only get attention for a *live* baby. You should have had a *live* baby, doofus!

Thank heavens for the 'pro-life' brigade, who are there for you when you lose your baby. They hold your hand, wipe away your tears and bring you flowers and a nice cup of tea. They seem to be the only ones who understand that your baby meant something to you. They are the ones who raise funds for miscarriage-prevention research. They weave kete for your baby so you can take their remains home with dignity, and not in a plastic pottle that looks like a poo-sample container. They run the well-resourced network of miscarriage support groups across the country. There is a legal requirement to offer counselling for abortion,[2] and they are the ones who lobbied for this requirement to be extended to miscarriage, too.

Ha, ha, ha!

There is no counselling! There is no kete! The 'pro-life' brigade doesn't care about you! They are the ones who stand outside the hospital waving the gruesome placards you have to pass on your way to get your dead baby removed.

You should have had a *live* baby, doofus!

Fern Rosalie

Fern is not five years old. Fern does not have red hair like her auntie. Fern does not love being pushed on a swing or counting logging trucks as they roll past. Fern is not better than all of us at finding the right jigsaw-puzzle pieces. Fern does not enjoy digging potatoes, watering the garden and picking berries. She doesn't laugh with delight at stick insects. She hasn't been scared to go to the toilet ever since Wolfie told her a crocodile lives down the drain.

---

2   'Information on abortion', Ministry of Health — Manatū Hauora, 21 June 2022, www.health.govt.nz/your-health/healthy-living/sexual-health/information-abortion

Fern was an embryo who became a 'chemical pregnancy' and spent long days weeping out of me in the style of miscarriage known euphemistically as a 'heavy period'.

Fern Rosalie is not memorialised in our garden. I was over memorialising dead babies by then. And I wasn't really even sure if she'd existed at all.

Inspirational quotes

'Lockdown was so hard for people with kids.'
— work colleague, delivered with a passive-aggressive glare

'Women who don't have kids tend to go a bit strange.'
— elderly artist in a community hall where I was the life model

'She was only 40 when she died — and it's particularly *tragic* because she was a *mother*.'
— general gist of any media story about any mother's untimely death

'Duke and Duchess of Sussex announce their baby joy!'
— international news released on International Pregnancy and Infant Loss Awareness Day, 15 October 2018

'The choice to not have children is selfish.'
— Pope Francis (who himself does not have children)

'When I watch from afar and see events such as this today, it's not as a politician. I see them just as a mother.'
— Prime Minister Jacinda Ardern

'There should be more writing residencies for people with kids.'
— person on Twitter

'Not having kids means you occupy a slightly excluded space in society.'
— my husband

Parents would definitely be rich geniuses if they didn't have kids

If parents didn't have to spend all their hard-earned cash on their kids, they would be rich. So rich! They would wear ethically made loungewear, and fly around the world, and laze beside hotel pools while drinking colourful cocktails. They would invest in NFTs and drive Teslas and have Scandinavian furniture and designer dogs.

If parents didn't have to spend all their precious energy on their kids, they would achieve all their goals. All of them! They would write novels, run marathons, start businesses and save the planet — all before breakfast! They would get all the writing residencies — and all the art residencies, too.

Harnessing the vibrations of the universe
Sadly, I have failed to manifest what I want.

It is true that I earnestly visualised receiving a writing residency — but I did not visualise it correctly, and was therefore condemned to writing communications for a district health board during a pandemic.

It is true that I pictured life with Wilhelmina — but I did not picture it properly, and was therefore condemned to watching my husband convert her nursery into his games room.

It is true that I have not bothered to envisage achieving great riches. Even this doofus knows that financial abundance is generally obtained through intergenerational wealth transfer, and not through positive thinking.

I am not standing on Lego
I am not trying to dry tomorrow's school clothes on a clothes airer in front of the heat pump. Wilhelmina is not chasing the cat around the lounge. The pile of laundry beside me on the couch is not as high as I am. Wolfie has not found a dog-eared corner of wallpaper that he is slowly ripping away from the plaster. Wilhelmina has not crashed into the airer, sending it tumbling onto Fern's head. I am not leaping to come to Fern's rescue, the soft arch of my foot crunching down onto a piece of Lego. I am not yowling words that I'll regret later. I am not standing on Lego.

Words
There are lots of words in this world. It's good to put the right words in the right order.

Improved marketing slogan:
'Fun for the whole family!'
'Fun for everyone!'

Improved 'getting to know you' question:
'Are you pregnant?'
'Where are you from?'

'Where are you really from?'

'When are you having kids?'

'Where did you go to school?'

'Are you going to have more kids?'

'Do you have grandkids?'

'What do you like to do in your spare time?'

More accurate names:

Midwife (from the Old English, 'with woman')

Midbabe (from the Old English, 'with baby')

Infertility Support Group

Group For Women Who Have Had Kids But Who Are, For Some Reason, Still In This Group

Pregnancy Help

Anti-Abortion Group That Provides No Actual Pregnancy Help As I Discovered When I Saw Their Office Sign And In Desperation Wandered In Saying Help My Baby Is Dying Help Help

If you thought words could be bad, check out these terms:
- Products of conception
- Spontaneous abortion
- Evacuation of retained products
- Dilation and curettage (D&C).

See also:
- 'Children are a gift'
- 'Blessed with children'.

If people with children are blessed, am I cursed?

Everyone down at the mall, people on meth, Kim Kardashian, Ivan the Terrible and Caligula had kids.

Why not me?

What moral failing do I have that Ivan the Terrible did not?

Did he just eat more pineapple?

I am not trying to get through the evening without losing my shit
I am not driving home with pounding temples and an aspiration to crawl into bed, only to discover my husband lying on the couch under a duvet claiming to have a cold while the kids run amok. I do not swallow two painkillers and open the fridge door to see a bunch of silverbeet, half a cabbage and some bok choy staring limply back at me.

I do not try to ignore the piercing sounds of screaming children as I chop and fry these godforsaken vegetables, roll them into pastry logs and put them in the oven. I do not walk into the laundry to see that even though my husband has been home for two and a half hours, he has not put on a load of washing. I do not close the door of the laundry behind me, sink into a crouch and put my head in my hands.

Good ancestors
#notallparents:
- Drive SUVs
- Eat meat
- Buy plastic crap
- Watch TV

Me:
- Insufferable
- Changed the Holidays Act.[3]

Good for me. But who will want my wedding photos when I die?

The magical superpowers of motherhood
Even if you have raised a defenceless creature from infancy and loved him fiercely, even if you have felt the full range of human emotions, and even if you have an excellent imagination, the sad fact of the matter is that you will never know true selflessness and empathy until you are a mother.

(So. Get. Out. Of. The. Way. Of. Their. Damn. Strollers.)

---

3   To enable people who have endured pregnancy loss to take bereavement leave. See Tess McClure, 'New Zealand brings in bereavement leave for miscarriages and stillbirths', *The Guardian*, 25 March 2021, www.theguardian.com/world/2021/mar/25/new-zealand-miscarriages-stillbirths-bereavement-leave

Facts of life

If I were a cow or a sheep, the farmer would have killed me by now.

I am in a work meeting

I am in a work meeting with a woman I haven't met before, and she is very beautiful and very pregnant. I'm sure she is older than I am. She is wearing a lovely maternity dress and it reminds me of the dresses I bought, and then gave away. The baby blanket I bought, and gave away. The copy of *Don't Puke On Your Dad* that I got for my husband, but gave away. I think about how upset my husband was last Father's Day. I think about all the milestones we'll never share. I think about customer engagement! And measurable goals! And search engine optimisation!

The pitter patter of little carbon footprints

Reasons to have kids:

- Because you just want them
- Because you want someone to look after you when you're old
- Because everyone else is doing it
- To provide a temporary sense of purpose
- To pass on your genes
- So you'll have grandchildren one day
- To carry on your family name.

Environmental effects of having kids:

- Annual 58.6 metric tonne carbon footprint per kid (the average car emits 4.6 metric tonnes of carbon dioxide annually)[4]
- 5500 disposable nappies per baby[5]
- etc.

---

4   Seth Wynes and Kimberly A. Nicholas, 'The climate mitigation gap: Education and government recommendations miss the most effective individual actions', *Environmental Research Letters* 12, no. 7, 074024 (12 July 2017), https://doi.org/10.1088/1748-9326/aa7541 and 'Greenhouse gas emissions from a typical passenger vehicle' (overviews and factsheets), United States Environmental Protection Agency, 30 June 2022, www.epa.gov/greenvehicles/greenhouse-gas-emissions-typical-passenger-vehicle

5   Anne Beston, 'Up to our knees in disposable nappies', *New Zealand Herald*, 17 February 2006, www.nzherald.co.nz/nz/up-to-our-knees-in-disposable-nappies/J5L33GW76WZJRADJHSWB35DPZU

~~Popes~~ People love to say that not having children is selfish. Not having children is selfish because:

- ?
- ?
- ?

Definitions

Cambridge Dictionary: A mother is a female parent. A parent is a mother or a father.

Oxford Dictionary: A mother is a woman in relation to her child or children.

Merriam-Webster Dictionary: A child is an unborn or recently born person.

Am I a mother?

It's very important not to upset people

Just because you're upset that you had three miscarriages and zero kids doesn't mean you have the right to express that sadness and make everyone else feel bad.

That's why we prefer you wait until you have *had* a child before you write your essay about infertility. That way we can reassure people that it will turn out all right in the end!

So the Duke and Duchess of Sussex announced their pregnancy on International Pregnancy and Infant Loss Awareness Day. So what? That's not on them and their team of public relations professionals. If you feel triggered, that's on you![6]

So you had to walk past a row of baby booties for sale on the way to your D&C consultation. So what? Why *wouldn't* a hospital sell baby booties in the gynaecology department?

Now shut up and organise that baby shower for Sharon.

It is not Christmas

It is not Christmas and we are not sitting in the lounge in our pyjamas. There isn't a Christmas tree so tall that the star Wilhelmina made brushes the roof. There is no pile of presents for the kids to dive into, no scents of coffee, pine

---

6 But please don't post your baby-loss story on social media — what a downer on Harry and Meghan's special day.

and pancakes, no sound of wrapping paper being ripped, no festive music on the record player, no squeals of excitement. Wolfie doesn't give me a jellyfish he made from an old yoghurt container. Fern doesn't cry because she's jealous of Wolfie's new T-Rex lamp. Wilhelmina doesn't hand me a badly wrapped parcel that contains a horrible scarf. I don't pull her into my arms and whisper 'I love you' into her ear.

Shame

How did I get so far into this essay without writing about shame? Shame is the grimy shroud that smothered me after ~~I lost~~[7] Wilhelmina miscarried. A shroud so dusty I couldn't breathe.

Shame stems from the humiliation of having violated a social norm. Not because miscarriage isn't normal — it is. Not because infertility isn't normal — it is. But because we're conditioned from childhood to believe that we'll have children of our own. We sense that childlessness is strange and suspicious.

Culture — like history — belongs to the victors, the dominant group.

I am on the phone

We're in Covid-19 lockdown and I answer a number I don't recognise. It's the embryologist from our fertility clinic. After the last miscarriage, years ago, we said our final and almost certainly defective embryo could go to research, into the bin, whatever. We were done. But there is obviously a glitch in their system. The embryo still exists, and now the embryologist is ringing me about it. We have to sign some papers so he can dispose of it. Why is he ringing now, years after we put all this to bed? He emails the papers through, and I ignore them. Push it down, down, down into a little box beneath the floor. Down, down, down towards the earth's core.

Definitions II

I am a mother of dead things.

Conclusions

I asked a friend to read this essay. 'I think it could do with a narrative thread that binds the whole piece,' she said. 'At times I wasn't clear on the argument or the lasting impression you want to leave.'

---

7   I didn't lose her.

This is excellent feedback.

There are many beautifully written essays about infertility,[8] and I thought this would be one of them.

I published beautiful essays about my first round of IVF. But when I turned in the series about my second round, the editor ghosted me. The second series was never printed.

My hunch is that without a baby, the second series (injections, egg harvesting, implantation, hope, miscarriage, grief) was just too similar to the first. Because without a baby, nothing changes.

There is no conclusion.

There is no moral.

No thesis.

No narrative thread.

It just is what it is — a small injustice that will never be resolved, and a kaleidoscope of emotions that range from sadness to relief.

But anyway, have I told you about my cats?

I am not on a beach

I am not sitting on the pale sand at Long Beach beneath a blue and white striped sunshade, looking at Wilhelmina and Wolfie as they run into the water. They are not tumbling through the waves, splashing one another and laughing at the oystercatchers. I am not watching as my husband makes Wolfie shriek with delight at his sea lion impression. I am not rubbing sunscreen onto Fern's back and adjusting her hat. I am not on a beach.

---

8   You know, the ones that conclude with babies being born or otherwise procured.

No car, no kids

ANDI C. BUCHANAN

t's never a good idea to let local community Facebook arguments keep you awake at night. I keep swearing I'll block the group — maybe delete the app entirely — and yet here I am, when I could be doing something nice with my time, arguing with the local NIMBY who has decided that families cannot live in townhouses and each need at least three parking spaces if one of their children plays sport. I rehearse arguments on the way to the bus stop, conceding there's a reason — other than my argumentative personality — that they're getting to me. The local NIMBY is, of course, ridiculous — as am I, for caring what they think — however the consensus that parenting is very difficult as a non-driver seems to be more reasonable.

I've lain awake at night thinking about how I would manage it if I had a kid. There's a school and a kindy just down the road, but what if they didn't have spaces for more kids? Or we didn't like them but felt stuck just because they were close? There's a GP within walking distance, but it's run by evangelical Christians and I'm non-binary and have green hair, and so I'm registered elsewhere. If we needed to go to after-hours, how reliable are the taxis, who are the people we could ask for a ride and how frequently? What if our child was disabled in a way that meant we couldn't take them on a bus or in a taxi?

It's a variant of a conversation I've had with myself over the years, as

I watched friend after friend finally pushed to get their full licence by an impending baby. I once went to a play where someone told a story of having an abortion because they weren't ready, and later having a baby when they were, and having a car was a key feature in that readiness. That was a valid choice, as all personal reproductive choices are. A mature and thoughtful one, even. But it's amazing how linked cars and babies are. And now I'm not far off 40, and I'll never drive and, as it turns out I'll never have children, either.

※

I didn't have a very car-centric childhood. My parents did both drive, but we lived in a small town and were often collected from school or taken to the library on foot. Using public transport was always associated much more with freedom than limitation for me. In my teens I got used to crashing on friends' floors if it was too late to catch the last bus; eschewing the taxi of Mum and Dad, at least sometimes, was another step towards independence. A few years after I left home, they abandoned the cars and moved to a city known for its train network; when I visit I'm lent a train pass. My dad, mostly retired now, sometimes occupies himself by sitting on the platform of the station near IKEA to watch what people try to load on the trains.

What I'm saying is: my hypothetical child would cope, and so would I.

But my worries about raising a child without a car come with a far wider range of questions a disabled person thinking of possible parenthood might ask themselves. Could I run fast enough to catch my toddler? If I can't play catch with them will they just not develop motor skills? Could I tolerate the whole noisy, mess-making unpredictability? The sleep deprivation, when even one bad night makes my chronic pain flare? Could I use the pram as a mobility aid, or would I push it one-handed and use my crutch? Would I even be able to steer a pram — I'm pretty bad with supermarket trolleys, and don't get me started on luggage trolleys at airports. Could I learn to talk to other parents, or would they hate me? Oh God, what if my child was into sports?

I don't think you actually need to be able to drive to have children, or even to be a good parent. People raise children when all kinds of circumstances aren't ideal, and they're fantastic at it. Some people have children and then a curve ball hits them. Being able to plan with knowledge of the things I can't do is far from the worst situation, and I think my own limitations have made me more inclined to look for solutions and to find ways around things, in ways that others might struggle with.

could say I was lucky not to have experienced the sort of pressure to have children that many others do, and in some ways I am. But beneath that is the sense that not only are people like me not supposed to have children, but also maybe we shouldn't.

It's 2023 and eugenics is back! (It never went away.)

In a spectacularly titled article in *The Spinoff*, 'Plunket's founder was an awful person obsessed with eugenics', Emily Writes touches on how deeply embedded eugenics is, not just in how we think about having and raising children but in the institutions that support it.

It's not a thing of the past either. People are probably mostly being thoughtless when they claim that people should have IQ tests before they're allowed to parent, but I notice it. As I was writing this essay, Newstalk ZB presenter Kerre Woodham was attracting controversy for encouraging a caller who was suggesting that we breed out the 'undesirables'.

But perhaps the most pertinent example for me is the vast amount of money poured into identifying the genetic traits that underlie autism — with the goal of preventing the existence of future autistic people. Money that autistic people have so, so many ideas for how it could otherwise be spent to make our lives better.

It would be a very bad idea to have children to make a political point, and when you're disabled, when you're queer, sometimes it feels like everything's a political point — just being alive is a political point.

I want to tease out the nuances. To say that people who are disabled in the same ways I am can be, and are, amazing parents, while at the same time acknowledging it's OK to factor in how that disability affects my life when it comes to my decisions about parenthood. We just don't live in a world that makes room for nuance very often.

It's hard to discuss the complex ways disability affects our decisions to parent or not to parent when every choice seems like fodder to illustrate the idea that people like us can't be good parents and maybe we shouldn't parent at all and worst, what if your child is like you?

Not having children is a good decision for me, and for my partner, and for our cat who thinks she is the only one who should get our attention ever. But in a world swirling with ableism and eugenicist ideas, where we cannot be just individuals but are held up as representatives, it's never going to be quite that simple. It's something I've had to learn to navigate. It's something I'll maybe always be navigating.

There's a particular sort of family that does seem permitted to not just live but thrive without a car. They mostly seem to be blonde and the papers take pictures of them smiling on their bikes, the youngest child in a carrier on a parent's cargo bike. They have ditched the car for a more eco-friendly lifestyle, and they're loving it! When you read the accompanying article there are usually all kinds of exceptions, like 'We borrow my parents' car for supermarket trips' and 'We can always rent when we go on holiday.' They do Great Walks during school holidays, while on a very good day I can manage the 45-minute loop track near my house.

These people — or at least the way the media portrays them — make me feel more alienated than the average two-car family. I don't have borrowed cars as an option to fall back on. I can't ride a bike. And there's a good chance any child I had would be disabled in some of the same ways I am and also not able to ride a bike.

And yet, and yet, sometimes I want to show people I could do it. That people like me can be good parents. The issue isn't a lack of evidence that disabled people can parent well, that autistic people have feelings, that people with chronic illness can plan to ensure everyone's needs are met. It's an unwillingness to believe it.

Still, sometimes it nags at me that by factoring disability into my decision to not parent, I might be letting the side down. Am I saying 'Yes, there's something to this?' Almost all the difficulties I'd have could be ameliorated by good planning and money — they're not something inherently wrong with me. Another person could have written this and concluded with 'And now I have children, and it's harder in some ways but I've found ways to adapt and manage things, and I've never been happier.' And that person could have been me.

☀

Ultimately, I could list half a dozen reasons my partner and I ended up without children. I'm not sure if any of them are covered in this essay. The decision was settled in my mind when I dreamt we were expecting a baby and I was trying to section off a corner of the dining room with blankets to make a nursery, rather than give up the bedroom I've converted into my very nice home office. It's not that I actively don't want kids, I just want other parts of my life more.

It's a good decision. On balance, I'm happy with my life. I just wish it had been an easier choice, not in the sense of being clearer cut, without mixed emotions, but in the sense of being without so much baggage attached.

As it is, I seem to be attracting toddlers who want to be friends. It's partly because I have a dinosaur sticker on my crutch. It's probably also because I have a hat with dinosaurs . . . OK, the dinosaurs are a thing. Anyway, we make friends on the train. They're delightful. I wouldn't get to meet them if I drove. I wave them goodbye at the station. I'm glad I get to hang out with them. I don't want to be responsible for them. I sure as hell don't want to give up my home office for them. They have good taste in dinosaurs, though.

Benevolent deadbeat baby-daddy

JANIE SMITH

t was the abs that did it.

As shirtless Ross Poldark swung his scythe, his rippling six-pack shining under the Cornwall sun, my ovaries started to ache.

It wasn't a metaphorical ache caused by my fevered imagination. It was the cumulation of a couple of weeks' worth of hormone injections to pump up my ovaries with mature egg follicles until they resembled grenades on the ultrasound.

On the morning of my egg collection, I'd made the mistake of watching *Poldark* — specifically the episode where the curmudgeonly-yet-smouldering Ross doffs his top to tackle his fields with a large blade.

My overstimulated ovaries couldn't handle the heat. *Exemplary genetic specimen detected!* screamed my horde of extra hormones. *Deploy eggs! Reproduce now!*

A friend had nicknamed my egg collection day 'the Harvest Festival' and we'd joked about wreaths of flowers, pumpkins and ears of corn. The reality was my husband driving me to the fertility clinic early while I was doubled up with pain, with nary a butternut or gourd in sight.

My fertility specialist, who would perform the procedure, popped in to see me as I sat curled awkwardly in a plush armchair.

'You'd better be bringing drugs,' I told him.

'No, but I know a guy,' he replied, cracking himself up.

Luckily for both of us, his 'guy' delivered. I was sedated rather than completely knocked out, but later I had no memory of the procedure that had netted 31 eggs — an impressive number by egg-collection standards, I was told.

I was afraid that I might have rambled nonsensically under sedation, but I was too embarrassed to ask. Did I babble about abs? Did I confess that I secretly called my specialist the Harry Potter of fertility because he's a wizard, but very youthful-looking? It's probably best that I'll never know.

My eggs went off to be fertilised by a man I'd only met once — the medical equivalent of a one-night stand — and the physical part of my egg donation was done.

※

The idea of becoming an egg donor had been hanging around in the back of my mind for a few years before I signed up. It first came up at dinner with friends, when the conversation turned to fertility issues. Someone mentioned that there was a longer waiting list for egg than for sperm donors.

A little lightbulb switched on in my head and I thought, I could do that. At that point I didn't have children and my husband and I were on our own meandering, often ambivalent fertility journey, but I liked the idea of helping someone else.

I'm not especially sentimental and I didn't think I'd have any problems handing over my DNA to someone who needed it. I couldn't imagine feeling connected to someone else's child just because I'd contributed a few cells to their production. I understood why people might feel uncomfortable about potentially giving someone else a child that was biologically half theirs, but I didn't share those reservations.

In fact, the opposite was true. The thought of technically reproducing without doing any of the hard work involved appealed to me. I could potentially impregnate someone and walk away responsibility-free, like a benevolent deadbeat baby-daddy.

※

This would be a tidier story if I'd contacted the fertility clinic the very next day and signed up to hand over my eggs, but the street map of my life is not laid out in a grid formation. It's a convoluted mass of intersections, crescents and loops, with a few cul-de-sacs thrown in.

The idea of donating sat dormant while my husband and I worked, travelled and continued to debate the merits of having our own children.

I've never been a 'kid person'. In fairness to kids, I'm not really an 'adult person', either. Adults have a slight edge by being generally less likely to poop their pants in public or scream for the duration of long-haul flights. But we were fairly confident that we would love our own public poopers.

As it happened, it wasn't as simple as chucking the contraceptives and playing a lot of Marvin Gaye. We discovered that we had what is medically known as 'unexplained infertility'. Nothing much was wrong with us, but for unknown reasons, our DNA refused to combine.

We reluctantly hopped on the fertility carousel. A laparoscopy, rounds of clomiphene to induce ovulation, a go at intrauterine insemination (IUI), visits to a naturopath — nothing made a difference. In vitro fertilisation (IVF) was our best option and we had to wait a couple of years to get on the waiting list for funded treatment.

When we finally got to the top of the list, things started going wrong. I was unexpectedly made redundant at work and my husband took a pay cut to change jobs. I started a fixed-term position in a different kind of role, but quickly realised that I didn't want to stay. The thought of trying to have a baby when other parts of our lives were uncertain was overwhelming.

A conversation with a colleague put egg donation back in focus. She was about to do a round of IVF using donor eggs and encouraged me to sign up when I said I'd been considering it. Walking home from work that week, I had a moment of perfect clarity. I didn't want to do IVF at that time. I wanted something else.

※

'What do you want to do?' asked my husband when I got home and revealed my epiphany.

'I want to see polar bears in the wild,' I said.

I also wanted to try egg donation. We went out for ramen to celebrate our decision and start planning for bears and eggs.

The next day, I phoned the fertility clinic and asked to be taken off the IVF waiting list. I also made an appointment with Dr Harry Potter to find out if I could be a donor.

The process involved health and genetic screening, a counselling session for me and my husband, and my favourite part — the non-identifying profile. I was provided with potential recipients' anonymous profiles, and if I was happy to donate to them my profile would be sent to the recipient to see if they were interested in my eggs.

I right-swiped everyone. Donors can put conditions on who gets their genetic material, but I figured that anyone who was willing to go down the potentially complicated and expensive route of using donor eggs would treat any resulting child as a cherished magical unicorn.

My only stipulation was that if it was successful, the child had to be raised knowing that an egg donor was involved in their production. Donor-conceived children can request information about their donor from the age of 16 and I didn't want an upset teenager turning up on my doorstep, feeling like half their identity was a lie.

I wrote my profile with extreme candour because it was important to me that recipients knew what they were getting. If they were looking for a quiet, serious, athletically gifted child, my eggs were not for them.

I wrote in detail. Maybe too much detail. I refused to describe myself in generic terms, like 'loving' and 'caring'. You could be a serial killer with a necklace of human ears who absolutely adores your 12 axolotls and still call yourself caring. I wanted to give a true sense of myself.

Perhaps because of — or despite — my radical honesty, a couple right-swiped me back. We opted to meet for a joint counselling session.

☀

Meeting strangers to decide whether you want to reproduce with each other is a strange feeling, like a high-stakes blind date. My personality was pretty well covered in my profile, but my looks were only described in basic terms — height, weight, eye colour, hair colour. They might have met me and thought, heck no, we don't want to have a child with a very off-brand Anna Paquin who eats her feelings.

We were all relieved to get along well from the start, to the point where the counsellor could hardly get a word in and joked that we didn't need her there. We agreed to go ahead with the egg donation — a wildly successful result by first-date standards.

But first, I had polar bears to see. My husband and I jetted off to Churchill, a small town in Canada, to stare at the apex predators from a safe distance and snorkel with beluga whales in the freezing waters of Hudson Bay. I came back refreshed and ready to get the baby train rolling.

Egg donation involves two people each doing half of an IVF cycle. I did the first part — hormone injections and egg collection — and my baby-mama did the second part — preparing to have an embryo transferred to her uterus.

Ten of my eggs were considered too immature to use (I imagined the embryologist making fart jokes to determine which ones made the cut) but the remaining 21 went to the gamete dance party to meet some sperm. Nineteen of them initially fertilised and 12 went on to become viable embryos.

I was open with friends, family and workmates — anyone who would listen, really — about what I was doing and the reactions were largely positive. There were a couple of people who thought I might regret donating or feel differently if it was successful.

I also discovered that a lot of people had no idea what donation involved. Some thought I was donating all of my eggs, rather than a very small fraction. Many people wanted to know how my husband felt about it. He felt that it was my choice, and he thought it was great.

❉

Recipients are not required to stay in touch with their donors, but mine rapidly became friends and we exchanged phone numbers and email addresses. They told me when the first embryo transfer didn't work, and when the second one did.

They let me hitch a ride on their pregnancy rollercoaster. I went to the anatomy scan, where we found out the baby's sex together. I introduced them to my immediate family so they could see the potential genetic variations their child might have, and to prove that traits like natural athleticism, musical talent and skinny legs do exist in my gene pool, even though I didn't get them.

I felt hugely privileged to visit them, days after the baby was born, to meet our beautiful collaboration.

While their baby dream was coming true, I had taken a year off from all things fertility-related after donating to enjoy not injecting hormones into my stomach rolls and to appreciate the fruits of our group labour — especially the part where I didn't have to experience actual labour.

Once the year was up, we decided to try to board the baby train ourselves.

This time, I wisely avoided *Poldark* ahead of my egg collection, and my ovaries remained calm. We only managed to produce three viable embryos, but two of them turned into children. I still mostly escaped labour by producing enormous babies who required surgical removal.

✻

The egg-baby is a school child now and their creation is still the best group effort I've been part of. I don't know who they'll grow up to be, but helping to give them the chance to be, in general, is pretty rewarding. I'm an 'other' in the best sense of the word. A valued biological contributor. A rogue scion grafted onto another family's tree.

Visiting Churchill's polar bears was a chance to see a species that may well disappear in my lifetime, but donating eggs helped to create a life that will hopefully last long after I'm gone.

The child

SHANEEL LAL

am afraid I will wake up one day and my youth will be gone, and I will have missed out on all the experiences that take place when you are young and only young. I am afraid one day all I will feel is nostalgia for opportunities I could not take.

I am not smoking cannabis, I am not dancing in a club till 3 a.m., I feel afraid to post a shirtless selfie to Instagram, I do not engage in the queer hook-up culture, I am not on Tinder, and I have never been to a Sunday morning brunch with the gays.

It is not the acts of smoking cannabis or dancing in a club or hooking up that matter. What matters is that, at 23, I feel I am not allowed to be young. There are consequences for me where there aren't consequences for others.

☀

was born to an Indian and Fijian family in a little village in Fiji. My being a boy would have no doubt made everyone very happy. Boys continue the family legacy. Boys grow up into men who marry women and have children, preferably boys, who then repeat the cycle. The legacy is merely creating people to create more people. The task sounds benign, but the duty is enforced strictly, and those who do not uphold it are treated like failures.

Little did my family and community know they were in for an unpleasant surprise. I'll give you a hint: I turn out to be gay. The family legacy will hang by a loose thread. I will not marry a woman and after the childhood I have, the prospects of having children myself become slim. Does the family legacy end with me?

My life had an idyllic start. I spent my early days playing with dolls with my sister and our neighbour's daughters. Badminton and hide-and-seek. I ran from my house to the other end of the village barefoot on the muddied grass footpath, greeting every household.

I was about seven when my friend Neha brought nail polish to school, and I painted my toenails with her. It was a joyful experience, but my English teacher was aghast. She whacked me across my calves with a metre ruler and told me boys do not wear nail polish. Why not? I was not told, but it was made clear there were certain things only girls could do and certain things only boys could do.

I liked doing too many things that only girls were allowed to do: paint my nails, play with dolls, sew clothes for dolls, dance. Be feminine. I did not understand why 'only girls do that' was a good enough reason to stop me from doing the things that made me happy. I was so feminine for a boy; it verged on rebellion. And my rebellion brought me to the religious leaders' attention. One day they dragged me into the temples and told me that if I did not change, my family would disown me, my community would banish me, and I would burn in hell for the rest of my life. My family and community were all I had ever known and loved so I had no choice but to accept the treatment my elders visited on me.

I lost my entire childhood to conversion therapy. Where I should have been a carefree kid roaming the streets of my village with stray dogs, I was praying to God to heal me or kill me. When the prayers did not work, I wore the enchanted bracelets that were meant to rid me of the evil spirits that were making me queer. I had to snap myself with a rubber band every time I had a queer thought or feeling. There were exorcisms and whippings and beatings.

I was kept away from the girls so that I would not become more feminine; I was kept away from the boys so that my femininity would not spread to them. If my queerness was not treated like an evil spirit, it was treated like a virus.

※

When I escaped conversion therapy and moved to New Zealand, I thought life would change drastically. I had lost my childhood, but I had the entirety of my youth ahead of me. I thought I would have my first kiss in high school, and hold hands with someone I childishly thought I was in love with. I thought I would be caught foolishly smiling at my phone every time I got a message from 'the one', that I'd bunk classes to hang out with someone I liked. An infatuated teenager. I thought I would lose my virginity, if that is a thing, in high school.

I thought I would have a few normal teenage years. But I guess that was not part of the plan. I was volunteering at Middlemore Hospital reception in the summer of 2017 when a church leader walked up to me and offered to pray my gay away. I refused, so he looked at me and said, 'It's hot, but do you know what's hotter? Hell.' I'd been under the impression I escaped conversion therapy when I left Fiji, but it was following me.

I made my most powerful — and later, regretted — decision: I was going to see conversion therapy banned, no matter what it took. At 17, I joined the movement, and I had to immediately omit from my life all of the things that brought me joy and happiness as a young person.

I could not have any flaws if I wanted to be taken seriously as a young person in politics. But flaws were unavoidable, because being young itself was seen as a flaw. Without realising, I sacrificed freedom, peace and joy to the movement to ban conversion therapy.

☀

I have missed out on so many basic experiences that I might have to spend the rest of my twenties trying to catch up on them. In particular, I have been so caught in the chaos of being young and queer, being active in politics and chasing a career that the thought of having a child hasn't yet crossed my mind.

Becoming a parent is a big achievement for some. I don't feel it would be for me. For me, it would take a lot of extra unnecessary work. First, there is the discrimination against queer parents. I don't want to raise a child on my own, so that adds the task of finding a partner into the equation. It is incredibly difficult to find a man serious enough to want a monogamous relationship during a time when queers are plagued by hook-up culture. If I do find someone, it will take years before we find ourselves in a position to seriously consider if we want children together. Maybe we won't get to that stage, but if we do, will he want children, and will he agree to adopt? You can see how this gets very complicated very quickly.

Becoming a parent is not impossible for me, but I feel I don't know who I am. Having children will not fix that. Your teenage years are when you are supposed to start developing a sense of identity and finding a purpose, but my entire identity revolved around the movement to ban conversion therapy. When we banned it in 2022, the movement was gone and so was the identity I had built around it. I felt homeless and — frighteningly — I also felt that my time was up, that I had nothing else to offer.

By 23, I had led the movement to ban conversion therapy, made it to *Vogue USA* as a model, been named as one of *Forbes* 30 Under 30, started writing for New Zealand's largest print newspaper, written my bestselling memoir *One of Them*, and become Young New Zealander of the Year.

I am so proud of what I have done, and I imagined that my family and community would boast about my achievements. Instead, the pressure of continuing the family legacy hangs over my head. But having children is not a legacy I am committed to. How could becoming a parent compare to all I have achieved?

The movement to ban conversion therapy saved lives and it will continue to long after I am gone. I do not accept that creating new life is more important than saving those that already exist. That is my legacy.

✳

When I was 19, I travelled to Canada, and within hours of arriving, I had a stranger in my bed. I thought I was ready for intimacy, but the first time we kissed, I felt nauseated.

When I was in conversion therapy, I was required to snap myself with a rubber band every time I had a queer thought or feeling. My queerness did not elicit pain but snapping myself with a rubber band did. After multiple pairings of my queer feelings and thoughts with snapping myself with a rubber band, my queerness started eliciting pain.

I was trying to figure out how I could even have intimacy. It required consistent positive queer experiences to break that bond between my queerness and pain. Every negative experience took me back to square one. What finally broke that bond was joyous sex. What replaced it was a new bond of queerness and love, and joy and thrill.

There is so much for me to undo. I need to heal from the prayers, the enchanted bracelets, the social isolation, the whippings, the aversion therapy and the exorcisms.

There is a gentle — frail, even — part of me that can't keep going on the way I am without confronting my past. Fighting for the freedom of queer people is a blessing but so is living for yourself. I have lived the former, and the latter feels overdue. One day I'll run away to a little town where nobody knows me, lie shirtless under the sun by a body of water, fall in love, have passionate sex, maybe feel heartbreak, dance a lot, sleep forever, eat everything I can, party like there is nothing more important than spending time with the people I adore, make memories I'll cherish forever and live life.

A traumatised kid lives within me. I need to heal so I can rejoice in the love that surrounds me. When I stop to think about the kind of family I want for myself, I feel that I am the young person that I need to raise again from the time I was a baby, to a rowdy toddler, to a rebellious young person, to a kind and intelligent adult. It will be a joy to retrace my steps through life with autonomy this time. That will be my otherhood.

Departure from the motherland

LINDA COLLINS

'm making a pasta dish, something I did when I was a mother of a living child. It's the first time I've cooked pasta since my daughter died several years ago, aged 17. I put a pot of water on to boil for the durum wheat pasta — the best wheat for pasta, as Victoria well knew. She had been an avid devourer of cookbooks. I'm using shell pasta, a shape that reminded her of a cat curled up asleep. I make a white sauce. The basic kind with flour and milk, not even cream. I beat it with a whisk to rid it of every glug of glutinous flour. This is for you, I mutter. My beautiful daughter. Victoria Skye Pringle McLeod. The smoothest ever.

We never knew what really lay beneath her glossy surface, I allow myself to briefly think. I say briefly, because to not live in the present is to invite introspection, which leads to questioning, self-blame, and the image of her body, lying on a pathway beside an apartment block. And the memory of me turning my gaze upward, to the ledge nine stories above, from which she propelled herself on the first day of a new school term. Then down, to her closed eyes. I thought she looked regretful. Peaceful, my husband, Malcolm, says. I'm going to need to grate parmesan.

When Victoria was alive we used to have pasta in one form or another several times a week. I haven't eaten it since. I avoid most meals that we used to eat then. One reason is that the memories are too painful. The other is that I can't be bothered. I get fried rice or fishball soup from the canteen at my office, or takeaways from a hawker centre, a name that nostalgically references the food pushcarts of the past. There is one up the road from the Singapore condominium where we live. The food court offers plenty of choice, from the mild and light boiled soups of China to the spicy stuff, like sharp papaya salads from Thailand, and vinegary adobo chicken of the Philippines.

Yet in our apartment back when our little family was intact — me, Malcolm and our Victoria — we used to make hearty, Western dishes suited to feeding farmers hungry from a day outdoors shouldering fence posts: stews, scones, beef-mince lasagne, meat roasts. The time-consuming preparation of this fare turned us into pale pillars of melting fat in our sweat-box of a small kitchen. A fan twisting and turning in a corner was no match for the flames surging from the gas hob or the waves of heat from the electric oven squatting on a countertop. As is common with Singapore kitchens, there was neither a built-in oven, nor hot water. Yet there we were, in temperatures over 32°C, spooning meaty juices over joints in roasting pans, laboriously peeling expensive Japanese sweet potatoes (as they were similar to the unobtainable kūmara of New Zealand), while boiling water in a kettle to wash endless pots and pans. All this, for a taste of home.

I open a drawer in my kitchen to find the old recipe books I've used since the time Victoria was a toddler. I had planned to pass them on to her one day, with the hope she would in turn have children to pass them on to. Some are glossy hardcovers by popular chefs of the day: Nigel Slater (Best-ever Mash was the go-to in our household) and effusive Sophie Gray (Chicken Pie with Cobbler Topping). Then there are simple books of comfort food, given to me as gifts by New Zealand relatives: Alison and Simon Holst's School Lunches and After School Snacks (Onion Dip Spread), or Ewing's Phone People IX: The Best of the Recipes (Mary's Nothing Pudding), from my mother.

Also in the cupboard are ancient stapled scraps of paper, repositories of recipes handed down from great-grandmother to grandmother to mother. So there's a sort of sacredness to them: the ancestors took a lot of care to preserve them — on a par with the family Bible. I had duly lugged them to Singapore even though the hot, energy-sapping climate doesn't call for such hearty fare, Bible included, some might say.

Today I peer at comments pencilled next to the lists of ingredients: 'Bill's favourite shortbread', or 'Add tsp more baking powder', or simply 'Nice'. This is disappointing. The notes are not at all revelatory in a personal way that would make me feel more connected to the women who cooked. Why was it so important that Bill liked that shortbread? Why do most of the recipes have filling fare that doesn't cost much? Were they poor or did they actually like that stuff? And what of Māori and Pacific Island cuisine? Where's the boil-up recipe for pork, broth and local vegetables? How about something with coconuts and juicy papaya? There are only hybridised recipes for toheroa soup and pāua fritters. The lovely shellfish is minced, disguised.

And there's another question, a clincher for any woman after the 1960s: Didn't you get fed up doing all that cooking for all those menfolk?

Among these tatters of culinary history is a New Zealand staple, a butter-stained, disintegrating Edmonds cookbook. It has recipes that my grandma and aunts cooked, including pressed cow tongue of a violent mauve colour that I was made to eat as a child: 'It's good for ya, girlie.' We kids would poke out our tongues and imagine cutting that off to eat. Yuck!

Victoria loved the macaroni cheese from Edmonds. I can hear her voice reassuring me, 'Mum, I really used to love it.' She preferred it absolutely plain, with no vegetables in it, and just a sprinkle of breadcrumbs on top. It was a carb-loaded comfort-food classic. I only made it because she liked it. I didn't enjoy cooking it, but I was, at times, a drudge back then. I think I got too tired. I never made her eat cow tongue. I do console myself with that.

Getting the steel grater out of the bottom kitchen cupboard has become an unfamiliar action. It lurks among chopsticks, old baking paper and other bottom-kitchen-cupboard stuff. I find it eventually. Tiny bits of mouldy cheese are caught in its sharp nubs, from when it was last used, the night before Victoria died.

※

Our last meal was spaghetti bolognese. We ate it on a Sunday evening, crammed together on the sofa, watching Annabel Langbein, whose show screened on an Asian food channel. 'Sooooo delicious,' Victoria said, imitating Langbein's weirdly plummy vowels, a contrast to the cook's jeans-clad portrayal of Kiwi informality. We laughed, and soon the living room was echoing with us all saying 'Soooo delicious'. Vic helped with washing-up afterwards, engaging in a tea-towel flicking contest with Malcolm, which she won. Later, I tucked her up in bed, kissing her good night. Early next morning — before I got up to cook breakfast and get her ready for the school bus — Victoria slipped out the front door, and never came back.

When the shock went away, and when loss was replaced by absence, we were left with ourselves and our redundant roles and identities. Victoria had been our only child. Without her, was I a mother? And what was it about our lives that led her to think it was better to be dead? We had believed our little unit to be a happy one. We loved her to bits. Tried to do lots together. Went for trips back to New Zealand to see relatives and friends. But it was not enough. It seems the child we thought we knew did not exist.

Yet, there are known facts: Victoria was of European New Zealand parentage. She was kind-natured and sensitive. She had a dreamy kind of attention-deficit disorder. We never saw dreaminess as a deficit.

She loved going back with us each year to our cottage in the South Island. She talked of going back to study in Dunedin once school finished.

But she also loved Singapore. Her favourite food was a hawker dish: Hainanese chicken, with rice cooked in the chicken broth.

She baked a beautiful pavlova. It was her Christmas ritual.

Suspected facts: She probably hated the chore — and pressure — of baking it every Christmas. But she would have wanted to please the family, and indeed, it did please me. I treated Victoria's pavlova-making as if she had passed some rite of passage into Kiwi adulthood, and this was of my doing. I was imparting the knowledge of baking a proper pavlova — from my mother to me — to her.

After our daughter's death we came to know the other Victoria by talking to friends and reading the extensive diaries that we discovered on her laptop. (I've shared them with researchers into suicide and teen anxiety, and her writing has now made it into two books). After reading her diaries, I realised that Victoria was wise to the shallowness of pavlova achievement, its woeful inadequacy for helping her find an identity amid challenges arising from social media, globalisation and isolation from a close community that could enfold us.

Facts to face: Vic was consumed by fears of failing exams, of losing friends, of changing countries, of life in a country she had never properly lived in. She was afraid of her future. All those visits back to the motherland, the watching of Annabel bloody Langbein, all that separating of yolks and whites for the pavlova, all those roasts and potatoes, had not given her an anchor at all.

The reality was that this nostalgia for the food of my homeland anchored me in a delusion. It took me back to my childhood, to food cooked with my own mother's love (perhaps the only way she knew how to express any fondness towards me), to known ways of behaving and being in a world. Unlike Victoria, I was rooted in a steady, familiar world of belonging utterly to one tribe, an amorphous muddle of dairy-farm folk, the descendants of Dorset dwellers turned early globalisers, riding the sailing-ship wave. (Or so I thought. After writing this essay, I faced up to the fact my mother mostly did not love me, and a DNA test showed that most of my ancestors are from County Cork in Ireland, an inconvenient finding that family members declare cannot be true.)

With my own child, I had felt so happy — kidding myself that I was doing something worthwhile with my life, nourishing her. That's what parents are supposed to do, aren't they? Among all the other things, a proper mum cooks and stirs and stands in the kitchen and gives her family spoonsful of love. Or was that a message I had absorbed from my family, from society, from judgemental expat mums at the school gate? And also, from the friendly expat mums when we occasionally met up during the school day for wine-fuelled lunches? And then, there were the women's magazines with food stories that are endless variations on *how to feed your family fast nutritious food they will love you for.*

On the other hand, my Singaporean friends and colleagues had no expectations of me as a mother-cook. My main identity to them was framed in terms of my economic contribution to their society. This pragmatism is a relief now. It is an uncomplicated identity. Being a mother is irrelevant, though they have always been curious about my cooking, asking if I baked 'meaty foods' such as shepherd's pie and lasagne at home, which places me as a foreigner and raises its own issues of personal identity beyond that of motherhood. At first, I used to see this as their seeking confirmation of the colonial habits of the Other. But it is more complicated than that.

Once, in the time long before we lost Victoria, a Singaporean-Chinese colleague at the newspaper where I worked as a copyeditor asked what food I missed from my homeland. We were gathered around the food table at work — it is common in Singapore offices for some makeshift space, even the tops of file cabinets, to be commandeered as a communal dining space. Someone had brought back goodies from a trip to Japan. (Another tradition: if a colleague from your department goes away overseas, they bring treats to share with fellow staff.) While being urged to try dried sour plums, which I don't like, I blurted, 'Oh, bread-and-butter pudding.'

I don't know why I said that, as it is not a particular favourite. Perhaps it was to end the conversation — I might have assumed my colleague did not know what it was. But she smiled and said: 'Oh, I miss it, too. I used to take it at halls during my study years in Britain.' Then she added: 'It was such a treat. So beautifully cooked. They used brioche. And there would be added sauce on the side in a little jug, beautifully fine vanilla crème.'

I didn't know what to say. It confused me on many levels — was she seeing me, a New Zealander, as a quasi-Brit? Are we just interchangeable white people who look and behave and eat alike? And then there was the class thing. Was she not aware that at that time, I had never even been to university? My family couldn't afford it. Hers was not the bread-and-butter pudding of my Kiwi childhood. Mum cooked it as a way to fill us up when there wasn't much food to go round. It also had the advantage of using up stale bread, and could be made with ingredients to hand — butter, milk, a few raisins, maybe grated lemon peel. It was of the mend-and-make-do, Depression-era approach. It was as far removed from high tea at Oxford as I could imagine.

But my colleague was looking at me hopefully. I realised that her comment was an offering, a kindness to acknowledge she understood I didn't like the sour plums and that she, too, had experienced the awkwardness of being a foreigner around food. It was a comment to do with a different kind of 'class', that of inherent good manners. Should I squash that with an uncouth rant about the economically gutted, neoliberalised New Zealand that had led me to seek work in her country?

I blinked and said, 'Yes, with vanilla crème. That's what I miss.' As I spoke, I tried to imagine the fine privilege of her vanilla crème coating my tongue. But the image that came was of crisped triangles of breadcrusts atop a sugary lumpen-ness in a Pyrex cooking dish, and my mother's look of triumph and weariness as she plonked it on the kitchen table. And, I now realise when I look back, a simmering, barely contained anger and resentment. So much for the imagined comfort zone of the motherland.

The bread-and-butter pudding incident is irrelevant to me now. I have little interest in food, let alone cross-cultural culinary confusion. I'm not cooking. I'm not the old me. It's not just because I never liked cooking. It's because I am no longer defined by motherhood, and no longer have to meet the expectations of my tribe and Western society. I'm not cooking, even when we go back to New Zealand to visit. It is Malcolm who does the cooking. He grills mutton chops for his elderly widowed mother, who seeks memories of the high-country kitchens of her youth, of joshing rabbiters with their bundles of floppy fur, of larking shepherds home from the mighty muster. At least, that's how she rosily recalls it in her suburban house in Ōamaru, staring out at her rotary clothes line with its unsettling, beseeching iron arms. A garden-centre statue of a Greek goddess crouches nearby, frowning. Victoria, in a filigree-framed photograph, winks at me.

I've cleaned the grater and rubbed the block of parmesan against it until there is a soft, airy bundle of strands ready to be sprinkled over the pasta and sauce. I don't even know why I am making this dish. Perhaps it is the desire to recreate something of my past that is palpable. I pat the strands of parmesan. They bounce like curls of hair. I would brush Victoria's bouncy hair for ages. She loved that. In the coffin, it felt stiff, like strands of uncooked spaghetti.

As I drain the little pasta shells and the hot steam hits my face, difficult thoughts squeeze through. My role as nurturer should have included asking the awkward questions to find how a child really feels inside, instead of simply filling that inside with food. To find out more, even though she is dead: *Victoria, when you ate that spaghetti bolognese on the sofa with us, did you already know it was your last meal? Why did you pretend everything was normal? Why couldn't you have just been real with us and told us that you were so worried about your exam results that you wanted to die?*

And now I've read her diaries in her computer, I'd like to know: *Did you sick up that last meal later in the toilet?* I want to know, so I can face the fact that the food I slavishly cooked to nurture her was being vomited up and flushed away. It was the complete rejection of all that stirred, salted, whisked, basted love. I had not fed her after all. In any way. I was not enough of the mother she really needed — not simply a cook and organiser and occasional hugger, but someone else, I don't know quite who. Perhaps it is bigger than me. Perhaps it was several mothers that she needed. And aunts, as well. There, in Singapore, not far away in New Zealand.

※

Small triumphs: I have managed to not burn the meal. However, while I have been standing here thinking about cooking, motherhood, cultural identity and death, the parmesan and slithery sauce have congealed in an unappetising way. What was I thinking? I'm not hungry. And Malcolm's not here to eat it. He has taken one of his Patrick O'Brian books and gone to the nearby hawker centre. The eighteenth-century world of battles at sea, the comradeship of men at war provide for him a passage through his sadness. There, he'll sit among the diners, get out his book, and tuck into the Malay stall's roti prata. He'll have checked out all the other offerings, simple street food: the chicken rice, the pad thai, the dim sum, the wonton mee.

But it is always the Malay stall Malcolm goes back to. The Muslim hawker knows him. They chat and laugh as the round of dough is spun and slapped down on the hotplate, and as the halal lentil gravy is ladled into a plastic side dish. And then Malcolm will find a place among the swirl and chatter of diners from all over Asia — they are Malay, Chinese, Indian, Bangladeshi, Filipino, Indonesian.

This enjoyment of food from Asian cultures is something that will make Malcolm feel at home when we eventually return to New Zealand. The life we created for our daughter by cooking food from our childhood was based on a New Zealand that no longer exists. Most of the fare at this hawker centre can be found there now, along with food from the Pacific — indeed, from all parts of the world. And the stodge of our childhood has been rebranded 'Kiwiana', a quaint retro treat for anyone from anywhere.

I didn't go with Malcolm to the food court as I hate sitting in the humid air with only a fan to cool me. And being stared at, the only Westerners there. It didn't use to bother me, but it does now. It is not the fact that we stand out as different. I wonder who they see, beyond the whiteness. A foreigner, yes — but worse, a lonely older woman with no family, marooned with her husband at a circular plastic food-court table. Him, reading a book. Her, imagining her dead daughter alive, imagining her placing an order of chicken rice, pointing to the cooked chickens hanging with hooks through their necks, telling the hawker in Singlish (Singapore's English-based creole) to take the skin off and 'Chilli, mei you (cannot)'.

Yet at the other tables are old folk surrounded by an enviable real life — laughing children, teenagers, cousins and neighbours. I, on the other hand, am clearly not part of any sort of loosely connected group. I don't belong to a discernible tribe making its presence felt. It must be puzzling for them to observe this woman eating among them, without the support and protection and enfolding love of an extended family. Any family.

Besides, I'm not hungry. I always cooked food for Victoria's sustenance, not mine. There's no child left to sustain. There's only Malcolm and me, and there's no Kiwi comfort food for what we are going through. A 'Kiwiana' pink lamington sponge stuffed with whipped cream isn't going to do it, though I am tempted to try. The only recipe I need is one on how to survive this. But there is nothing in my grandmothers' cookbooks. No pencil marks recklessly urging, 'Bill's favourite. Then add rat poison.' (On a visit to the family farm, I found my grandma crying. Her nephew Bill, a beefy man-child, was sitting on the porch cleaning his shotgun, having culled all her beloved stray mummy cats and their kittens.)

No, the margins are empty. I was foolish to have looked for directions from them for any of what has happened to me. Their world is gone. As has mine. If only my world was that imagined by my Singapore colleague, one of vanilla crème — uneventful, smooth on the tongue. But then again, she had mentioned her high-tea memory to me while savouring sour plums. That is what I must learn to do.

This is a lie

LORI LEIGH

I could give a monologue about my lack of maternal instincts. I could talk about my childhood and how while other kids were changing the Betsy Wetsy doll's nappy I was loading my Super Soaker with urine to chase my sisters around the house.

The one time I was gifted a doll, her short life ended in a science experiment with the ceiling fan to test the rate of decapitation.

I had nightmares about being Ellen Ripley from *Alien*, with an Alien Queen embryo growing inside my belly, waiting to erupt.

Even my pet hamster ate its own offspring.

※

Number four on my street is a perfect family of four. Even number. Divisible by two. Mum, Dad, Avery and Marley.

I live at Number five. Number five has one resident. Odd number. One is the loneliest number — or it would be, if it wasn't for Dooley, the miniature dachshund mix who belonged to my mother.

When I hear Dooley bark, I know Avery and Marley have come out to play. A favourite pastime is defacing our suburban cul-de-sac with sidewalk chalk. As I walk to my carport, I try to avoid their pastel body outlines that look like crime scenes, afraid they are plotting my murder.

Marley and Avery leave 'artwork' under my doormat. I don't want their scribbles. It's an embarrassment. The only abstract stuff I like is Jackson Pollock.

Kids eat their boogers. It doesn't matter if you explain it's yuck. They're going to do it because their little taste buds have booger cravings. I don't want to see that, or hold your hand afterwards.

Kids have no sense of personal space. Once I told a kid that I needed some privacy to go to the toilet, and they asked why. I said because I needed to do a number two. They challenged that by saying they needed to do a number three. Now that's just messed up.

They're always listening. Countless times I have been with a parent-friend and they make some kind of subversive eye contact mid-conversation, motioning towards their child and mouthing, 'He hears everything.' That's just creepy. Does he work for Google?

I don't want to share my Nintendo Switch. That's my gaming system, and it's always my turn.

Kids don't even know where they came from. 'I came from Mum's tummy.' No, kid, you came from her uterus — the small pear-shaped organ between the poo hole and the pee sack. Stop being a subject of the patriarchy and learn about women's bodies.

I don't want a kids' profile on my Netflix. I only want one profile, and it needs to be full of sex in corsets.

I'm not getting a basic-bitch cheese pizza. Unless I'm on a tight budget and need to order from the kids' menu.

I want to open my Settlers of Catan board game and find all 95 of my resource cards and 16 wooden cities. If a piece is missing not only is the game obsolete, there's also going to be hell to pay.

It's B-A-N-A-N-A-S in Pyjamas, not 'Llamas in Pyjamas'. Learn how to talk. And while you're at it, learn how to spell.

I don't want to listen to Anika Moa or 'The Wheels on the Bus'. Like, I get it, the wheels go round and round. I don't want to hear about it, much less sing about it. 'What colour is the grass, Anika Moa?' It's whatever colour my cannabis dealer has that week. It might be green, but it could also be Orange Bud.

※

My mom used to go on about how much she wanted grandkids. That's why she got Dooley. She would even go so far as to buy toys for the non-existent grandkids. After she passed, I cleaned out her garage. The rocking horse she'd bought was covered in cobwebs.

The truth is, I come from a generation of non-breeders. While some families have mottos like 'Honor et virtus' or 'Force avec vertu', the creed of my sisters and I may as well be 'Sine Liberis'. Roughly translated from Latin, that's 'Childfree' or 'With no children comes much liberty' or 'From kids we have hid'.

At Halloween, my older sister turned out all the lights and hid with her husband because she didn't want to deal with trick-or-treating children. She just wanted to eat pizza and watch *Sleepy Hollow* in peace. My younger sister shares memes of people wiping their childless tears with wads of cash.

There's no heartbreaking story of loss here, no political platform of population-reduction strategies.

We just don't like kids.

I just don't like kids.

But this is a lie.

✷

I have heard women talk about their longing for vaginal labour. This is a concept I cannot fathom. If, by some miracle, I end up with a living being trapped inside of me, by all means rip me open and get it out, as soon as possible.

There is a breakdown in my urge to be a baby-birthing machine. I don't have the constitution. My biological clock doesn't tick. My biological clock is a smartwatch without that app installed.

I could, maybe, get into the idea of a water birth. I would like someone to install a little swimming pool right in the middle of my lounge and fill it with warm water. I would submerge myself in front of a small audience of loved ones. From there they could watch me transform into a demi-god, splashing around while yelling obscenities at them.

I could really embrace the challenge of 'eating for two'. I want it to be an unreasonable hour of the night when I turn to my lover and say, 'Go get me a jar of pickles, a tub of chocolate ice cream and a vanilla Coke-zero,' and then force her to watch me eat it on all fours like a farmyard pig who's been starved for six months.

It would be nice to park in those reserved expectant mother spots at New World.

But I'm not breaking up with my seared tuna sushi, or my double-cream brie or my chocolate martini any time soon.

I would like to pass on my genes. I just want to do it like a man does it. Drop my load in someone else while I climax during sex, and then politely remove my body from any further processes. Nine months later, violá! Little Timmy has my eyes!

I just don't want to be a parent.

But this is a lie.

※

My GP used to ask me, 'Is there any chance you could be pregnant?' I would squirm a bit. 'No.'

GP: 'Are you having sex?'

Me (smugly): 'Yes.'

GP: 'Then how do you know you're not pregnant?'

Me: 'I just do.'

GP: 'But how can you be sure?'

Me: 'OK, you see, when a woman and a woman love each other very much ...'

But the conversation also reminded me of the ever-present fact that I'm never going to accidentally get knocked-up.

Sometimes I joke with my lover. I prop myself up on a pillow, look her in the eye, and with my best fuckboy voice say, 'I hope I don't get you pregnant,' or, 'If you're pregnant, I want a paternity test.' These jokes aren't very good. They are masking some deep-seated pain. I would like to make a baby with my lover. I would like to see my partner's stunning eyes again for the first time. I'd like to hold a hand that mirrors mine, in miniature. I dream we fall asleep in each other's arms with a new life between us.

I want a mistake. I want to cry over two lines on a stick that isn't a positive Covid test and feel earth-shattering overwhelm. I want to make a mistake and then spend the next 18 years realising it was not a mistake at all, but one of life's magic tricks where perfection is pulled from the hat.

But I can't make a mistake. No heat-of-the-moment blunders where passion grips us and we're not thinking about tomorrow.

I am always thinking about 'tomorrow' when I think of having a child. It's always tomorrow. I have to plan, methodically. Research. Finance and fund. It feels earth-shatteringly overwhelming. I wanted to get my PhD before having kids. Tick. I wanted to get a stable job. Tick. I wanted to own my own home. Tick. This is how my biological clock ticks. I wanted to have the right partner. Tick. Untick. Tick. Untick. Have kids so my mom could be a grandmother. Untick.

I've somehow woken up middle-aged and motherless. I have no mother; I am no mother. I sit on the threshold of impossibility, the dream of having a biological child slipping away at the speed of sound. I grieve my mother all over again.

I'll never pass a piece of myself along to a child.

But this is a lie.

※

I open my door to find a gift from Marley and Avery. On my doorstep is a little jar of pink gerberas with a handwritten note, 'We want to share this with you.'

I have put every piece of art they've ever given me on proud display on my fridge. I could see their artwork sitting comfortably beside a Pollock.

Marley and Avery call me Aunt Lori. When they went away at Easter time, they asked if I could put a note on their door letting the Easter bunny know to come back when they got home. I texted back a picture of Dooley dressed in his bunny outfit. Marley and Avery came home to find Easter bunny baskets filled with chocolate eggs, crayons and stickers. They said, 'It must've been because Aunt Lori wrote to the Easter bunny.'

With Marley and Avery, I can be five again. I can fill kids with wonder. I remember I'm worthy of art and flowers.

Marley and Avery light up whenever they see Dooley. But sometimes when I look at him, I remember my mother is not here anymore. One of the incomprehensibles of life is your mother dying, that this magic that birthed you could end, that your origin could disappear.

I look at Dooley and know he is the last piece of my mother that I have left.

But this is also a lie.

※

There are pieces of her everywhere — in the arcs of my fingernails, in the silhouette of my smile, and in the moments when I feel like the mother I may never be.

I'm staring at her hands as I look down to see mine stroking Dooley's dapple-patterned fur, making the same shapes she used to make to stroke my head.

In the moments when I am with kids, I feel my mother more and more. I sense a tensile force and pull. I think about the uterus and how we are, at one time, attached to our mother through a physical cord.

I wonder if my uterus, like a wandering womb with a phantom cord, is searching for attachment. It's a kind of grief I feel for my unknown or unborn child. Then I remember that when a child is born, the cord rots and must be cut.

Different ties bind us to the people who care for us, give us magic, play with us, love us. This is its own kind of lineage, a passing on of all we are and all we came from, not through genes or birth, but simply through the joy of living connection.

This is the truth.

No kidding

LINDA ROONEY

I t was Mother's Day 2014, an unusually warm, sunny day in May. I was lying in a hospital bed post-hysterectomy with the windows wide open, and I could hear chattering families getting in and out of cars outside. My husband had visited earlier. My surgeon's nurse had also popped in, happily chatting about the meal she was about to have with her family. I felt very alone. No flowers, cards or chocolates for me. Never my favourite day, Mother's Day, but this year I felt even more isolated than ever.

It was more than 10 years earlier that the door had closed on having children, on my forty-first birthday. There was no party, no special dinner. Only a sad, tear-blurred drive home from the clinic where a last-ditch diagnostic test had surprised me with its finality. After years of trying and losses, I was not going to have children.

※

I was a feminist from way back, even before I had ever heard the word. Growing up on a farm, with no brothers, meant that I never felt that girls were inferior. My sisters and I drove tractors, rounded up the sheep, and threw around hay bales just like any farm kid in New Zealand. Help inside the house was compulsory, too. None of it was gendered.

The feminism of the 1970s and the gains of the 1980s confirmed my belief that we were equal, and we all had the right to choose how to live our lives. I met my husband at university in Christchurch and we married young. But I wanted to embrace the opportunities that presented themselves to young women in the 1980s, and children were not something I thought about in my twenties. So, I was surprised when, in my mid-thirties, I actually felt ready to start trying for them. I was even more surprised by the devastating sense of loss I felt when I discovered I would never have children.

Coming to terms with this was not easy. I had to learn to accept this news, and then rebalance. I had to adjust my perception of what life might be like. I could not think, *My kids would look like this*, or wonder if they would be clever, or musical, or sporty, because it just was not going to happen. It was too painful to think about the 'what-ifs' and 'should-have-beens', so I didn't let myself.

I had to deal with the guilt I felt at having a body that denied my husband and me children. I had to deal with the feelings of failure at not being able to do something that everyone assumes they can and will be able to do — 'the most natural thing in the world' as some people put it, or 'the reason we are here on earth', as a friend once said to me. And I had to deal with my fear of judgement from family, friends and acquaintances. I say 'fear of judgement' because a lot of that judgement was in my head. But not all of it.

Like everyone in my position, I had to make this adjustment while surrounded by fertility and pronatalism. Pronatalism is when parenting is prized over non-parenting, and as a result, those who parent are awarded a superior status over those who do not. Friends and family were creating and raising families, the ever-present emphasis on motherhood in the media seemed to grow, commentators and advertisers alike made me feel invisible, and of course, politicians focused on 'the average family' and talked about 'your children and your children's children' in election campaigns. It was almost impossible to escape the feeling that I was in some way considered marginal to society, 'other' or 'less than' because I wasn't a mother.

It was very painful to hear ad nauseum — sometimes blatantly, often subliminally — from society at large that I was not as important, that my life had less value, that I didn't know what love is, and that I wasn't a 'real' woman. (Someone actually said this to a friend of mine. Ouch.) Many women really struggle with this. Throughout their lives they have been conditioned to believe it. There is so much shaming involved. Men get similar messages.

'C'mon, be a man, get your wife pregnant,' my husband's brothers said to him. At first, my own thoughts parroted these ideas back to me.

But fortunately, with my innate sense of logic, I came to see how false these thoughts are. There are examples in the news every day of people who are parents but should never have had children. They have not been judged 'worthy' to be parents — biology simply allowed them to be — just as I have not been judged unworthy.

As I learnt to dismiss those internal negative voices, it became easier to dismiss the loud, external voices too. I came to see that unhelpful and judgemental comments told me more about the person making them than they did about me. Most fell under the category 'How to tell me you don't understand without saying you don't understand'. The ignorant 'just adopt' comments; the cruel 'Here, have my kids' said while laughing uproariously; the dismissive 'At least you can <fill in the blanks>' comments that either came from a degree of envy of my freedom, discomfort at my situation, or a wish to silence me because it just made the conversation too awkward.

Oh, and on top of all that, we are told we are selfish. Yet many generous, giving people do not and cannot have children. And many selfish people have them.

※

I gradually managed to develop an inner belief in myself, rejecting the messages and judgements that were all around me. An online community I joined after my first ectopic pregnancy loss was enormously helpful in making this transition. Talking to others who understand was, and always is, immensely helpful. We shared our fears and our victories, gained hope from those who were a few years ahead of us and provided hope for those coming behind us. We had a lot of fun, too. If I couldn't sleep or was upset in the middle of the night, there would be someone up and ready to chat in Coventry or Dorking or Indiana or Vancouver.

As the years passed, we became firm friends. Some of my UK friends travelled here, and I travelled there. Together with other volunteers and users, we celebrated the organisation's 10-year anniversary at the House of Commons in London. These online and now in-person friends and I ate cream cakes, looked out the window at the Thames and educated British MPs on ectopic pregnancy.

Back then, online support was relatively new, and people didn't understand it. But if you don't have friends and family in real life who have been through similar experiences, then many people need to look online. However hard some of my friends tried to support me, they were never going to 'get it' at the same level as those who had been through it.

Of course, in real life, many people do not even try to understand, don't broach it with us, and don't in any way acknowledge our lives without children. They worry about upsetting us (even though silence is always more upsetting), they think it is easier to ignore the issue or they suggest adoption as if that is easy (it isn't) and solves everything (it doesn't). I was once at a women's business networking lunch where a woman next to me asked if I had children. When I said 'no', she muttered something and turned her back to me — for the rest of the lunch, which was supposed to be all about business networking. Sadly, this reaction is not that unusual.

Deep down, I knew I was not to blame, that my life was as valuable as that of any other individual and, most importantly, that my life would still be good, despite the societal messages that seeded guilt and doubts when I was at my lowest. I came to accept the hand I'd been dealt, even if at first I didn't like it, and I felt like acceptance was a betrayal.

In the midst of my early grief, I sat on a clifftop looking out over the Tasman Sea on a bright summer's day, listening to the waves crashing below me. I felt the sun on my back. It made me smile, and I knew even then I would be OK.

Over time, I found renewed joy in life. And I was lucky. My friends were mostly professionals, had their kids at different ages, and always felt that being a mother was part of who they were, but not the only thing. It made it easier to spend time with them, because we always had other things to talk about — politics, books, travel, work, houses, art, wider families, fashion, social change, you name it. Perhaps inevitably, one or two friends dropped away, as they increasingly spent all their time with the friends they had met through their children's schools or activities. It hurts to be dropped. But that was their loss, too, as we would have gladly supported them and their kids in those difficult, growing years.

❋

My husband and I became that classic cliché of a couple without children, travelling internationally. I had wanted to travel since I was a child, it had been a large part of my career, and it was one of the things I had looked forward to doing with children. But now we had to do it alone. It wasn't that we had a lot of extra funds. A friend once talked about the fees for her daughter's private school. 'See, that's my annual travel budget,' I pointed out.

During one trip, on a gorgeous island off the Queensland coast, we were talking about where to go next. We could hear the waves lapping against the beach as a gentle tropical breeze cooled the balcony where we were enjoying a lunch of beer-battered barramundi and champagne. How could we top this? 'We need to put together a ten-year travel plan,' my husband suggested. My heart lifted. I set to my task with enthusiasm, and over the next 10 years we saw many new places and had many new experiences. Every cloud has its silver lining.

Life was good. I had left full-time employment and was thoroughly enjoying freelance consulting, serving on boards, chairing a government-owned company and volunteering for the ectopic pregnancy charity's online support services. After six years my volunteer role ended, and I looked for a way to replace that. I found several women blogging about being childless. There are a vast number of supportive communities online that bring people together, provide valuable information, and offer an understanding ear. This was certainly true of those who were involuntarily living life without children. I had found my tribe.

In 2010 I began blogging myself, as *No Kidding in NZ*. I was perhaps the first person blogging in New Zealand about living a childless life and accepting it. Others were still trying to conceive, and even now, newspaper or TV articles tend to focus on people who hope that they will still have children. Then there are the stories that end in the 'miracle baby'. They are the exception, not the rule, but they disproportionately dominate infertility stories in the media. Because the idea that you might not have children when you want them seems to be too awful, too final, for both media and the public to confront. We are everyone's worst nightmare, and those going through infertility find it almost impossible to believe that we might be happy. But for exactly that reason, it is important to talk about our stories, the tough times, and even more importantly, the good.

So, I blogged. At first I wrote under a pseudonym, but I have since nervously spoken out in several articles, internationally and nationally, under my own name. I was receiving well over a thousand hits a week to my little blog, so I knew I was reaching people. I talked honestly about the positives and the negatives of my life. My mantra is 'I'm not kidding' (pun intended). The feedback from people who needed to hear that they were not alone, and that this life can and will be good, made sense of the isolation that I used to feel, and the loss that I had endured.

Because that's the thing that is rarely recognised. There is ongoing loss, no matter how well I have healed, no matter how much I am enjoying my life, no matter how it seems that I am now 'over it'. A friend once said, as I was losing my second pregnancy, that I hadn't had anything, really, so I hadn't lost anything. This was a common refrain. But it didn't feel like that. I miss the lives that my children would have had, their growth, difficulties, victories, their future. I miss their interactions with their cousins of the same age.

Every Christmas, I decorate my tree on my own. I donated the Christmas stockings I had bought in hopeful anticipation at a market in Thailand years ago. I will never teach a child how to bake, knit, crochet or sew, how to swim or play netball, how to play the piano, or introduce them to the joy of books, languages and travel. I will never fall about laughing with my child over something ridiculous. My husband and I celebrate major wedding anniversaries and birthdays alone. We travel alone. And when we cared for our elderly parents through illnesses, distress and confusion in their last years, we felt the gaping future loss that we won't have children to be there and care for us in the same way. Don't ever tell me I haven't missed anything! I love my life. But it has come at a cost.

By the time I was in my late forties and perimenopause was making its presence known, I was not afraid. For me, it was a great leveller. It was a shared experience with women in the way that motherhood had never been. An experience that gave me permission to focus not on the differences between mothers and non-mothers, but on our similarities.

✺

After that difficult Mother's Day in hospital, there was real cause for celebration in my hysterectomy. Some women find it devastating. They question their own womanhood. But by the time I had surgery, I had already done the hard work. I had long dismissed society's gaslighting, refusing to accept that an issue with my body meant that I was in any way a second-class woman. For more than 10 years I had dealt with the issue of who I was without being a mother. I knew more about myself, about other people, and about my personal values. Working as a volunteer with women had taught me about resilience and growth. Writing had led to deeper thinking, sorting out my values and beliefs. Maybe this was simply a result of being in my fifties and knowing myself better. If I'd had children, I would have undoubtedly changed, too. But going through those years of loss and rediscovery led me to a new stage of self-knowledge and understanding.

So, for me, my hysterectomy was a welcome liberation. After all, my uterus had — it seemed — actively conspired to kill me, first with not one but two ectopic pregnancies, and then with fibroids, leading to urgent blood transfusions. It had never been of any use to me, and I did not miss it when it was gone. I knew that a uterus, or what I might have done with it, did not define me as a person, and definitely not as a woman.

This meant that I could move into my fifties and the rest of my life feeling confident and free. Menopause, for me, meant that my reproductive status was no longer relevant. That was liberating. It came at a time when friends and family were facing empty nests and were more available to socialise. (Although this is not the same as being childless!) Our respective reproductive status is, for the time being, completely irrelevant.

Of course, my husband and I are now also beginning to think about our old age. Caring for his parents taught us much about the preparations needed, and the mental and physical declines that we may experience. Unlike many who are parents, we can't ignore it and leave it to our kids. It is easy to be afraid. Most childless people worry, 'Who will look after me when I'm old?' There will be no one else around on a day-to-day basis to help us. So, we need to prepare. We've seen too many elderly people, both with and without children, fail to do so. It causes angst — for them and their carers. We know that we need to decide where we will live, and what help we might need. And crucially, we need to act before it is necessary, because by then it is already too late.

That is an unexpected advantage of ageing without children, I think. We are less complacent. We cannot afford to be. We know life does not always go to plan. We know we cannot leave it to someone else.

Even writing wills as a childless couple is more complicated. I made this admission in front of a friend who clearly found it too much detail or saw it as a complaint, and — although I was already 50 — responded with 'Well, you could still adopt!' But there are so many questions to answer. Who will have power of attorney? Who will be executor of the estate? How well do we know all our nieces, nephews and great-nephews? Do they need our help? Do we want to leave a legacy in other ways? For us, the answer to that last question is yes, and we have made provision for scholarships and medical research grants among other things. But it isn't simple.

Almost 20 years on from that drive home from the clinic on my birthday, I am happy with my life without children. Mostly childfree now, rather than childless, I can see and embrace the positives of life without children. If I did not, if I simply mourned the life I never had, then I would have lost two lives — the life I wanted, and the life I have now. The only way to honour my losses and everything I have been through is to grasp this life, appreciate it, and thrive in it. I owe it to myself, and to my husband. I am not kidding.

I was asked recently what gives meaning to my life. I talked about my husband, my writing, and how I have been able to help others also on this path. But ultimately, my answer was that the most meaningful thing in my life is simply my life itself — living it, enjoying it, feeling gratitude for it. Shouldn't that be what gives every life meaning?

Another good year

MICHAELA TEMPANY

When I was a child, my mother framed an important religious document and put it on the wall of our living room. It was called 'The Family: A Proclamation to the World'. It hung over the fireplace, right next to the bookshelf and the piano. It was like a disembodied god, looming over us, always watching.

It begins like this: 'Marriage between a man and a woman is ordained of God and the family is central to the Creator's plan for the eternal destiny of His children.' It was written in 1995 by Mormon prophets, and it says things like: 'We declare that God's commandment for His children to multiply and replenish the earth remains in force.' A father's role is to protect and provide for their families. Mothers are primarily responsible for the nurture of their children. The Family Proclamation is a source of Mormon pride. It perpetuates a long-held belief that families can be together forever. It is a map for happiness. Follow the rules and you (and your posterity) will be blessed.

I was raised to follow the map. To be a good girl. I could fold myself neatly and obediently inside Mormon ideals, the way one might fold origami into a desired shape: a hat, a jumping frog, a little boat. When people asked me what I wanted to be when I grew up, I said, 'A mother.' What else was there for me to be? Motherhood was my divine destiny. I was as sure of this as I was about ice cream on a hot day; wearing a skirt to Sunday sacrament; the squishy, sweet-smelling skin of a newborn. At night I'd imagine all of my future babies. I'd give them names and feel purpose fill me up from the inside out. But I didn't understand loss then. I didn't understand that a womb can be treacherous, hostile, fickle. Like an Old Testament God, or a religion gone wrong.

☀

Both of my parents were converted to the Mormon faith. When my father was eight years old, a pair of missionaries knocked on my grandparents' door, and his entire family was baptised. My father was sent to a church boarding school in Hamilton, and at 19 he went on a two-year mission in the South Island. In his mid-twenties he met my mother. Mum was not religious; she was 21 and searching. It was an intense courtship. She loved my father, but he gave her an ultimatum that seemed as natural to him as his beliefs. 'I'll marry you if you get baptised,' he said, which is exactly what happened.

My mother's parents threatened to disown her, afraid that their daughter would become a religious zealot who walked around barefoot and had lots of children. I try to picture this image: my mother lumbering through a supermarket with no shoes on, a baby strapped to her back, toddlers at her ankles, her belly big and full and heaving. The image isn't far from the truth. My mother got baptised in secret. She married my father in a small ceremony that her parents didn't attend. They had six children, one after the other. We are so close in age that I wonder when my mother had time to take a breath.

If there is one thing that I can remember from my childhood, it's this: I wanted to be just like her. Mum was my centre. I was a planet orbiting around the vastness of her body. She made big pots of porridge on cold winter mornings, which she would let us douse with brown sugar, peaches and cream. After school, there would be a batch of fresh muffins and hot chocolate steaming on the stove. In the evenings she would play the piano, and music would drift sleepily around the house. At night she would do the rounds, putting us all to sleep, one by one. She was a massage therapist, and she would rub our feet, massage our faces, the knuckles of our spines.

The joy of my childhood is hard to describe. My community of siblings. A father whose laugh was so loud and booming that he was chosen every year to be Santa Claus at our church Christmas parties. But there was something happening inside my mother, something invisible. As the church pianist, she sat at the head of the chapel and watched us, her six children, lined up on the pew in front of her. We joked around, started calling her 'The Hawk' because she had stopped smiling. Her face was pinched and sad looking. Except, it wasn't funny. Suddenly, she was prone to rages. She stopped getting out of bed. There were days she didn't come home.

Now that I am older, I can finally make sense of what was happening to my mother. She had dedicated her entire being to our livelihood, to a religion she had been persuaded to join and that no longer made sense to her. After years of fulfilling her divine purpose, she grew tired. Mum, who once told me that women without children were selfish, shucked off these beliefs and moved away.

I was 18 when she left. Young enough to reel from the fallout: weren't families meant to be together forever? She took my youngest sister with her, but the rest of us chose to stay with our father, a man we felt sorry for because he could no longer look at us without crying. If I'm honest with myself, shamefully honest, I believed that leaving the church made my mother 'bad'. I can admit this now because I would also go on to leave the church. The catalyst? My own failed attempt at motherhood.

✻

I am 26 years old when I meet my husband. We marry in a Mormon temple in Melbourne and hold a ring ceremony beneath a eucalyptus tree. It's a balmy December afternoon in 2016. We hire a Mexican food truck and eat tacos on picnic blankets, drink sparkling grape juice from paper cups. It is one of the happiest days of my life.

From the very beginning, I am desperate for a baby. It takes me a while to convince Andy that we are ready to have kids. We're still in university, broke, living in a small apartment with a car we've borrowed from his parents. It doesn't seem ideal to bring a child into the picture, not when we're not sure whether we can provide. But my excitement spreads, and soon we find out we are expecting.

I streamline through the first months with a blundering, hopeful faith. I know that miscarriages occur, but no one ever talks about them. I have no idea how common they are, that one in four pregnancies don't make it to 12 weeks.

At 11 and a half weeks, I start bleeding. It's faint. I google it. The bleeding gets worse, so I book myself in to see a doctor. But before the appointment, we lose the baby. It is indescribably painful. Messy. I sit on the toilet in the early hours of the morning, while Andy, 23 years old and unsuspecting, mops up the blood with an old towel. He holds me while I cry. We cry together.

When the doctor's clinic opens, I sit in the waiting room with a hottie on my stomach. My name is called and I hobble into a little office, where a doctor I have never met before says, 'Babies usually die around nine weeks.' He refers me to another clinic, where I lie on a table, naked from the waist down, my legs in stirrups. It is the first ultrasound I've ever had. No one tells me that you are supposed to drink water beforehand, so that the bladder expands, becoming a window for the baby and its organs. The nurse looks at me sadly and says, 'We are going to have to do this vaginally.' She lubricates a little wand and inserts it inside me. Andy grips my hand tightly as I shut my eyes from the pain.

As the nurse pokes around my womb, she stares at the space in the monitor where a baby's foetus should be. 'I'm struggling to see anything,' she says. Then, 'Are you sure you were pregnant?' The words are so matter of fact, so incriminating, that even now it is hard for me to write them.

'Of course I was pregnant,' I say. Then, with hesitation, 'I think.' Remembering the positive test result, the six weeks of nausea and vomiting, the sore breasts, the tiredness, the indigestion, the wild mood swings, the shooting pains up the backs of my legs, the blood.

We leave the clinic in silence. I sit on the couch in our apartment and try not to stain the fabric. I'm propped up on a mountain of towels. A friend comes over, to hug me, to bring me a packet of underwear from Kmart because mine are all covered in blood. The doctor calls me a few hours later and tells me that I have experienced a 'complete miscarriage'. I hadn't known that there were different types. I search it on the internet, learning that a complete miscarriage is when the baby and everything else comes out at once. For most women it is painful and generally shocking. I do feel horrifically empty after, and in the weeks, months, and even years following, I completely fall apart.

I read a book about grief. It helps. It tells me that grief doesn't come in stages. It is an unforeseen visitor, never knocking, just pouring in from every window, every crack, even in moments when you least expect it. The book tells me that anger is normal. And I do feel anger, a lot of it. It tells me acceptance will come, and it has, slowly. Time heals, it says, and it does. But it says nothing about faith. It does not tell me that I am about to be shuttled towards a junction, one where I am at odds with my body, my identity, my womanhood and my religion.

✳

Not long after the miscarriage, Andy packs up our home in Australia and moves us back to New Zealand. He believes that I need family around me. He doesn't say it aloud, but I hear it all the same: he has no idea what to do with me. As I reel from the loss of a baby, he is reeling, very quietly, from the loss of his wife. All I do is cry. I develop a fear of going to the toilet. I can't sleep. Suddenly, my life is filled with bulbous bellies, fat ankles and glowing faces. I had been pregnant at the same time as my twin sister, my little sister and two of my sisters-in-law. They all give birth to beautiful, healthy babies.

A few years later, they give birth to another round of beautiful, healthy babies. It is hard to describe my happiness, my sadness, my constant comparison. Invisibly, the shame is burrowing in. It is the shame of not living up to my divine purpose, of believing that something is inherently wrong with me. It is the shame of not being happy for my sisters, of being so envious of their babies that I avoid photos and baby showers and birthday parties. I feel unbearably broken and permanently empty.

Several months after the miscarriage, I book an appointment with a Chinese acupuncturist. He puts needles in my abdomen, my ankles and my hips. He leaves me there on the table and I can hear my whole body begin to gurgle. Is this my body letting go? Afterwards, he gives me a casual reading of my horoscope. He tells me that I was too stressed to carry a baby. 'Two thousand and eighteen,' he says, 'wasn't a good year. Two thousand and twenty-one — that will be a good year for you. And two thousand and twenty-three. Another good year.'

Everyone tells me to try again. 'It is so good that you were able to get pregnant,' they say. I recognise that this is well-meaning and filled with love. But I feel incapable of doing this. Instead, I throw myself into my studies. My goal is pure survival: make it through the day, one day at a time.

Andy and I attend church every Sunday, but it is getting harder and harder to go. On Sunday mornings we wake up and look at each other, feeling the heaviness, the dread. We put on our holy undergarments, our Sunday best. Sometimes we talk about it, usually we don't. We don't have the words for it yet. We drive to church and sit side by side in the chapel on a hard wooden pew that digs into our backs.

As a male, Andy holds the 'Priesthood', which is a direct power from God that allows him to pray over me, to bless the Sacrament, to receive superior revelation for his family (me). I am aware that this is sexist, traditionalist, but it has never bothered me till now. The Family Proclamation has taught me well. A man's role is to protect and provide. Mine is to have babies.

As hymns are sung, as the bread and water is passed, I am filled with such debilitating worthlessness that I can't breathe. I don't feel God's love. I am far, far away. If I cannot have a baby, Mormon theology no longer makes sense to me. If my womb doesn't work, I will be powerless and worthless forever.

※

Twenty twenty-one passes quickly, catching me by surprise. I think of the acupuncturist and wonder if I have let the window of my womb close up. But it is a busy year. I am preoccupied with finishing my master's programme, which requires me to write a novel in nine months. I am so stressed I can barely think. A few months in I call Andy from the university library.

'I'm done,' I say.

'Really?' he says. 'The novel?'

'No. Church. I don't think I can go to church anymore.'

Radio silence. Then, a tiny intake of breath.

'Oh.'

We have been on this journey together, but my declaration still shocks him. To help you understand it, I have to try to explain the pain that belongs to a faith transition. It's like being dunked in a pool of water but never being able to come up for air. It's the love of a community, and then the loss of it. Severed family members, like cut-off limbs. The prejudice, the isolation, the fear. But this is what I knew: that I was so deeply unhappy I no longer knew who I was. One of us had to make a choice and it was always going to be me.

We stop going. Just like that. In November, I hand in a finger-thin manuscript — I have barely achieved the word count that is required to pass. My novel is about sisters and mothers and fertility and intergenerational trauma. My protagonist is pregnant and at the end of the book, she gives birth to a baby. Looking back, I know that I am writing about my own unborn child. I am trying to give it back its life.

On the weekend before submission, Mum had flown up from Wānaka to help me with the final edits. My mother is a different woman now. She smiles again. She walks robustly, with a sense of freedom that I envy. She talks loudly about sex and happiness and authenticity.

Mum read my entire manuscript in one sitting and told me, gently, what it was really like to give birth. She helped me restructure the ending, and I felt a deep love, watching her. When I handed in my thesis, she hugged me. 'Well done,' she said. We have always had a good relationship, but it took leaving the church for me to understand all the choices that she made, and to finally forgive her for them.

A few months later I receive feedback from an established author. I take a while to read it because I'm scared of what it might reveal. I am right to fear it. 'This book is about bodily feeling,' the author writes. 'It is about womanhood and its great ambivalence, about reproduction. But where is the happiness? Where is the joy that comes from motherhood, and sisterhood, and bodies?'

The feedback is hard for me to bear; I am looking past her words and deep into myself. Is she asking me whether or not I love my body? Am I the only one who has experienced motherhood and sisterhood in this way?

Suddenly, I am walking around in a daze. I lift my arm to put away a cup and think, *I am lifting this cup.* I crane my neck to stare out a high window and think, *I am looking up.* At the end of a long day, when Andy wraps his arms around me and asks if I'm OK, I think, *Am I OK? Is it possible to come back from this?*

※

I never know what to tell people when they ask if I want children. The answer varies. Lately I say: 'I'm struggling with my fertility.' The internet tells me that I'm a liar. Infertility is 'The failure to achieve pregnancy after 12 months or more of regular unprotected sexual intercourse.' Is it possible to be trying for a baby when you are still using birth control? I am trying, but not in the way that people think. I'm trying so fucking hard to *want* to be trying. In the five years since our miscarriage, I think daily about having a baby. Whenever my period comes, I still feel the hangover of grief.

There is a loneliness in me that I believe only a child can fill. And yet, the thought of trying to get pregnant floods me with adrenalin, gives me panic attacks in the middle of the night. If Andy tries to bring it up, I walk out of the room. Over time, as the awful fog lifts, I've discovered that I am deeply averse to anything that might take me back to these emotions. I can't help but question it — surely my sanity is more important than children?

Whenever I voice these emotions, people tell me, 'You can't live in fear!' So I stop voicing them. I begin making up new ideas, new identities for myself. I tell people I no longer want children. I tell people I want to adopt. I tell people there is so much good that I can do in the world as a childless woman.

I cannot fool my husband. He is careful around me. He watches me with his big, kind eyes. I know he wants kids. I see him with our nieces and nephews; he has a knack for it, this parenthood thing. But he is patient. Like a chess player, waiting for me to make the first move. And sometimes, that makes me angry. I am angry at him for his patience. For having a body that won't expire the way mine will. I am angry at him for his graciousness, the way that he loves me so completely, for being calm and stoic and good, all of the fucking time.

But really, I'm just angry at myself. I have fought so hard to have a say over my body, and yet, where is his choice? What if I can never give him what he wants? This terrifies me more than anything — that I will fail, over and over again. And here is another thing I don't tell people: that I am afraid I will be successful. That I will get pregnant easily and give birth to beautiful, healthy babies. Then I will be just like my mother, who spat out a volley of children and lost herself to them.

※

Twenty twenty-three rolls in. According to my acupuncturist, it is another good year. I am on a flight to America, where my twin sister lives, and where I will be living for the next three months. I am here to help her navigate a tough life transition. It's a radical, spontaneous move on my part; I have never been away from Andy for this long. I feel saintly, flying halfway across the world to attend to my twin's needs. But there is something selfish about my decision, too. I am on the hunt for purpose. I have just quit a strenuous job and my novel lies untouched, gathering dust, my aspirations of becoming a writer ridiculous and far-fetched. I am 33 years old and career-less, childless, shapeless.

It's the beginning of February and Seattle is cold. I throw myself headlong into mothering my sister's two small children. I believe that, somehow, my service will make me worthy. I am crying again, at night in the dark. I find myself reaching for another book. This one, by Kristen Neff, is called *Self-Compassion*. I read it slowly, over the course of three months. I read it like a bible. I wake up at 5 a.m. just to turn its pages, searching desperately for something to make me feel whole. It dawns on me that for the entirety of my life, God has externally validated me. My worth has been predicated on his love, on my commitment to his commandments, on my ability to be a good girl, to procreate. I no longer trust God. The person I do trust is oceans away. It feels both cheesy and monumental to write what I am slowly starting to learn: that the only person left to love me is myself.

Every morning in Seattle, I take my two-year-old nephew for a walk around the lakes. It's the middle of winter and sometimes there is snow on the ground. We wear gloves and puffer jackets. I will never forget his little face, peeking out of his hood, his pale skin ruddy in the icy air. We walk past blueberry fields, through pine forests. Most days we end up at Phantom Lake, my favourite of all places. We sit on the jetty and watch the ducks. These are some of the happiest memories of my life. His little arms around my neck. The utter silence, except for the gentle slap of wind on water. This, a gift of being childless. To help my sister in need. To be a mother, if temporarily, to this little boy, who I know loves me in the way that only children can. He gives me a gift, too — I feel hope, gathering at my edges, trying to get in.

❋

I've been back in New Zealand for two months. My husband and I move into a beautiful house in Wellington's Khandallah hills. I go to the doctor to talk about my fertility. It's a big step. She tells me in a half-crazed jumble that New Zealand doesn't put iodine in salt, and spends a weird amount of time talking about volcanoes. I don't mind. There is something graceful about me now. I'm taking prenatal vitamins. We're not 'trying' but I take the pills religiously. One is tiny and white, the other a yolky orange.

Maybe, one day soon, I will wake up feeling brave. I will run my hands over my beautiful, lovable body and thank it. I will say, 'Thank you, body, for working so hard.' And maybe, one day, I'll have kids. Maybe I won't. I understand now that I am worth something, no matter what.

Weaving a life horizontally

CAROLIJN GUYTONBECK

'Can you come to my birthday party? I'm going to be four!' I received the request with both delight and trepidation. Delight that this little boy liked me enough to invite me to his party, and apprehension about my ability to fit in and enjoy the experience. I need not have worried.

I had only just met this little guy. He had come to visit with his parents and baby sister. He'd been asleep in the car when they arrived, but later emerged, groggy and timorous, hiding behind his mother. My warm inclusion of him in conversation soon had him out of his shell, and he displayed an excellent vocabulary; unsurprising given his mother is a writer and an English teacher. He had dark eyes and a mop of hair, as you can imagine a boy with an Italian father would. As we walked around my rural property visiting the animals and orchard, he danced about with the kind of enthusiasm for life that has a magnetising pull. We played, he chasing me with his toy dragon and creating mini scenarios. He walked alongside me as we all returned to the house, animatedly talking of all manner of things, including, with much excitement, his upcoming party. As the family was preparing to leave, his request came . . . followed by, 'You can come if you have children.'

I felt dual disappointment and relief, along with a lack of surprise. After all, I had lived my adult life without invitations to children's birthday parties, baby showers or twenty-firsts. I never quite understood this. There seems to be an implicit belief that people without children are not interested, do not like them, have better things to do. Is that the parents projecting? Do I not interact well with children? Am I a scary witch?

My confusion about this phenomenon of missing invitations is further amplified by close friends wanting me to be interested in their children — they know I care, and I, in turn, know they care about me. 'You are their godmother, unofficially' — I don't remember being asked — 'so if anything happens to us you will look after them.' A statement not a question.

❋

Living where I do, I have limited family. My parents were immigrants, hence I missed out on extended family. I especially envy people who have grandparents. My greater family are on the other side of the world, and are very European in their sense of history and connection. My father's younger brother later joined my parents, seeking a life here in Aotearoa. He married a New Zealander and had two sons, my dear cousins. There were four children in my immediate family and we two families, being all we had, were close, sharing events and celebrations together — even as we children reached young adulthood, even after both sets of parents had separated. My siblings left Ōtepoti.

My younger brother, while still young, was thrown into fatherhood and a difficult relationship. My niece spent a great deal of time with me as she grew up. She lived in other towns but visited for school holidays and when her parents needed breaks. We've remained close, but she, too, lives in another country now. It is as if diaspora is in the blood, although one could say that for many families of Aotearoa.

My older brother settled in Thailand, and he and his Thai wife adopted their twin nieces after their biological parents were killed; after separating from his wife came a third daughter. My older sister married in Melbourne and had three boys. I have no doubt that had we all lived in the same place I would have joyfully received regular birthday party invitations. Of my two cousins, one never had a family, but the other married and had two children. Still, it is as if it never occurred to them that I might like to be included in events important to the children as they grew, despite my interest in them and their fondness for me. Their friends with children participated in the birthday parties. But not I, the childless; not I, the 'other'.

This term, the 'other' is used in many varied ways. The concept seems so ingrained in Western ways of seeing that we can forget to question it. Until we are on its wrong side — even, at times, in white, privileged worlds. Our lives are ruled by views of the self, the ego, our identity. As we grow through our childhood years, a sense of unease develops, like dust in the sunlight that begins to settle on our bodies. Who we are, where we came from, who we belong to. The occasional schoolyard taunt or bitter retort (in my case, 'You Dutch came and took all our jobs', even though my parents had difficulty getting good work), and soon we have teenage angst. We are all 'other' in some form or another, that becomes clear, or at least it does if we possess a level of self-awareness.

I came out of university an independent, self-willed woman. My arts degree was not taking me into a specific career, and as unemployment at the time was high, no serious arts-related jobs were available. So, like many of my brethren, I fell into various types of work. With my siblings departed, my ageing parents needed my support, and leaving my hometown did not seem to be a viable option for me.

I met my partner, who, like me, came from divorced parents and had no clear career path to follow within those years of New Zealand's neoliberal economics. He set up his own business and later I joined him in that. We were a team, but all our eggs were in that one basket, and times were tough. In my early thirties I fell pregnant, and my partner persuaded me that now was not the time to have children.

We were both forcefully aware of what was then referred to as 'global warming'. A threat that, for us, was on the heels of the threat of nuclear war. What world was this to bring a child into? We lived in a cold, damp rental house. My parents needed care. How could I care for a child when I was caring for them? My feminist and pro-abortionist doctor told me that there was no obstacle that could not be overcome, should I wish to become a mother. I dearly loved children and did wish to become a mother. Yet all the arguments weighed on me and, most strongly, I did not wish to have a child whose father did not wish to be a father. My choice was clear, but it was a deeply painful one, especially when I was sent for a scan and given a photo of the foetus (my doctor was angry on hearing this).

A powerful moment in my life was waking from my termination and seeing my partner's face as I opened my tearful eyes. At that moment, he knew the regret of the decision we had made. That moment was immediately followed by another: the termination experience was a production line. Nurses got us out of our beds one by one and we lined up to see the medical professional who had performed the procedures, a well-meaning doctor no doubt, as he chose this work.

As I shuffled up, trying to put on a brave smile, I was met with one that was grim and worn-down. I was handed a packet of contraceptive pills and told to take them. The short conversation was loaded with the message that I should take the pills and not get pregnant again. I had felt in control of my life; post this event, I felt like life controlled me. Were men in charge of my body?

Life, of course, went on, and although my partner had softened, all our other reasons for choosing not to have children remained. If I were faced with it again it is likely I would make the same decision. We went on to have a lifestyle block parenting many animals and trees, and built a warm, dry home. I was no stranger to birth and neonatal care — we had decided to breed Hereford cattle. Over the years, I was midwife to many births, at times up to my armpits repositioning badly presented calves, and often frantically working to keep mother and baby alive. In our care for these beautiful animals, it was not long before my partner and I became vegetarian; with our already-existing concerns for global warming, our breeding days were brought to an end.

My niece and parents also required a lot of attention, and while I was childless, I was still very much a caregiver. I cared for both my parents through their ill health and was with them when they died, and I helped get my niece through university. Then I could care for myself. While continuing to work, I studied part-time for a second degree in what was my original love: art history and theory. With the little money my mother left me, I got to visit my family in the Netherlands, beloved despite the distance between us. My caregiving has extended to mentoring artists, teaching at university, working with disabled students and, for a while, caring for a troubled young homeless man.

Women are often caregivers, even those who, like me, don't have children to show for it. At times it has exhausted me, at times I have felt the loss of a life that I could have had were it not for the sacrifices I made. My caregiving has not been that of motherhood and has made me other.

※

During the course of writing this essay, I've become acutely aware of how much motherhood, parenting and the desire to have children is written about. Jumping out at me weekly on Literary Hub and *The Guardian* were titles such as, 'My four miscarriages: why is losing a pregnancy so shrouded in mystery?', '"Infertility stung me": Black motherhood and me', 'I'm childfree by choice: should I feel guilty about ending my line?', and many more, all touching on deeply felt personal situations.

In a refreshing take, Andrew Porter, author of *The Disappeared*, wrote on Literary Hub that after becoming a parent he felt things in his life, mostly intangible, began to disappear. He felt as though he had been accumulating things and people. When children came along, much of his known life drifted away, freedom pointedly being one of those things that left. On becoming parents, a division is drawn between those with children and those without. Those who do birthday parties and those who don't. His book, he felt, was his way of making something, of adding, of reclaiming the things that get lost. 'The human heart,' he writes, 'resists it, after all, the notion of things disappearing. That's why we tell stories . . .'

I have survived life without children, and I will survive life without grandchildren. As a dear childless friend says when asked about children, 'Oh! I forgot.' My life is not enhanced by little wriggling bundles of joy, emblems of hope and a future, yet my life is not defined, or lacking, by being without them. When my mother died, I was a woman both motherless and childless. But I still had close family connections through my siblings, cousins and close friends — I am a happy unofficial godmother.

I am a thread that weaves horizontally, but not vertically. Some will think that producing a future generation is their legacy. My partner and I went another way. Along with 12 cows (in retirement), we share our lives with nine Muscovy ducks (who flew in), one domineering cat (who needed a home), numerous rambunctious native birds, and other wildlife. We have planted small native forests along the two rivers that run through our property — thousands of trees, shrubs and grasses. We are helping in the battle against climate change, and we are leaving our world a better place, a legacy for generations to come. The trees will grow roots that connect with each other, and they will grow vertically for me, some for decades, some for centuries. I will never stop longing for the little life that might have been, but my maternal love, my otherhood, has found its worth in many other ways.

Trunclehood

SAM ORCHARD

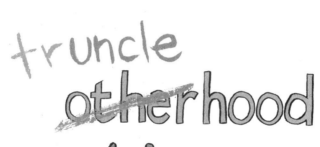

Yes – it's **really** important that you help advocate for better healthcare for trans people who actually do want to be parents (or need access to abortions).

Trans parents need access to safe and inclusive care, whether they're the birthing parent or not.

And there are **heaps** of trans parents out there. And reproductive justice is essential for all of us!

Read 'Warming the Whare for trans people and whānau in perinatal care'.

Sorry. Where was I?

I don't want kids of my own but I'm really grateful to have heaps of incredible kids in my life.

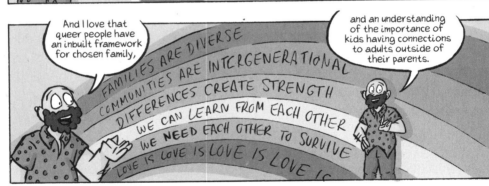

And I love that queer people have an inbuilt framework for chosen family,

and an understanding of the importance of kids having connections to adults outside of their parents.

FAMILIES ARE DIVERSE
COMMUNITIES ARE INTERGENERATIONAL
DIFFERENCES CREATE STRENGTH
WE CAN LEARN FROM EACH OTHER
WE NEED EACH OTHER TO SURVIVE
LOVE IS LOVE IS LOVE IS LOVE IS

Having kids in my life helps me to be a better adult in this world.

So yeah – unclehood, or gunclehood,* or trunclehood,** or otherhood ... is what suits me best.

* gay unclehood
**trans unclehood

The happy wanderer

RAINA NG

Dreams are the guiding words of the soul. Why should I henceforth not love my dreams and not make their riddling images into objects of my daily consideration?
— Carl Jung, *The Red Book*

Sometimes my dreams come back to me vividly. In one, I was stuck in a stuffy cabin among too many strangers, trying to find a way to escape. I had begun searching for my shoes in the swarm of them by the door, when I heard a singing voice. Convinced it belonged to someone who had my shoes, I followed it:

I love to go a-wandering, around the mountain track,
and as I go I love to sing with a backpack on my back.
Valderi, valdera, valderi, valdera-ha-ha-ha-ha-ha . . .

The voice led me to another cabin. When I knocked on the door, the voice answered, and I looked up to see a uterus. She claimed to be mine. I demanded she give me my shoes, and we, this uterus and I, began fighting over them.

The uterus, or hystera, has long been villainised as a restless, greedy animal. In an ancient medical document called the *Kahun*, the wandering womb was discussed: it is said that a dissatisfied uterus displaces itself and embarks upon a journey toward fulfilment.[1] Plato believed the womb, in its search for fruitfulness, would cause disease by wandering through the body.[2] A sixteenth-century German-Swiss physician by the name of Paracelsus thought the womb could turn 'unfavourable', resulting in the contraction of the organ. He wrote, 'if such contraction takes place in the veins of the whole body, vapour and smoke come out of the womb to the organs around it. And it touches the heart.'[3] This condition, he said, manifested itself in a 'dance which we find in whores'. The condition was known as uterine hysteria.

Medically, the woman had been painted as a being obsessed with the need to fill her womb. I often wonder about the effect of such a picture, implying as it does that a woman's life cannot be full outside of motherhood. This picture, which I never thought to question, clouded my full enjoyment of being single.

Years after I had that dream, I was diagnosed with a sick womb; it was by then enlarged and misshapen by fibroids and adenomyosis. I bore my sick womb with shame. As the likelihood of conceiving or bearing a child was small, the doctors supported a hysterectomy.

In the months before the scheduled hysterectomy, the dream about the singing uterus came back to me. I never had a harmonious relationship with my uterus. In many ways she endured the brunt of the hatred, disgust and shame I had carried about my body. I needed to give her a farewell. As the anaesthetist's countdown began, I found her beaming with her knapsack on her back. When she saw me, she waved and thanked me for the shoes.

'Before you go,' I called out to her, 'what is a woman without a womb'?

'*Valderi, valdera, valderi, valdera-ha-ha-ha-ha-ha . . .*'

She was gone.

＊

1   Lana Thompson, *The Wandering Womb: A cultural history of outrageous beliefs about women* (Prometheus, 1999), www.profkramer.com/assets/wandering-womb-intro-1-and-2-f07.pdf, 4.

2   T. A. McCulloch, 'Theories of hysteria', *The Canadian Journal of Psychiatry* 14, no. 6 (1969): 635–37, https://journals.sagepub.com/doi/pdf/10.1177/070674376901400614

3   Thompson, 5.

What is a woman without a womb? I had thrown that question around a handful of friends and one answer that came back felt like an assault: *A woman without a womb is barren.*

Barrenness has long been associated with a curse: the withholding of a gift.[4] Throughout the Bible, we see the women they called barren carrying infertility with shame. Hannah was 'taunted' because 'the Lord had closed her womb'.[5] The way the story was told, so zealous was her praying and weeping, she looked to others as if she were in a state of drunkenness. She kept up the fervent prayer until God finally 'remembered' her, and she bore a son.[6]

Infertility, and the ending of a family line, is also seen in Chinese culture as a sort of curse upon a family. I remember overhearing a remark made by a friend's father that the choice not to have children is a selfish one. It is sort of a duty, Confucian filial piety, for the younger generation to carry on the family honour and name. I got that lecture, too.

I caught up with a friend on a trip back to Kuala Lumpur. He was then expecting his third child, one he said they had much difficulty conceiving. He'd consulted a monk at a temple who told him it was his destiny to only have three children. While musing on this, he realised he and his wife had already had three: there had been an abortion early in their relationship. He was told that in order to have the third child, they would have to pay penance for the abortion. It was after a long series of good deeds they conceived their third.

'Karma,'[7] he said.

I must have something I need to pay penance for.

✺

We are new beings made from old beings. My mother has poured everything that is her being into me: her deep love, her kindness, her desire for goodness. But in giving her all, she's also given her pains. Within me are her fears, her anxieties, her anger, her trauma, her insecurities,

---

4   Cynthia R. Chapman, 'Barrenness', Bible Odyssey, 28 February 2023, www.bibleodyssey. org/people/related-articles/barrenness, accessed 6 May 2023.
5   'I Samuel 1:4', the Bible, www.sefaria.org/I_Samuel.1.4?lang=bi, accessed 6 May 2023.
6   Lillian Klein (Abensohn), 'Hannah: Bible', Jewish Women's Archive, n.d., https://jwa.org/ encyclopedia/article/hannah-bible, accessed 6 May 2023.
7   Ven. Mahasi Sayadaw, 'The theory of karma', www.buddhanet.net/e-learning/karma.htm, accessed 20 May 2023.

her prejudices. All the things that accompanied me in her womb.

As a child, I often dreamt I was pregnant, in my 10- or 11-year-old body. I would be on a journey somewhere, and would suddenly find myself pregnant and very distressed. I now know these dreams came from my mother's fears. All the talk from my mother about sex and puberty were cautionary tales of exploitation and teenage pregnancies. I learnt that the sexual act was shameful and disgusting, and the woman's body was a burden. To my mother, nothing would bring more shame to a woman than teenage pregnancy.

But it happened when I was barely 17. Both sets of parents made the swift decision to do what they believed would be in our best interests. My mother flew with me to Bangkok, where his parents had arranged everything. It went smoothly: I saw the doctor, put on the gown and was wheeled into the operating theatre where the nurses were warm and comforting. When I awoke in the sterile hospital, the whole thing was done. Swept under the carpet, it became a blip in my memory. Something I managed to almost forget about — until it showed up again, several years later, in another recurring dream.

※

I dreamt of a little girl in a garden who was painting on a giant canvas. I would chat to her as she painted, and when I took a peek at the canvas I would find it blank. After painting, we would have tea and cake, and as we chatted it would dawn on me that she had no face.

Waking the third or fourth time after having this dream, I decided to name her Sarah Jane. For a long time I believed Sarah Jane to be the child I never had. In these dreams I would ask her if she wanted to come home with me. She never wanted to.

I recently came upon that garden and the canvas in another dream. While walking through the garden I began to wonder if Sarah Jane was really a version of me. One that could have been if I'd had the baby. Whoever Sarah Jane was, a choice was made — and as a consequence, she remained an idea that had been conceived but never realised. She remained faceless because she was never born. Yet she left that canvas for me to paint on.

※

Recently, I had a dream about my cat, Millie. I walked into a roomful of cats, all ginger and white like her. I found her, and when I picked her up, we began flying.

Millie came to me a couple of years before the surgery, on a blue-skied November day. On the morning of her arrival I had set out to the local bakery for fresh croissants, which I planned to have with coffee in the sun. As I anticipated her arrival I wrote to a friend, telling her I was anxious about having an animal inside the orderly, clean house.

'What if,' I asked, 'I hate her? Or she hates me, with my slight cat allergies and slight fear of cats?'

Like most prejudices, cat prejudice is inculcated gradually. My mother is obsessive about cleanliness and squeamish about all things furry. Over the years I have come to understand her prejudices were just fears and anxieties. But fears are easily passed down.

I savoured every bite of the buttery croissant in the quiet calm with those thoughts. When the croissant was done, I set aside the anxiety, ready to receive Millie with all I am.

She was a ball of nervous energy when she arrived. She ran for cover the minute her crate door was opened, and found the unreachable corner behind the washing machine. That first week was spent coaxing her out of all our dark hidden corners. As she emerged from a tight ginger ball to queen of the house, my fear of cats turned into love.

Biologically, the female body has the ability to give space within herself to another. We will never be connected, joined, to another in the same way we were our mothers. Now that I'm free from my sick womb, I am physically incapable of achieving that feat. And yet, I never felt as myself as I do now.

I spent most of my recovery from surgery on a sofa bed with Millie curled up next to me. I am so proud to be her ally in this big, scary world. What my little sidekick has shown me is that I am capable of doing what my mother has done for me: connecting, giving, nurturing and, most importantly, yielding space for another to be.

❋

One night I was picked up by a flying horse. It took me over the roofs of several houses to land in a bedroom. I picked up a picture frame, and the person in the picture spoke to me.

'Fullness,' he said.

In his *Letters to a Young Poet*, Rainer Maria Rilke wrote, 'I think that there is motherhood in man too, bodily and spiritual motherhood; his begetting is a kind of bearing, too, and bearing it is, when he creates out of his innermost abundance.'[8] This became evident to me at an intimate Jonathan Crayford and Patrick Bleakley concert at Suite's Wellington gallery. I was seated comfortably in the corner as the rich notes stretched themselves under me like a magic carpet, ready to carry me places. Watching the musicians absorbed in their instruments, I was struck by an awareness: as these men poured their hearts into making these tunes, they were pouring their love into life. They birthed something new each moment they filled with their music.

※

A dictionary definition of the word barren is: 'empty of meaning or value'. But this is not true for me. My life, whether full or barren, is still a story that is being written.

My fullness does not depend on what I do not or cannot have. The fullness of my life will depend on the choices I make each moment. It is dependent upon what I choose to do with what I have. I want to pour love into each moment of life. Whatever I do not know, I will learn along the way.

I am not barren, I am Raina.

---

8   Rainer Maria Rilke, 'Letters to a young poet, letter four', The Rainer Maria Rilke Archive, 11 March 2023, rilkepoetry.com/letters-to-a-young-poet/letter-four

Another birth

GHAZALEH GOL

No fisherman will find a pearl
in the hubble stream that pours into a pit
— Forough Farrokhzad, 'Another Birth'[1]

On a dreary Monday morning in Tāmaki Makaurau, I sit in a tiny radiology department waiting my turn for an ultrasound. That word seems to be synonymous with pregnancy but ironically, I am here to see if everything is as it should be in that area or if 'something is rotten in the state of Denmark'. Rotten. Barren. It took me 40 years to learn that 'womb' is not an actual scientific word, but one taken from Old English, possibly Old Norse. Womb, also known as belly, bowels, heart, uterus.

᳂

I got Covid in the second year of the virus. As with many things, we were late to the party here in Aotearoa. I got the 'vid while living with flatmates, one of whom was about to start a very important stint on reality television,

---

1   Forough Farrokhzad, *Let Us Believe in the Beginning of the Cold Season*, translated by Elizabeth T. Gray Jr. (New Directions Publishing, 2022), 73.

so I moved in with a friend who lived alone in a posh part of town: a newly renovated house with minimalist white décor and capsule coffee. We spent the week feeling sorry for ourselves, watching terrible (weirdly satisfying) reality shows about young people sexing it up on yachts in the Med, and '90s music videos with questionable mullets.

Like many others, my Covid stuck around, like an unwanted houseguest, mooching and haranguing me and my body for months after. Its first target was my hormones, sending them into a chaotic orbit. I missed one period. Then they came every two weeks. It's an odd and disruptive feeling to spend the majority of your life terrified of it being late, then welcoming lateness because the alternative is not getting it anymore. The big M looms around the corner and it's even more ghastly because for me, for someone who now wants a child, it symbolises a type of death. There is no specified time to mourn the death of your expectations; the death of your body and its abilities; the death of something you never thought you wanted. But Death is in the business of snatching.

❋

Another month with no period. Lateness is something I used to excel at when younger. In complete opposition to my mum, who believes if you're on time, you're already late. I sometimes blame my appalling time-management skills on my childhood. I also blame my awkward shyness on being forced to learn a new culture, new language and new everything at six years old. Apparently, I was an annoying chatterbox back in Iran, but my inability to speak English here shut me up.

Being uprooted from Iran to Aotearoa New Zealand as a child also means I'm constantly in a state of limbo. Scholarly works on diaspora and exile note that liminal space exists between two worlds, neither here nor there, somewhere between the home and the new nation. This space can be a place of colliding cultures, where new identities are not only forged but are also in a continual state of development. A part of me has latched on to the idea that because I was put into a liminal place at that age, I will forever be attempting to catch up. Mentally I am always six years behind. Like a deranged Benjamin Button, I shall grow at a delayed rate. Currently I feel like a wannabe-Millennial: someone who buys period undies, has no real recollection of 9/11 and has had to say goodbye to her Harry Potter collection because, well, TERFs.

But sadly, my body never got that memo. This is the body of a 40-year-old.

She aches in random places, she's scarred from various dumb things her owner did to her and she's nearly ready to free herself from the menstrual overlords.

A few months later, it's period city. Every two weeks, another box of Countdown home-brand tampons. I'm constantly harassing my mother about when she went through menopause, convinced I am going through it early. She tells me to stop worrying. She's sure I'm normal. Regular, ordinary, natural.

❋

The waiting room is minimalist and sterile — no funky colours or Scandi furniture here. Luckily only one lone poster about pregnancy peeks out at me. It's non-intrusive, unlike the procedure I'm about to go through.

A nurse squirts cold gel then runs some contraption across my very empty belly. My experience of an ultrasound has been tainted by numerous films and TV shows that feature such a scene for expectant mothers. It's *always* a pregnancy scan. It's not a scan for *abnormal periods*, or *weird cyst thing in your vulva* or *unexplained woman troubles that we assume are uterus related but really we have no idea because we have 50 Viagra substitutes to work on.* It's eerie to look at the monitor and not have the nurse smile and relay some romantic speech about heartbeats. Instead she asks if I'm allergic to latex, then straps a condom on a long plastic thing with a camera.

❋

The last day I visited my favourite aunt in hospital was the day she passed away. She was too kind for the cruelty of the disease that ate away at her body. I left my aunt's overloaded ward in distress, devastated by the smells and sounds of decay and sadness. In the lift a woman was holding her newborn baby. A tiny thing, barely able to hold its eyes open, its skin fresh like a new flower petal blooming, completely untouched. It was an odd but moving moment, almost foreshadowing that old thing; a life taken and a new one given.

Sometimes this need for a baby depresses me. Other times, I feel a need to fight the sadness. To stand in its way and say, no, move on, find a new dream. Those are the days I wish I was back to being a six-year-old, stuck in liminality but far away from making crude life decisions; a magical place where you have limited choices to make but a lifetime of choice awaits you. Which doll would I take to my cousins? Do I want kebabs or an ice cream after my TB shot?

As a child I never wanted to get married and have babies (or baby; why is it always plural?) but I just assumed it was going to happen. Like puberty and taxes, like love affairs and heartbreaks. In part it was rebellion against societal norms. Growing up in the 1990s, feminism was undesirable and therefore anything 'feminine' was deemed so very uncool. Being 'girly' or wanting 'girly' things became clichés that I consciously fought against. But I played with Barbies and rewatched blockbuster movies. Hollywood and Mattel were both hero and nemesis. In the movies, growing dinosaurs in a lab was feasible, but showing an alternative lifestyle to heteronormative couples with blonde kids and a giant dog named Beethoven was beyond comprehension.

While the 1980s were atrocious for anything outside of the norm, the '90s at least attempted to try. *Sex and the City*, for all its faults, has one particular episode that rings true for me every time I watch it. The ladies must venture out to the suburbs to attend a baby shower for an old friend. Decked out in all black, they stand aghast: Carrie worried about a late period, Miranda disgusted by what she calls the cult of The Motherhood and Samantha deciding to hold her own 'no-baby shower'.

Years later, with three single friends in tow, we unconsciously replicated that exact scene — decked in black, drunk and bored at a baby shower celebrating The Motherhood Cult. It's depressing to think a show written by gay men about aspirational rich white women in NYC was my only source of influence for a long time. What's worse is that the show still gave in to convention by marrying off Carrie and Charlotte, and pushing Miranda out to Brooklyn, baby in arms.

Where is the alternative version in which the ladies buy a lush commune together where they continue to explore sex and sexuality deep into their twilight years? Where they help raise Miranda's kid as a tight matriarchal unit, where Carrie finally takes a writing course, Charlotte 'discovers' polyamory and Samantha heads the United Nations? I need more from my pop culture.

As I sat with the girls at another hip raw-paleo-keto only New York City restaurant, I couldn't help but wonder about the choices and 'unchoices' we have in life. Charlotte complains about how there is no option on Bumble for 'Don't have kids but open to single parents'; Miranda rants about laws that operate against single women trying to get government funding for IVF or adoption, to which Charlotte desperately replies, 'I'm aware I don't have choices anymore and this becomes another choice I don't have. I feel incomplete.' Is it true? Is the choice to be different to the status quo another problem we need to add to the list of problems faced by single women in their forties? Only Samantha finds the humour: 'Oh honey, no one's ever complete. That's what keeps you thriving, getting that cup filled.' We all laugh, except Charlotte.

※

S till in the radiology room, and 20 or so minutes pass, filled with long silences, beeps, clicks and dry sheets being scrunched as I stretch to look at the monitor, fantasising that miraculously there's something in there. But the nurse dashes all hope of a miracle baby: 'It's a cyst on your right ovary. Should be fine. Come back again in three months.'

※

T o this day I still find the idea of a baby shower abhorrent, but over the years becoming a mother slowly etched its way through my mind. I'm not sure why or when, but the joy I experience meeting a friend's little one or the daydreams I have of growing my own awesome human have become much more vivid. Probably a few years too late. Once again, my body has become a victim of my mind's tardiness.

A therapist once told me to imagine a life without children. To see the positives and really see what my existence would be without them. The main word there: imagine. Because in this world we have yet to see that alternative as a norm. The role of women is still intertwined with motherhood. Early feminists struggled and fought for choice but that, as with most things, has been tainted and overtaken by capitalist patriarchal values of having it all or having nothing. Third wave feminists gave voice to this conundrum: it's not enough to want to be a successful career woman or a stay-at-home mum; you must want to become both — and look good while doing it. Otherwise you are incomplete as a woman and punished. It is a desire that cannot ever be fully fulfilled — classic capitalism.

The Guardian recently noted that one in five women are childless at midlife.[2] One in five doesn't seem like an alternative to the mainstream. That same article notes how choice plays a big part in who is visible and who is not. For example, those who *choose* to be childless are now (rightly) being

---

2   Nicola Slawson, 'The chasm between mothers and childless women is widening', *The Guardian*, 7 April 2023, www.theguardian.com/commentisfree/2023/apr/07/chasm-mothers-childless-women-widening-motherhood-empathy

celebrated just as those choosing to have children always have been. But those who have no choice, or have had that choice taken away, are still shamed. Not having the choice is stained by some sort of mythical shame monster. Spinster, old maid, hag. In Farsi, the term is torsheedeh — something sour.

※

One of the greatest Iranian poets, Forough Farrokhzad, is revered in modern Iran and in the diaspora. Her turbulent life and tragic death at 32 helped her gain legendary status alongside her revolutionary works. For Forough, poetry and art was life. In her renowned poem 'Another Birth', Forough's female speaker is unapologetic for her desires. Whether they're for a lover or for poetry, she emboldens the reader to just go for it. 'No fisherman will find a pearl in the hubble stream that pours into a pit'.

I am not delusional, and like any good problem solver (is it even a problem?) I constantly think of different plans and back-ups. If having a child is not on my horizon, then what other desires can I chase? I search for childless heroes. I envision new adventures. I think of my own friends who are going along similar paths and how, collectively, we can help each other. Some are childless by choice, others like me have made the journey and gone through the tunnel and come out still shining in the end. A type of sisterhood baptism where you are, excuse the pun, rebirthed.

Perhaps now I need to prepare for a type of mourning but, like any kind of grief, try to convince myself that it will end. That end may give rise to a new beginning. It may not be the ideal but neither is motherhood — so I've been told.

Synchronicity

NICOLA BROWN

At first, I didn't get the job. When I interviewed for the role of clinical psychologist at the fertility clinic, one of the interviewers opened by asking me, complete with deep frown and rumpled brow, 'Why would you want *this* role?' The implication was that it was perplexingly inappropriate for a twenty-something newish graduate. It seemed hopeless before I'd even opened my mouth.

I wasn't about to say, but I knew exactly where my interest lay. I was aware I'd need help to become a parent — because I had a female partner. I had given a lot of thought to the intricacies of trying to conceive when things can't be left to chance. That wasn't my sole motivation for applying, but it definitely made the 'situations vacant' advertisement jump off the page.

I didn't get the position; the feedback they gave was that I needed more life experience. Which was interesting, as they didn't specifically ask what 'life experience' I'd had. Coming out in the 1990s when all we knew about the whole 'gay thing' was that it somehow related to Boy George, AIDS, and getting yelled at if we held hands in public — would that count? Or all that I'd learnt as a rest-home caregiver, sitting with people in their last days and weeks, tending to their fragile bodies and treasuring their stories? No? Oh, OK.

I trotted off, found another role, and applied again when the person they'd employed resigned within a year. This time, the job was mine.

❋

We had this dream that Ros would have a child, then I would. We both hoped to carry a pregnancy and, since she's nine years older than me, it made sense for her to try first. We wanted our children to be able to know their genetic origins and to have a relationship with their donor if they chose, so we needed a sperm donor we could have contact with. There was a similar process each time. We'd tentatively approach someone who we thought might be open to the possibility, and there would be sometimes easy, sometimes complex discussions with them, their partner if they had one, and whoever else needed consulting. At least once, our approach was rebuffed. That was tricky, but fair enough — it had to be right for everyone involved.

Once we had a possible donor ready to go, the next question was how to actually proceed? I was working at the fertility clinic by now, and was adamant I wanted to stay outside that process if at all possible. Having treatment at a clinic means surrendering to timeframes outside your control, lists of instructions to follow and intrusive procedures; I hoped the creation of our family could be an intimate experience, rather than a medical one. And I wanted to avoid being client and clinician at the same time; being both felt murky and complicated.

This was in the late 1990s and we were stabbing in the dark — so to speak — about how to maximise the chances of DIY insemination. AOL and Yahoo search-engine performance was mediocre when it came to this topic. Even if we'd had Google, what would we search for? 'How to get my lesbian fiancée pregnant'? The computer would have had a meltdown.

A couple of relevant books were passed around the Dunedin queer scene and, far from the pulse of fusion disco-feminist-country music at lesbian dances, quiet conversations were had with people who knew things. Ros and I equipped our bathroom with pink-lidded sterile plastic specimen cups and needleless syringes, started watch-parties for fertile mucus and We. Got. Excited.

Attempts were made. Then more attempts. Things would seem slightly promising — tender breasts, period late by a couple of days — or was it wishful thinking? Blood tests were had, results considered, adjustments made. After tough discussions and another round of appeals, we switched donors. Made further attempts. The novelty wore off pretty quickly when every month was carefully choreographed around likely ovulation peaks and making sure we and the donor were in the same place at the right time. Waves of hope and disappointment started with a gentle sway but when months went by, we — and each donor — got worn down. People's lives changed and even with the best of intentions on all sides, we started burning through donors like tealight candles.

※

Within my first week working at the clinic, I learnt many things. First, I didn't have an office. The clinic needed a counsellor — it was mandated to offer counselling to people going through certain treatments or offering to be donors — but it was space-poor. I turned up on my first day with four different coloured pens, a clipboard and a stash of lined paper in my bag. My stationery and I shuffled around the hospital while the service manager showed me possible places to perch myself, brightly prefacing each space with 'You might not get to stay here long.'

After a few upheavals I was planted in the finance department, not only in a different building to the rest of the team but also a seven-minute walk away. I drew myself a map to remember how to get there. I got kicked out of that office when someone more finance-y needed it.

Next, I was packed into a room where men provided their semen samples (mercifully for everyone concerned, not while I was there!). This room was the size of a peanut, so clients and I were pretty much sitting on each other's laps. Perhaps this was useful for developing rapport, but it was a little too intimate for comfort. Every couple of minutes the intensity was interrupted by the noise of the elevator shaft clanging right next door, and a prominent local radio announcer's voice saying 'Lift stopping, second floor'. If I had the mechanical engineering skills to dismantle the speakers, I would have done so.

In my first week in the role, I had to read books on infertility as part of my orientation. There was no such thing as online training then, but the books were enlightening. First, I learnt that what I'd been taught to call a vagina was technically a vulva. Whoa. The second useful piece of information was how a woman's hormones work throughout a monthly cycle, and when the most fertile time of the month is. Why were these facts not taught at school? They would have been of far more actual use to me than what I learnt in health and physical education, which was how many burpees I could do without projectile vomiting, and how to manoeuvre a condom onto a banana. I haven't used either of these skills since.

In the staffroom, I mentioned having a female partner. A couple of days later the clinical director — a gentle, compassionate man — called me into his office. We were surrounded by teetering stacks of academic paperwork and books. Hesitating, he brought to my attention that another member of staff had expressed concern that I was in a same-sex relationship. Given that I would be counselling people who were primarily in heterosexual relationships, was I an appropriate person for the role? I said, 'I don't know the sexual orientation of everyone on the team but if we follow that reasoning, should any health professional who's heterosexual ever work with gay or lesbian patients?' He thought for a moment, then said, 'Good point.'

※

After a few years of Ros trying to get pregnant, I bumped into an acquaintance at the supermarket. She asked me if we had any children yet. Just hours before, Ros and I had found out that yet another attempt had failed. I collapsed into sobs among the cans of chickpeas and cannellini beans. The acquaintance stuttered, 'Oh I'm sorry, I shouldn't have asked,' patted me sympathetically and scurried away.

By this time we'd been trying for around five years. Couples around us had popped out entire families — one, two, three kids — in the time since we'd started. It felt like we were being lapped on an athletics track, and then lapped again, but we hadn't even managed to locate our running shoes.

Our experience of infertility was one of having ideals and dreams that — gradually or suddenly, partially or completely — eroded in light of the brutal reality. There was a stream of heartbreaking conversations when we acknowledged we had to relinquish more elements of our vision. We had to accept we were getting nowhere doing this by ourselves, and we became patients of the clinic. Ros underwent round after round of clinic inseminations, with me by her side, chatting to colleagues who were now also our health providers. Slightly awkward but not terrible; my colleagues were as accommodating about it as they could be. It would all feel worthwhile, if only it worked! But still, no luck.

After months of this we walked up the Pineapple Track and found ourselves surrounded by the thick fog that inexplicably swirls in each time we decide to ascend a Dunedin hill. We found ourselves scrambling and sliding down a path we could barely see. As we walked we talked, and made the tough call to switch from Ros trying to me. I know the devastation I felt, and that it was so much greater for Ros. It meant once and for all saying goodbye to fulfilling her longing to carry a baby, with her own genes, in her own body. Until that point it had been beyond her comprehension that she wouldn't have a biological child. Her deep sadness was — still is — palpable. Neither of us wanted it, but it made sense. Head-sense, but not heart-sense.

❄

Having hundreds of conversations with people about infertility over the years, common themes emerged. The process can test even the strongest of relationships. There are multiple, ongoing layers of grief involved, and many of the losses are invisible. There is an almost universal need for people to understand *why* things aren't working; humans like things to make sense and to have hooks to attach meaning to. With infertility that's often not possible — sometimes this is just how it is and we won't ever know why. Self-blame, regret and a sense of being let down by one's own body are all common feelings not easily understood by people outside of this experience.

Usually, if a couple wants to have a baby, that's a decision between the two of them. With infertility, however, suddenly complete strangers and invasive tests and procedures are involved. There are also questions, comments and well-meaning but often misguided advice from friends and family. For example, there will inevitably be someone, somewhere, someday who states that if you just relax, it will happen. This will be followed by an anecdote about their colleague's friend's sister who went to Rarotonga, adopted a stray Rottweiler puppy and meditated 24/7 for a year, then miraculously found herself pregnant.

As a fertility counsellor, I suggested people prepare a response for this situation. Such as, that's lovely for your incredibly distant random mythical acquaintance. However, I'm allergic to tropical holidays, I'm not a big fan of ferocious non-housetrained canines, and meditation makes me want to hit you on the head with this fertility clinic operations manual. But thanks so much for your concern. (I wouldn't say that, obviously. Puppies are nice.)

Before Ros and I had our own infertility journey, I felt like I could empathise with the struggles, challenges, despair and frustrations of clients. I *thought* I got it, but after going through our own lived experience — days, weeks, months and years of it — I saw it had been more of an intellectual knowing before. The layers of understanding went so much deeper once it was my — our — reality, too. Clearly, I wasn't going to sit with clients and say 'Wow, yes, relatable!' but it became an embodied resonance, rather than a hypothetical one. Now, I *really* got it.

☀

After I'd tried for a baby for a year, there was one time it suddenly worked. I had constant anxiety; I'd almost stopped believing a viable pregnancy was possible. A few months before, I'd had a chemical pregnancy — this is where things look promising for a few days and an embryo has formed, but has either not implanted or has not continued developing. This time, the hormone levels kept rising. Pregnant. Every time I went to the bathroom I was terrified I would see blood. I was scared to tell people initially; it seemed we might be tempting fate.

One of the first people I told was a friend who was also a fertility counsellor. 'You've just exchanged one set of fears for another,' she said. Correct! I told another friend who'd known in detail about the years of trying. 'I'm so happy for you!' she exclaimed. 'You've always been so gracious about other people's pregnancies.' It might have looked that way, but I didn't necessarily feel gracious. Sometimes I would be smiling on the outside, imploding on the inside. Not that I wasn't happy for them, but part of me had been wondering, *It works for other people, why not us?*

It took months to allow myself to believe this might actually result in us having a baby. I mentioned to a friend how I knew all too well the many things that could go wrong with a pregnancy. Too much information is dangerous. 'Yes,' she said, 'but what if it all goes *right*?' This was the third trimester and it took that long for me to develop any enduring sense of optimism.

A thing I observed with clients, and experienced too, was the realisation that having a baby doesn't erase the pain and multiple traumas of the infertility process. After his birth, I would gaze at our son, Flynn, and wonder, 'Is this even true, and how can we be so lucky?' I was acutely aware that not everyone had this outcome, and felt (and still do) grateful for him every single day. But also, how could it be so hard, take four donors, an unquantifiable number of cycles, and seven years to get here? How did it soak up so much of our relationship's joy, energy, spontaneity and money? Where did all that time go?

By the time Flynn was four, I'd been trying to get pregnant again for more than a year. Ros and I were still chasing the dream of two children, but we didn't know how hopeful to let ourselves be. There had been more chemical pregnancies and a miscarriage, which sucked me into a vortex of grief for months. By now I was in my late thirties, so we stepped things up a notch to in vitro fertilisation (IVF). The process was a whirlwind of attempting to follow directions to the letter, and seeing how much more difficult this was in reality than in theory. A mistiming meant I had to inject drugs into my belly in the public library bathroom.

A few days later while staying away from home, I made a panicked after-hours plea to the nurse on call after realising that the 'fridge' in which I had stored the stimulation drugs was actually a freezer. Going through the scans, appointments, blood tests, medications and egg retrieval — only to end up with very few eggs — felt like an assault. Again, I got to experience what clients so often talked about.

We had one good embryo to transfer. On results day (the day when we'd find out if the transferred embryo had implanted and started growing) I clearly remember being at the Dunedin Botanic Gardens with Flynn. He was happily hoofing it along the path on his scooter, pelting ducks with grain from scrunched-up white paper bags. I was compulsively checking my phone. There was a telltale blood test prick in the crook of my arm. The phone call came just as we were about to pull out of the car park. I knew from the nurse's greeting that the news wasn't good — her tone made it clear. 'I'm really sorry, Nicola, it hasn't worked.' She checked if I was OK, but 'OK' is a relative term under the circumstances. I thanked her, knowing that delivering unwelcome news is a tough gig. And when it's your colleague, it can't be any easier.

Ending the call, I burst into tears. 'What's wrong, Mummy?' came from the back of the car. I turned; Flynn strained forward in his car seat and reached out his hand. When I could talk, I said, 'I just got some sad news.' 'Call Mum Ros,' he instructed. 'She knows how to make things better.'

I remember squeezing his hand, sobbing, and thinking, *You were the result of magic. I don't know how we managed it. What if it's a trick we can only perform once?*

※

Secondary infertility is the inability to become pregnant following the birth of one or more biological children to the same couple. My clients often struggled to articulate the deep sense of loss they experienced with secondary infertility, thinking that others without children needed and deserved help more than they did. But myths and assumptions about this form of infertility are as abundant, and as hurtful, as for primary infertility. For example, if you've been pregnant before, it must be possible again; if you have one child that must be a choice; at least it's not as bad as if you didn't have a child at all; and surely you should be grateful for the child you have.

Some of these have elements of truth — *of course* you're truly blessed with the child you have — but there are other, unrecognised layers of suffering.

It's draining for people who are caught up in trying for a subsequent child — while also busy with their existing child or children — to spend time swatting away unhelpful comments fired their way. There is emotional labour required to convey that, in fact, already having a child can underscore the pain of not being able to have another. It's tough to say out loud that you want this not just for yourself, or for your partnership, but for your existing child. It's especially painful if that child is asking every second day about a baby brother or sister, while you scramble to find words to convey the truth of the situation without burdening them with adult uncertainties.

It can feel surreal to be faced with daily reminders of your own fertility, right there in tiny *Toy Story* pyjamas, stealth-lurching into your bed each night. And you're now officially in no-person's land with regard to support. People in primary infertility support groups may not welcome you — and you can recognise that they need and deserve a reprieve from infinite reminders of pregnancy and children. But you also might not feel fully at home in the company of larger families. Complaints about teams of siblings injuring each other with hostile hula hoop battles are hard to take when your period just made an unwanted appearance yet again.

There are also damaging stereotypes about family size and children's wellbeing. The myth that single children (the term 'only' is inherently loaded) are spoiled and selfish originated from Granville Stanley Hall, the first president of the American Psychological Association. He is reported to have said that 'To be an only child is a disease in itself.'[1] Recent research suggests that the misconceptions about negative qualities in single children are unfounded.[2] But this knowledge hasn't filtered through to popular culture or

---

1 Chiara Dello Joio, 'Why are people weird about only children?', *The Atlantic*, 1 November 2022, www.theatlantic.com/family/archive/2022/11/are-only-children-worse-off-kids-siblings/671955
2 Ana Aznar, 'Myths about only children debunked', *The Conversation*, 8 November 2019, https://theconversation.com/myths-about-only-children-debunked-126127

school playgrounds, meaning that children in single-child families have other dimensions — stigma and judgement — added to their experiences in the world.

While Ros and I waded through secondary infertility, I again sensed my own experiences, and those of clients, were orbiting each other. No two stories were the same, and no one's reactions were identical, but there was a surreal quality to the interconnectedness. The ebb and flow; overlapping cycles of dreaming, deciding, planning, trying, succeeding, failing. One of the clinic nurses asked me, at a Christmas dinner, how I managed the inevitable crossovers. 'We talk about you sometimes,' she said. 'We wonder how you do it, and what it's really like for you.'

❅

Soon after the unsuccessful IVF cycle, I was at a preschooler's birthday party. Flynn and his fellow partygoers were outside, squealing as they chucked water balloons at each other in the insipid winter sun. In the kitchen I was trying to be useful; making cups of tea and talking to someone's great-aunt. We knew each other, and when she asked how I was I was honest. 'Not good,' I replied. 'We just had fertility treatment and it didn't work.' I said how relentless it had been, and that I wasn't sure how much more of it I could take. As bedraggled, frosty children galloped inside — they'd been told it was time for party food — the great-aunt looked at Flynn and said, 'I'm an only child. It's the worst thing in the world. You must keep trying. You MUST.'

I tried not to cry; at a four-year-old's party, surely tears are the prerogative of the person whose birthday it is. I stuffed down a few saveloys, even though I don't like them. I wished she hadn't said it, knowing it would be indelibly etched in my mind in the way stinging comments typically are.

As it turned out, we didn't try much longer. There were a few more attempts at home, but my hope level had pitched so low that it was messing with my mind. Even with all the knowledge I had, and all the support around me, I simply *couldn't* anymore. It wasn't just my decision, although since it was my body going through the treatment, I made the final call. There was no dramatic decision-making moment; just a gradual awareness that constantly striving and hoping for something I didn't have was depleting my ability to enjoy the life I actually *did* have.

I know — because I've had this conversation hundreds of times with clients — that infertility is unlike so many other elements of life. With many hopes, dreams and ambitions we can set goals, work towards them and maximise the chances of success. With fertility treatment, because of the mysterious inner workings of our bodies and the limitations of medicine, we can do everything humanly possible, but we cannot *make* it work. There is a time to give it everything. And a time to let it go.

※

T hroughout the years of actively trying — nine, in total — Ros and I became all too familiar with our own dance of dream and disappointment, loss and longing. Clients wouldn't have known, and we were doing different moves — but we were all on the dance floor together.

Auntie

PAULA MORRIS

I n 2004, four years after Tom and I were married, we moved to New Orleans. We thought we'd like to have children, but no children seemed to be forthcoming. I taught at Tulane University and had reasonable health insurance, so we booked appointments with different doctors at the same teaching hospital. Both doctors were pleasant and professional; they both subjected us to various unseemly and intrusive examinations and tests.

After a few visits, my doctor told me there was nothing 'wrong' with me. 'There rarely is,' he said, 'with my ladies.' Tom's doctor told him there was nothing wrong with him, either. 'You'll be back here in a few months,' he predicted, 'handing out cigars.'

But we didn't visit again. We bought no cigars. Some of our friends were waging wars against infertility, committed to the cost and discomfort and disappointment of round after round of IVF. We had little appetite for this. The next year, the year of Hurricane Katrina, I turned 40: maybe we'd left it too late. We decided to slink away from the battlefield.

Sometimes I wondered if one day I would regret not fighting harder, if I'd feel something crucial was missing from my life. We moved to another city in another country — Glasgow, the opposite of New Orleans in most ways, apart from its fervour for alcohol. I told my new doctor that we'd hoped to have children but seemed to be unable.

'Perhaps,' he suggested, 'you have a womb that repels sperm.'

I liked the idea of this superpower so much that I gave it to a character in one of my short stories. Of course, I wish I had a more useful superpower, something to do with invisibility and/or time travel, but in life you have to play the cards you're dealt.

We were dealt the 'no children' card and had to accept it. Instead of having our own children, we would take an interest in the children belonging to other people — nieces and nephews, the children of our friends. We lavished them with (sometimes unsuitable) presents. We helped them build things with blocks or sand. We coloured in with them; we cut out paper dolls; we read them stories. We took them to fairs and MOTAT and McDonald's. We pushed swings. We listened to their musical performances, observed their swimming lessons and cheered them on at school sports days. I watched my niece dance en pointe at the Glen Eden Playhouse. For a friend's two daughters, I sat through a whole day of the Eisteddfod in Carmarthenshire, where the only announcement in English was to ask the owner of the red Toyota to move their car.

We knew what this role involved because we both had childless aunts. Tom grew up in St Louis, Missouri. His mother's only surviving sister was Aunt Pat, who never married or had children. She lived a 20-minute drive away and worked full-time in regional logistics for Woolworth Co. Every Friday night she would move into their (very small) house to spend the weekend, sleeping on the sofa. During the day she played softball and baseball with Tom and his three siblings; in the evenings they played cards or board games. When Tom saw the sea for the first time, it was with Aunt Pat in Florida. They drove there squashed into her notoriously unsafe Chevrolet Corvair.

When Tom was 11, she took him and his older sister to Washington DC for five days. They travelled by Greyhound bus and stayed in a hotel, Tom's first. In DC they saw the Smithsonian, various monuments, JFK's grave in Arlington cemetery, a baseball game. They sat in on a House of Representatives session at the Capitol and visited one of their senators in his office.

All her life, Aunt Pat remained very close to her niece and three nephews. Mike, one of Tom's younger brothers, moved in with her after his marriage ended. Whenever we were back in St Louis, we'd hang out at her small condo or take her out to play mini golf. She liked beer and baking, romance novels and small decorative items like angels or shamrocks. Every so often she'd teeter down into the basement and return with a memento of Tom's childhood, like the 'Little Golden Book' he wrote about space travel, or a rocket chart he'd drawn, taping on an extra sheet of paper to accommodate the tallest rocket. These days we visit Aunt Pat in Saints Peter and Paul cemetery where we can see her name on a plaque rather than a grave. A devout Catholic, as well as the best of aunts, she had donated her body to science.

※

My grandparents lived in a big, draughty villa on the corner of Douglas Street and Ponsonby Road in Auckland. Across the road was a hat shop, Bhana Bros fruit shop and Tordoff's dairy, joined in 1964 by the now-famous Ivan's restaurant. This was the year my father, Kiri, returned from his OE with an English wife — a divorcée — and her six-year-old daughter. The house was large enough for all of them, and also for my father's only sister, Dawn. I was born into a house of adults and a world of aunties. Apparently I was an unaffectionate child, resisting hugs and kisses, and I wonder if this was intuitive self-defence: there were five adults and a big sister all trying to get their hands on me.

Dawn's full name was Dawn Rahui Te Kiri, and she was the mātāmua, the oldest child of the oldest child of the Te Kiri line of our hapū. When I was little, Auntie Dawn was in her late thirties, slim and dark and glamorous. Her bedroom was a stage set from a musical, with a curtained dressing table, wrought-iron umbrella stand and slippery bedspread. Every Saturday morning, she snapped on rubber gloves and mopped the wooden floor. She wore mules with pom-poms around the house and 'flatties' when she drove her Ford Prefect. A giant shower cap with a hose attached was her hairdryer, and she used the hot air blasting from the hose to dry her nail polish as well.

Dawn worked in retail, starting with a job selling gloves at George Court's department store. By the mid-1960s she was working at another shop on Karangahape Road called Lady in Waiting, selling maternity and baby clothes. She'd already lived for a while in Australia, and by the time I was five or six she'd returned there to live in Brisbane and work at the Myer department store. She spent the rest of her life in Australia. She never got married.

I remember small things, like sitting on Auntie Dawn's knee at the Formica dining table, eating a fried egg doused in black pepper. Lynn-Elisabeth, my sister, remembers more. Auntie Dawn was a doyenne of the Auckland Operatic Society and would take my sister to rehearsals on Grafton Road. She got my sister the one child's role in the musical *And So to Bed*, staged at the Town

Hall. Our whole family was musical-mad, singing and dancing around the radiogram or the piano. When I was a toddler, I could say, without hesitation, 'supercalifragilisticexpialidocious'.

The five adults of the house were all desperate for Lynn-Elisabeth to get the part of a royal princess in *The King and I*, so Auntie Dawn coached her audition number, 'Do-Re-Mi' from *The Sound of Music*. My sister was not a great singer and she had blonde hair. When my mother tried to dye her hair black, it turned blue. Still, Auntie Dawn took Lynn-Elisabeth to the audition and comforted her when she didn't get the part.

A few years ago, at a tangi at our marae, my cousin heard me singing and beamed at me. 'You sound just like Dawn,' she said.

My mother thought there were similarities as well, not only in our singing voices. 'You're selfish,' she said to me on numerous occasions. 'Just like Dawn.'

※

We moved to a new house in a new suburb out west when I was small, but still spent half our time at the house on Ponsonby Road.

Other childless aunts were part of our lives there, even after Auntie Dawn returned to Australia. My great-uncle Bob's widow, Auntie Alice, lived a short walk away on Winn Road. She was born in Blackburn, Lancashire; her mother was a cotton winder and her father was a ball warper at the dye works. The family migrated to New Zealand before or during the First World War.

Maybe Alice met Bob in the small factory on Karangahape Road, where he was a shirt-cutter and she was a machinist. They were married in 1920, when she was 19. Auntie Alice was small and kind, and in her looks and accent, my sister says, she resembled Minnie Caldwell of *Coronation Street*.

My grandmother had numerous sick friends who lived as invalids: she and I would visit them in nursing homes, and they all scared me, with their bruised arms and wild hair and whispered complaints. Auntie Alice was never sick; she helped tend to these 'malingerers', as my mother would call them. When I was five, to everyone's horror, she dropped dead on Anglesea Street.

Her jewellery was valued at $71 by a jeweller named Coltman in His Majesty's Arcade and placed for sale at Cordy's on Emily Place. I have the IRD form that reports all this, though I wish we had one of her rings instead. In my hazy memory, I see some of Auntie Alice's remaining possessions spread out on the double bed in my parents' old room in the villa, for friends and relatives to pick through. My mother and grandmother must have taken some things, and I suspect that I have most of them now, like Auntie Alice's wooden sewing box and a set of Uncle Bob's ribbed beer glasses.

There are so many things I have now that are of obscure provenance, possibly my grandmother's, possibly Auntie Alice's: cut-glass bowls, a silver-and-crystal toilet set that may have been a wedding present. I have a Bible that belonged to her, now falling to pieces, into which are tucked photos of her and Uncle Bob, along with a pressed four-leaf clover; an embroidered silk bookmark with the words 'Forget Me Not'; and a torn ribbon from the 1911 funeral of one Thomas George Croft Kenyon — another Blackburn ball warper — that says 'Gone but not forgotten'. A small card commemorating my parents' marriage in 1963 was sent to her from London, my sister thinks, with a slice of wedding cake. And there's a khaki-coloured leaf with 'To My Dearest Sweetheart Alice, XXXX Bob' on one side, and 'Aug 24 1917, Cape Town' on the other. He was 19 and on his way to fight on the Western Front. Alice was 16. These are the things she kept all her life.

Because they had no children, what remains of Alice and Bob's shared life is in my hands. I try to make sense of the pieces, knowing that those pieces are of no interest to anyone apart from me and my sister. Who will care about these things after us? Who will value our great-aunt's things, her goodness, her life?

I start a document on my laptop: it's called 'Provenance'. It's for my niece and nephew, my sister's children, so they know something about the things we've inherited. Still, I'm aware that sentimental value diminishes with every generation, especially when there are no direct descendants. After Auntie Alice died, my grandmother put this notice in the paper: 'The Morris family wish to thank most sincerely all relatives and friends for their floral tributes, cards, letters, telegrams and help in the sudden loss of a lovely aunt and sister-in-law.'

That was 53 years ago. Neither my brother nor I have children. Soon there will be no Morris family left at all.

❄

My grandfather had two brothers and one sister, Violet, who was born in 1911.

When I was a child, I thought Violet was unmarried, like Auntie Dawn. After all, she lived alone and had no children. I asked my parents why her last name was Comyns, not Willetts, and that's when I found out the following:

that in 1937 she got married to one Percival Comyns; that as a three-year-old, my father was a page boy at her wedding and forced to dress in white satin and, according to Auntie Violet, ruined all the photographs with his sulking and crying; that Uncle Percy was the projectionist at the Crystal Palace cinema in Mount Eden; and that after 20 years of marriage Auntie Violet decided she didn't care for men and their ways, and moved out. There seemed to be no hard feelings, my parents said, and decades later, when Uncle Percy bumped into Auntie Violet on the street, he called out 'Hello, Piggy!' — his pet name for her.

Auntie Violet outlived all three of her brothers, lasting so long that she was simply called Auntie by everyone, including all the mothers at the Mount Albert Playcentre where she took my nephew — her great-great-nephew — two days a week. Auntie loved children. I think she viewed Dawn as a surrogate daughter, much as Tom's Aunt Pat viewed his brother Mike as a surrogate son. I would stay with her sometimes in her tiny unit on Calgary Street in Sandringham. She would try and fail to teach me how to crochet, and we would walk up to the playground at Potter's Park. In the evening she'd steam a chocolate pudding, the kind that came in a tin and was the most special of treats at home.

She never had much money, but every Easter she would buy us an egg with chocolate buttons, and at Christmas we got things like small rubber balls, ideal for bouncing off the wall outside. For my twenty-first birthday, she gave me a glass cake plate that I still use. She made tea showers — as my sister calls them; I say 'fly cloths' — with crocheted borders. My mother got green and my sister blue, their favourite colours. I got multicoloured, because Auntie saw me as frivolous and flamboyant, I suspect. I still use that as well.

Back in 1964 Auntie was not so accepting of my sister, another man's daughter, as the rest of the family. My grandmother told her off about it. But 30 years later when my nephew and niece came along, Auntie was their devoted servant. 'She always carried a knife and fork in her handbag,' my sister says, 'so if we popped into McDonald's, she didn't have to eat with her fingers.'

Whenever my sister drove her home, Auntie would give each of the children a Shrewsbury biscuit half wrapped in a tissue for them to nibble. Rebecca, my niece, was only a toddler, but she remembers this clearly. Shrewsbury biscuits, she says, remain her favourite to this day. I emailed Rebecca to ask what she could recall of my own expert aunting skills when she was younger. I was thinking of the pink teddy bear she demanded, for which I scoured New York, pre-internet shopping; or when I escorted her to Jumping Beans — gym for toddlers — and let her wear lipstick and a skirt, much to the irritation of the staff; or the New Year's holiday when we took her to Tuscany when she was studying in Germany. 'I remember being in your kitchen in Wellington and waiting for the water to boil for Tom to cook pasta for dinner,' she wrote back. 'I think that might be the first time you said "fuck" in front of me.'

☀

I loved Auntie Dawn. My grandmother took me to Brisbane twice to visit her, once when I was seven and once for my twelfth birthday. Her flat was in West End, then a largely Greek neighbourhood. I played with my dolls and with the kids in the street; I watched the *Colour Machine* and *The Mickey Mouse Club* on TV; I slept on the sofa. On both trips Auntie Dawn took a day off work to spend time just with me. She and Grandma each gave me $2 towards my first Barbie doll; I paid the other $2 from my holiday money.

Auntie Dawn's life remained glamorous. When she came home from work at Myer in the evenings, she liked to have a beer and some cheese on crackers rather than eat dinner right away. She was still involved in light opera, though now as a director rather than a singer, and took me along to rehearsals. She had a boyfriend named George, who seemed incredibly old to me, but was probably in his fifties, not much older than she was. One night I woke up needing the loo and had to walk through her bedroom to reach the bathroom. George was asleep next to her in the bed. This felt scandalous. I never told my parents.

My mother was jealous of my relationship with Auntie Dawn. They'd never liked each other. Both were imperious women, and my mother could be stand-offish and suspicious: I never had a single friend she liked. I can't really assess Auntie Dawn's character in the same way because I only saw her, and remember her, through a child's prism.

My grandmother died in 1979 when I was 14, the week of my sister's wedding. Auntie Dawn had returned to New Zealand two years earlier for my grandfather's funeral but didn't come back for Grandma's. In fact, she never came back to New Zealand again. In my grandmother's will, I was left a bracelet made from sovereigns, given to Grandma by one of the sick friends, Mrs Birch. It was to be held by Auntie Dawn and given to me when I was 'of age'. My mother was adamant that this bracelet should not be sent to Australia, where it might go missing: Australia could not be trusted. It was too valuable and should be held in safekeeping by my parents.

At the time I was only vaguely aware of the international incident this argument created. I wrote regular letters to Auntie Dawn, and my mother told me to include something in the letter I was writing about the bracelet — how we shouldn't argue over this, and it was best if the bracelet stayed in New Zealand. I was 14. I did as I was told.

Auntie Dawn didn't reply to the letter. She made no contact with me at all for 13 years, until Auntie Violet told her I'd got engaged, and she sent me a congratulations card. By then I was living in London. She'd become a stranger.

Auntie Violet told me that I wouldn't recognise Auntie Dawn: when she'd last visited Brisbane, Dawn was white-haired and crippled with arthritis. I don't remember if I replied to the card, which means I don't think I did. By then I'd lived almost half my life without her. Everything about the bracelet dispute made me annoyed with my mother and annoyed with my aunt. They didn't like each other, but they should have kept me out of it. Auntie Dawn should have forgiven me for the letter, should have realised that I was a stupid kid who was made to write those words.

Although I've been 'of age' for decades, I don't have the bracelet now. I asked for it when I was in my twenties, but my parents didn't think London was any safer than Australia. Then their house was burgled, and it was stolen. My mother felt guilty about this and spent some of the insurance money on an expensive piece of pounamu for me. It's beautiful but I rarely wear it. It reminds me of loss — not of the bracelet, but of my aunt.

※

I n 1995 I was working at a record company in New York. I'd got married in haste, so my English husband could move countries with me. He was eager to have children but I was dragging my feet, already aware I'd made a mistake. We separated in 1997 and I agreed to wait until his Green Card was approved before initiating a divorce. This took two years. He was bitter and upset, and it took him some time before he found a much nicer, more suitable second wife. But she was older than him, and it was too late for children.

I'm still in touch with a number of my colleagues from those days, and I'm part of various work-related social media groups. When I look at the old photos of us carousing at conferences and sales meetings, I realise that only one of my close friends at work went on to have children. The rest of us form a parade of the childless. We were all obsessed with work in those days. Perhaps we still are.

In September 1995 I got a call at the office from New Zealand. It was my father, telling me that Auntie Dawn had died. She was not quite 67 years old. He hadn't seen her since 1977, or spoken to her in decades, but he and my brother and one of my cousins were flying to Brisbane for the funeral. There was something else he wanted to tell me. Auntie Dawn's Australian friends had placed a death notice in the *New Zealand Herald*, and this said she was survived by a daughter and granddaughter.

None of us knew anything about this. The story unspooled a little when my father went to Brisbane. He learnt that in the late 1950s, when Dawn was living in Australia, she had a little girl and decided to give her up for adoption. Her daughter grew up with a family in Hawai'i. Auntie Dawn returned to New Zealand. Her close friends in Australia who knew about this kept her secret.

My parents are no longer alive, so I can't ask them any more questions. What I remember from their reports: at the end of her life Auntie Dawn tried to find her daughter, and they were finally able to meet the day before Dawn died. My parents said it was lucky that Auntie Violet was dead by then, because she would have been heartbroken to learn that Dawn's child had been given away. 'Auntie would have wanted the baby,' my mother said. But we all knew those were different times, and there was shame around pregnancies outside marriage. And not all of us can be, or want to be, mothers.

The daughter, my father said, was the image of Dawn. She was friendly but seemed overwhelmed, with little interest in exploring the Māori side of her heritage. After the funeral she returned to Hawai'i. I discussed all this with my sister while I was writing this essay, and she says that once, when she was on holiday in Honolulu, she saw a woman crossing the street who looked just like me, and just like Auntie Dawn. Perhaps this was our cousin's daughter, or perhaps my sister was imagining things, wishing we'd had the chance to meet.

Auntie Dawn's daughter was the same age as my sister. Back in the Ponsonby Road days, when my sister arrived in the house — all-singing, all-dancing and embraced by our grandparents — it must have been difficult for Dawn. It must have been difficult working in a shop that specialised in maternity and baby clothes. And then I was born, ostensibly the first baby of the family, doted on by my grandfather, coddled by my grandmother and her battalion of sisters, sisters-in-law, friends and fellow members of the Māori Women's Welfare League. But Auntie Dawn was kind and loving to us both. In her will she left my sister a small ornament that, my father said, Lynn-Elisabeth loved to play with when they all lived on Ponsonby Road. It's a faceted glass ball, a prism that changes colour to reflect its surroundings. 'It's often purple,' my sister tells me. A suitably imperial colour, I think, for both my sister and for Auntie Dawn.

❊

I have no children and I don't own a house or a flat: I spent all my money on Lego pirate ships and hardback editions of the *Little House* books and meals for other people's children in Italy, France, Mexico, Latvia, Guatemala and so on. My niece told me once that when she inherits her parents' house, she will turn it into a dog sanctuary and I can live there as well, in the garage. That's my best-offer retirement plan right now, a garage with a bed, Netflix and a drinks trolley. Even smaller than Auntie Violet's final flat, and less well-insulated, but it sounds fine to me.

In the interim I'll keep working on the 'Provenance' document, telling the stories of the things in my possession. It's our fate to be forgotten, or at least to be shuffled further and further back in the pack, because memories can't be inherited. But stories can.

What our aunts gave us was love, an intangible gift. This is all I can give, too — not my genes, not my name, just love. Love is felt in the moment but not necessarily remembered, and it means nothing to subsequent generations. Still, there it is, an invisible superpower of its own, making our lives happier.

My favourite girl

JAZIAL CROSSLEY

The first time my partner's daughter says she loves me is after we've been to McDonald's for dinner. It's her dad's birthday, and we've had a fun-filled day. We just watched a soccer game live and the Phoenix won spectacularly, then we caught the train back with lots of other over-excited fans. Earlier in the day we ate lunch with her grandparents, aunt and uncle and her one-year-old cousin. I let her decorate the lemon sour cream cake with decorations she'd chosen herself to celebrate her father's thirty-ninth birthday — she stabbed edible sugary rainbows mounted on toothpicks and colourful round lollipop-shaped candles into the thick, white icing one by one, in a formation of her own design. She is four years old.

Now, as we walk out of the brightly lit restaurant at the end of this happy day, bellies full of fries, she asks if she can tell me a secret. I bend down so she can whisper in my ear. Her father watches on, a few steps ahead.

'Um um um,' she starts, gulping down air after each word. 'Um, um, I love you.'

I feel a drop as if I'm on a roller coaster, and I know I must say it in return. I place a hand on her back and whisper, 'I love you, too.'

※

D ating a man who has a young child is like being in two new relationships at once. There are two new people who are very significant in my life. We're getting to know each other over time. Bit by bit, day by day, a new family is building with every interaction we have.

Their presence changes what my life looks like. I no longer feel that I failed my life by not going ahead with the engagement I called off a few years before. I'm no longer just passing the time outside of work. I still spend some evenings alone, painting my nails, watching quiet foreign films and sipping peppermint tea . . . but there's more to my life now than just getting through it. The possibility of a new future spools out before me.

The opportunity for a different kind of life, one I never thought I would have, has opened up.

My new life arrived in a rush of berry-scented Trolls-branded detangling hair spray. My new life is accompanied by a pink flamingo soft toy that twists its long neck in time to fast-paced electronic music when a button on its side is pushed. My new life wears glittery gumboots that have coloured lights in the soles and a t-shirt that says 'Save The Bees'. She puts her hand on her hip and says 'OK, so' repeatedly when she's thinking. Her dad, my dream boyfriend, wears floral Vans and a band t-shirt for the nineties rockers Veruca Salt. He shares my love of Fiona Apple, New York City, Murakami and Henry Miller. He drums his fingers lightly on nearby surfaces when he's thinking.

In the back of my dream boyfriend's Nissan there's a booster seat, with a blue rug next to it that his daughter can toss over her knees and snuggle under on chilly mornings. Often there are crumbs from the crispy noodles she likes to snack on. There are always several assorted small soft toys around: a fluffy duck, a teeny tiny teddy called Teeny Tiny Teddy, a plush round ball with eyes and a unicorn horn, a small grey miniature schnauzer stuffed toy that I gave her — a replica of my dog.

❋

I always thought I wouldn't have children. When I was younger I was sure I wouldn't be anyone's mother because I'd seen my own mum struggle after having me at 17 years old. It is only as an adult that I've come to understand that raising me alone was the least of her difficulties during my childhood; my mum had other adult problems weighing her down. Still, the isolation and poverty we experienced were not something I wanted to risk recreating in my own life. Focusing on work and caring for my home and pets seemed like a simpler way to be an adult. Keeping my life smaller made me feel safer. I never expected that I'd want to contribute to raising a child, until I met this man and this child.

※

The first time I meet this child she is three-and-a-half, and I've been dating her father for a few months. Her dad takes us to a family-friendly pub in Upper Hutt. I need him to translate some of her toddler words for me. We share a mushroom blue cheese pizza that she gamely tries, then we order a dessert platter between us. We expect small samples of the sweet dishes on the menu to arrive but a large wooden board is delivered to our table with full-size portions of each of the dessert items. A hulking slice of cheesecake, banoffee pie, lemon meringue pie, sugar-encrusted churros and a slab of chocolate brownie with half a dozen scoops of ice cream flavours that are rapidly melting. We are mortified and get most of it to take away.

When I say goodbye, she stops her play and looks at me for a moment. Then she runs towards me at top speed and wraps her arms tight around my legs. With that hug, the tone is set: we're friends, delightedly so.

※

Dating a dude who has a daughter doesn't make me a parent. Even if we marry someday, I wouldn't want to call myself a stepmother. It feels wrong. 'Mother' is such a significant word and I haven't earned it. She has a mother. She doesn't need another parent-ish figure muscling in on how she should be raised. Her two parents care for her wonderfully, with great dedication.

All I can be for her is myself, and that's enough.

She started school this year. I finish work early on a Friday afternoon towards the end of her first term so I can join her dad in collecting her from the school gate. We arrive 15 minutes before the bell to get a good car park. When she sees us waiting in the crowd of caregivers, she squeals, 'It's my Jazial! It's my Jazial!' She turns to call her teacher to attention and says, 'Look! This is my Jazial!' I wave ironically at the teacher, embarrassed and honoured all at once.

※

One day early on in our relationship, my partner's daughter invents what adults would term a trust game. We are sitting on the sofa while her dad works away in the kitchen making jackfruit tacos with corn, carrot, avocado and tomato — a meal the whole of this new family enjoys — with added hot sauce for the adults. Ignoring her cartoon on the television, she stands up on the sofa and leans her whole weight against my shoulder.

Then she steps back and launches forward to lean on me harder. This progresses until she is running back to the arm of the sofa then leaping at me, knowing I will catch her. She squeals with delight when I make a noise as if she's surprised me every time. I catch her every time. She trusts me.

When I visit with a pack of Trolls temporary tattoos, she asks me to put them on her immediately. She wants them on her feet. One by one, I cut out each tattoo, place it on her foot and press a wet cloth to the back of the tattoo so its design will transfer to her skin, then we count to ten together. She's overjoyed when each one is revealed. 'One more,' she says, and I put another colourful image on her foot. 'One more,' she pleads, until the whole pack is gone and both her feet and ankles are adorned with the cartoon characters. She thinks this is hilarious.

We go to Rainbow's End in Auckland together and her dad waits while she and I ride the little roller coaster in the Kidz Kingdom for under-eight-year-olds. She squeals with joy the whole time. Afterwards she asks if I thought it was fun and tells me, 'I feel like a bursted heart,' spreading her arms wide and turning her face to the sky to demonstrate what the thrill of the ride feels like. 'Me too,' I tell her.

※

I decide early on that I will meet her where she's at. If she enjoys my company, I'll continue spending time with her. If she reaches out to hug me unprompted, I'll feel comfortable to hug her when I say hello or goodbye. I'll follow her lead. If she acts up or is unhappy with my presence during her time with her precious dad, I'll remove myself. Thankfully, she's always happy to see me.

She wants to know what the word is for our relationship. She asks her dad who she is to me because to other people in her life, she's a 'niece' or 'granddaughter' or 'cousin'. It's too complicated to explain there is no word unless marriage is involved because society is weird, so she makes up her own phrase: she's my 'favourite girl', officially and literally. It sounds much better and more accurate than 'stepdaughter' to me.

worry what will happen in the future. What if she starts to despise me when she's older and learns the trope of the wicked stepmother? What if her dad and I move in together someday, and it's confronting for me to share a home with a teenage girl who might have wild moods? I remember my mum's partner moving in with us when I was almost 13. I think about his generous willingness to accept every emotion I'd encounter through my teenage years. They were many and varied and often, I'm sure, very difficult to be around.

He never once complained when I played the most ferocious music Courtney Love has ever recorded very loud, over and over again. When Hole played at the 1999 Big Day Out, when I was 14 and obsessed with her (I'd bleached my own hair in imitation, of course), he took me to the show. He always let me be my own person, and would talk to me through any issues and concerns I experienced no matter how volatile I felt in the moment. He stood by my tears and my tantrums. We still talk to each other regularly, about all the things that really matter in life.

'Trust the child,' a friend tells me when I share that I worry about the future.

✳

Sometimes she gets overwhelmed. When we catch a ferry from Wellington to Days Bay in summer, her dad and I are excited about having an ice cream on the beach on arrival but she cries, hiccuping red-faced sobs on the boat. We thought she'd love the journey; her mood is baffling.

'I want my mum,' she wails, and pushes me away with force when I offer her a drink of water.

Another passenger, also travelling with children, is watching us. They give her a muffin and she calms down after eating, as if it had been cast with a spell.

I feel rattled for the rest of the day, but she shows me how resilience works: after swallowing the last of her muffin, she asks to go on the open-air top deck that had terrified her moments earlier. Her dad holds her as she looks out at the ocean all around us and feels the wind. 'I'm a happy girl now,' she says, 'I was sad before but now I'm having a good day.' For the rest of the day, she is bubbly. She enjoys her Goody Goody Gumdrops ice cream and wades in the water up to her knees. I decide we'll always have snacks with us when we go anywhere with her from that day forward.

I understand it must be so difficult to be a child, to experience so much that is new and confusing without the words to articulate how you feel —

sometimes without the comprehension to understand yet why you feel the way you do. You have so little agency as a kid. You get dragged from place to place, you get fed whatever someone else decides to give you. It must be so confusing so much of the time to be a young child in this complex world.

✳

'm wonderful at being patient. I don't get angry or have explosive reactions, but I do feel affected by seeing her upset. I get quiet, not knowing what to say. I overthink what the 'right' thing is to say, so I end up saying nothing at all.

When we take her to see snow for the first time at Tongariro, she's distressed by how cold it is but also determined to make a snowman. The fabric on her gloves, socks and scarf begin to bother her once she feels frustrated by the new environment. There are lots of other people around. She's never seen snow before in her life. The low temperature is shocking to her. Everything about this moment is overwhelming, and I understand that.

I don't know what to say when she tears off her gloves then wails that she's too cold. Her dad is calm as always, but he, too, is unhappy at seeing her so uncomfortable. It isn't easy to watch someone you love suffer, no matter how irrational you might judge their emotions to be.

Later that night she takes a bath and I make us pasta. She calls out for me from the bathroom, where her dad is supervising. She's sitting in the warm water with her knees drawn up to her chest and a serious expression on her face.

'Jazial,' she begins, and I say 'Yes?' She takes a big breath, thinking through what she wants to say. 'When Baby Yoda grows up, is he still called Baby Yoda?'

She's moved on from all the fear and frustration she felt earlier. She's learning to be a person and that presents her with so many mental, physical and emotional challenges to work through every day. She's bounced back. She always does.

'That was tough,' her dad says later, referring to the whole day. It was, and we got through it. I stayed by her side throughout all the emotions she experienced that day, from fear to joy to exhaustion. I'm proud of myself, and proud of her, and proud of her dad. I'm proud of all of us.

✳

My colleagues aren't sure what to make of my family situation. Most of the people in my team have young children and I often talk about my partner's daughter. They're confused when I explain we don't live together. I bought my house a few weeks before I met my partner and it wouldn't have been right to move in together quickly anyway, when his daughter is so young, I explain, but I see them wondering what my role is. We're not married. We don't live together. If I'm not her stepmother, what am I? I talk about her when they share stories of their own children but, what? She's just a kid I spend a lot of time with?

One of my workmates asks me what she calls me. I tell him she calls me by my name.

One time she and her dad and I are at Zealandia bird sanctuary watching kākā and apropos of nothing she tells a stranger who is standing near us, 'That's not my mummy, that's my daddy's friend.'

Everyone I know always asks me about her mum. They want to know if she and my partner get along. They want to know if she and I get along. Sometimes I think people seem eager for me to share some drama. The subtext to their nosy questions seems to be, *Is she a bitch?* We all get along well, I tell them honestly — her mum's lovely. For my partner's daughter's fifth birthday, her dad and I, and her mum and her new partner and his two kids all went out to dinner together. A happy extended family. People seem disappointed how simple that side of it is. I'm overjoyed — I couldn't be in this situation if it had any vicious or unresolved elements.

✳

We're at her grandparents' house, and she pulls me away from where I'm chatting to her dad on the deck. I leave my glass of rosé behind and go along with the game she's just invented for us to play: first, I have to follow her movements. Walk in slow steps, raising my knees high, then freeze when she says stop. Then she tells me there's a one-eyed monster behind that tree over there.

'OK, so,' she starts, hand on hip, 'you have to get two pine needles.' I dutifully pull two needles from the tree. 'Now THROW THEM at the monster.' We both throw our two needles into the air. She pauses in amazement. 'Did you see that? All four of the pine needles went into the monster's one eye. We defeated it!'

Later, she describes how she can see — just pretend — a sabre-tooth fox.

We have to run away from it, she says, so we sprint across the grass. My dog follows us. She squeals that the sabre-tooth fox is on her head. The magic to defeat it is fresh mint, handily growing in a pot beside the garage. 'Get some mint! Quick!' she directs, and I run to take a few leaves from the plant. She relaxes when I place them on top of her head. 'We defeated it!' She dances in victory. We're a good team.

※

I still think I probably don't want children of my own, but I don't exactly *not* have a kid — I'm not a parent, but I'm not quite not a parent-ish person, either. I spend a lot of my time participating in her childhood by playing with her, cooking for or with her, and simply sharing life with her. She loves eating at restaurants and cafés, and so do I. The Mongolian barbecue place where she can select her own vegetables, noodles, meat and sauce is her favourite. She gleefully tried the yakitori sticks I ordered at Tanuki's Cave when we visited Auckland. She's good company, this kid.

I don't like the word 'stepmum', but I understand it's a societal shorthand for what this is. I don't want to be celebrated on Mother's Day, because I'm not her mother. I'm not any kind of mother. I'm her Jazial. She's my favourite girl. Dating a man who has a young child is like being in love twice, in two different but complementary ways.

I don't need to say the 'right' thing to her; there's no such thing as the right or perfect thing to say. I think in the harder moments that I don't know how to be a parent, or how to be the not-quite-parent-ish person I am in her life, but I do know how to be compassionate and kind to another human who I care about, and that's enough. I'm pretty sure women who grow children inside their own bodies don't know what to say to their kids sometimes, either. We're all parenting imperfectly whether we're related to children by blood, by marriage, or simply by love.

Being myself, I'm slowly learning, is enough. Giving her my time, love, attention and interest is enough. Maybe when she's 14 she'll feel free to tell me something that bothers her, perhaps a worry about her friends at school, because she's learnt I'm a safe person.

Or maybe when she's 14 she'll hate me for a while, because she's 14. That'll be OK, too. I'll think back to how I chose to breathe deeply instead of screaming on the snowy mountain. I'll always try to make the best choices I can to help her through her life, putting her needs ahead of expressing the more childish fleeting emotions I might still feel inside sometimes. She's teaching me how to grow up, too.

I'm here for her, however life turns out. And no matter what name society puts on our relationship.

DINKs on a plane

ALIE BENGE

used to worry as I aged that not only did I not have the things I was meant to have by 27, 29, 31, but also that I didn't want them yet. The 'not-wanting' felt like the real lack, like there was a mechanism in me that was halted, something stuck in the wheel.

When I finally admitted what I didn't want, I felt set free from time, free to reach my mid-thirties, free to see grey hair shining on my temples. I felt an expansive sense of time. There was so much of it. Tick tick tick and it's all mine. I collect years, they don't collect me.

The question was never whether I wanted kids. I knew the answer to that. The question was, would I? Should I? Am I supposed to? I can hear a voice in my head that says, *What's a bit of extra money and travel when you could have made a person?* and that makes me question what gives our existence a purpose.

I think I'm asking what it means to live a good life.

꙰

n Capri, we walked through streets that looked like a Pixar movie. Sprays of pink bougainvillea burst over bright white walls, which parted occasionally for a glimpse of sparkling ocean. At night the cobblestone lanes were lit by strings of fairy lights. We ambled back to our Airbnb after dinner, and I noticed how puckered David's t-shirt was with the holes I'd mended over the last three months of travel.

The next morning, we caught a boat to an isolated cove, passing through a neighbourhood of superyachts, some the size of small cruise liners. We were led to our allocated beach chairs and lay down next to women with deep tans and unnaturally plump lips. Behind us, the small beach angled up into a sheer mountain face. We were in the most beautiful place we'd ever been, feeling that soon someone would be along to tell us we weren't fancy enough.

'It feels like we're not allowed to be here,' I said to David. His eyes were half-closed as his mouth ranged around for the straw in an Aperol Spritz. It seemed impossible that two people travelling on savings and freelance incomes were able to see all this, swim in this water as warm as a bath and later watch the sunset over the Gulf of Naples, near the bay where Jay-Z parks his yacht.

I learnt the term DINK (double income, no kids) before we left New Zealand. Apparently it's a retro concept, from when it was unusual to see childless couples and they needed a name. It's a useful term because it's easy to forget, when we change our plans last minute to incorporate a road trip along the coast of Spain, or fly to Istanbul for the weekend, that there's a very simple reason we can do this. We're often telling each other how lucky we feel, and we are. But we have this life because we made choices.

We're also lucky to have come of age in a culture where DINKs are no longer a rare species. Ninety per cent of my friend group are childfree couples. I'm rarely asked if I have kids. My parents have never asked when I'll be giving them a grandchild, though I think they would have liked one. David, on the other hand, has been an uncle since he was 13, and on his side, there is such an abundance of grandchildren that no one seems to have noticed we've not produced one.

☀

I have doubts sometimes, of course I do. But then I remember the strained-looking mother on our flight to Sicily trying to fit five bags into the overhead compartments with a child screaming at her about which parent he loved the most, while I put in my noise-cancelling ear buds and started editing a manuscript, which doesn't make me a lot of money, but enough for two adults to spend two weeks in Sicily.

In a village in the Atlas Mountains, I briefly lost David and found him patiently doling out high-fives to a crowd of children, who squealed with laughter as they jumped to reach his hand, and I thought, that's a man who should be a father. He'd be a good one: fun and fair. I, on the other hand, don't have it in me. I know in my heart I'd be a bad mum. I just don't have the energy or the interest. I can't cheer on a child as they do 50 million shit cartwheels. I can't listen to endless facts about dinosaurs. I want to sleep in on a Saturday morning, then cross the road to buy the newspaper I will spend a whole day reading. I want that more than I want a baby. Even if it's different when it's your own, even if there's no love like the love you have for a child.

❋

When we were moving to London, we talked about getting a dog, and I started to picture what I thought might just be a perfect life. A little flat in Hampstead, a job at Daunt Books, and taking the dog for a walk on the Heath. This vision lasted about a month. But then I remembered, dogs leave fluff everywhere. And we'd need someone to look after it when we went on trips. And we'd have to walk it every day. Even if it's raining. And that's why I know I'd be a bad mum, because even a dog requires something beyond the limits of my care.

I know that to have made this decision means there's a chance I'll be lonely at the end of my life. David has the immune system of a sickly Victorian child. The chances of me outliving him are high. Loneliness is, to me, the worst of feelings, but I can't use the fear of being alone to justify having a child to look after me. What if they refuse that role, as they have every right to do? When I'm tempted to fear this loneliness I feel even more resolutely that I want to live a good enough life now that when I'm alone, maybe lonely, it will have been worth it.

❋

When you look at the natural world, entities exist to propagate themselves, and in doing so, gain a kind of immortality — not for themselves, but for some essential thing about them that carries on down a line — a second death coming only with the extinction of their species.

Growing up religious means being wired for infinity; to value things for their eternal consequences. My inner critic is a self-flagellating, hair-shirt-wearing radical fundamentalist who tells me that a life spent in pursuit of pleasure is a wasted life. *What is any of this compared to the creation of life and the continuation of your lineage?* To have a child is to make yourself eternal. The voice says pleasure exists only in its own moment, thus it's the antithesis of infinity and is worth nothing, thus my nice life is worth nothing.

A life with children that involves sacrifice and a loss of sleep, and never having quite enough money and having to work harder for the things I want, feels more noble and therefore more meaningful. It stores up treasures in Heaven which, I've been taught, are better than treasures on Earth. But I want my treasure now.

Having a child just to make something that will outlive me doesn't seem a good enough reason, just as breeding a carer for the end of my life isn't a good reason. In fact, I don't know if there is a good reason, except not having a reason at all — simply wanting a child seems the only good justification to have one. Perhaps having children, while the world heaves under our weight, is just as selfish as not having them.

※

The first time I was called a spinster I was 30 or so. It was in an effort to explain to me why I could be thoughtless sometimes, why I struggle to compromise. 'Sometimes, people like you — spinsters,' and here they put their palms up as they said the word, trying to soften it, 'you forget what it's like to have to consider other people every day. You can become a bit, you know. Selfish.' Maybe there's something in this. I experience so little inconvenience in my life that I've become sensitised to it. Everything in our flat is at the right height; everything lives in a sensible place. I don't have to unlock baby-safe drawers or climb over guard rails to get down the stairs.

My slight noise sensitivity has grown to full-blown misophonia, so that I could murder the motorcyclists hooning down my street at night. Maybe the inconvenience of a crying baby would be good for me. Perhaps it would make me a kinder and more patient person. Maybe it would make me less selfish.

What does it mean, this flavour of selfishness? It isn't like not sharing the toys in the sandpit. The colleague who said I was selfish for not wanting kids also expected me to gleefully cover her many days off when her son picked up some grotty infection at day care, seemingly every week.

Every time one of us in the workplace had a birthday, we'd buy them a caramel mud cake from The Cheesecake Shop. We'd gently encourage all the customers to leave the shop so we could eat it in the storeroom, and spend the rest of the day trying not to shit ourselves because it was so dense and rich.

Birthdays in the shop were an event because of that cake. On this colleague's birthday, the one who called me selfish, our boss snuck off to buy the cake and we paraded it into the storeroom. This colleague, however, took the cake without a word and put it on the counter, then went back to her phone.

We hovered, waiting for her to open it. Throughout the day, we'd pop in to check the cake's progress, shaking our heads at each other across the shop floor to indicate that it was still on the shelf, sealed tight. At the end of her shift, she put the unopened cake box in her bag and went home. The rest of us laughed, bewildered. Does she not know how cake works?

Selfishness implies taking something from someone, hoarding something that should be shared. I'm not hurting anyone, or taking something anyone else is owed. I only want my life to be my own. Is my selfishness that I refuse to give up my life for another? Is my life that caramel mud cake from The Cheesecake Shop, secreted away to enjoy later on my own? But I share my life with plenty of people. I share it like I'd share a birthday cake. I love plenty of people, but I'm not in service to any. Does that make me selfish?

☀

In primary school there was an Exclusive Brethren girl in my class called Ingrid. I felt sad for her because she wasn't allowed to do the things the rest of us did. We once left her crying in the classroom with an activity book because she couldn't come with us to the Life Education van. When I heard Ingrid's mum died, I bought a Mars Bar with my pocket money and sellotaped it to a card. Her two aunts began picking her up from school; like Ingrid, they had long braids and wore full-length dresses. I remember the braids because they swung over me when her aunt found me a few days later in the playground, put her hands on my little shoulders and thanked me, holding back tears, for giving Ingrid the Mars Bar.

I don't think I said anything back, mostly confused about this reaction to such a small thing, and now realise that I've stored that memory away until I was old enough to understand it. I can see now what I didn't see then: a woman who'd taken up a role she didn't choose; a woman who lost a sister and became a mother in the same moment. Because someone has to do it, don't they? Because not everyone needs a child, but everyone could do with a mum. If I understood then what I understand now, I would have given the Mars Bar to Ingrid's aunt.

They say there's no love like the love you have for a child, as though one love is measurable against another; as though there is a limited pool of love and it's rationed out like sugar in the war. If it's 'different when it's your own', what does that say about Ingrid's aunts, waiting outside our classroom every day? How can we say their love is less than anyone else's? And do I have less love because I haven't had to do that? Because I would if I had to. I'd wait outside the classroom if someone needed me to, and no, it wouldn't be the life I'd have chosen for myself, but of course I'd do it, of course.

☀

There was a moment after meeting David when I realised how curly our kids' hair would be. After that I had a dream in which David asked if I wanted kids and I said, 'Yeah OK.' And it was that easy to have a different life. That dream stuck around and I wondered what I'd say if David really did ask that. I always thought that if I fell in love with someone who wanted kids I could be persuaded, but now I am in love and I don't think that's true. Now I live in fear of accidentally imbibing grapefruit. How would we decide things like schools and religion, and what to tell them about Santa? And I'd have to get a different job, or no job at all. We'd have to move to a cheaper flat, and there are so many places in the world left to visit. And can you both go to a three-hour movie if you have little kids? It's a lot to give up just for curls. I became nervous that David might decide he wanted that life after all so I asked him, 'Are you sure you don't want kids? You won't change your mind?' What he said surprised me: 'I never said I didn't want kids. You didn't want kids. I'm just not that fussed.'

Not that fussed. Oh, to not be fussed. I exist in relationship to motherhood whether I choose it or not, because it's what I'm expected to do. To do anything different marks me as unusual, it makes me harder to categorise. While he's not fussed, I had to *decide*. I had to write a long essay, then edit an anthology, then find that there was still more to say, that I still need to justify it to myself. David said at the end of that conversation, 'Not having kids isn't something I need to write several long think pieces about.'

The question that comes back to me, which I've not been able to shake even now, which followed me to Capri and Morocco, through Spain, and moved in with me to my London flat, is this: Is it OK? Is it OK for us just to have a nice time and care for each other and when we're done with these lives, to leave nothing behind us? Is it OK to go on little holidays and read in bed all morning and work hard but not like, crazy hard? Is that enough? It feels like enough.

About the editors

Alie Benge (she/her) is a New Zealand writer who lives in London. She was the essay editor for *takahē* and has been published in *The Spinoff*, *Turbine | Kapohau*, *Pantograph Punch* and more. She was joint winner of the 2017 Landfall Essay Competition. Her debut essay collection, *Ithaca*, was published in 2023.

Kathryn van Beek (she/her) is the author of two children's books and the short story collection *Pet* (2020), which is also available as a podcast. Her work has appeared in *Overland, Landfall, takahē, Newsroom, The Spinoff, Sunday Star-Times* and *MiNDFOOD*. She contributed to *Misconceptions*, a web series about miscarriage available on the *New Zealand Herald* website. Kathryn was the 2023 Robert Burns Fellow.

Lil O'Brien (she/her) is the author of *Not That I'd Kiss a Girl* (2020), a beloved Kiwi memoir about coming out during her years at Otago University, among other things. Lil is currently working on the screenplay of *Not That I'd Kiss a Girl* with South Pacific Pictures. She's an award-winning freelance copywriter by day, and has had essays published in *takahē, The Spinoff* and more.

About the writers

Amie Taua (Pata Falelatai, Apia, Sāmoa, English, Clan Gunn) was born in Tāmaki Makaurau and raised in Ōtepoti. She divides her time between working as a creative partnerships advisor in local government, making memories with her large aiga, filling the Google calendar she shares with her partner and enjoying good food, great coffee and the exceptional company of her friends.

Andi C. Buchanan is a writer, mostly of science fiction and fantasy, who is based in Te Awa Kairangi ki Tai Lower Hutt. Their cross-genre novella *From a Shadow Grave* — inspired by a local ghost story — won the 2020 Sir Julius Vogel Award for best novella/novelette. You can find them at https://linktr.ee/andiwrites.

Anna Borrie is an environmentalist and artist who engages and encourages communities to listen to and create their own narratives around environmental and social wellbeing. She is also an expert in navigating health systems and has accumulated an archive of inappropriate and average medical advice.

Carolijn Guytonbeck is a humanities tutor at the University of Otago. She tutors writing papers and works with disability students. Her life centres around providing a home to cows, ducks, native birds and a cat. Her website, Bice Grace Lapin, 'advocates for us all to have self-fulfilment through expression'.

Donelle McKinley is a freelance information professional based in Ōtepoti Dunedin. 'Selfish' is from her memoir-in-progress, which follows the light through 30 years with undiagnosed bipolar type II and explores the importance of home and place and the role of cultural heritage and the arts in her quest to maintain a steady state of being.

Feby Idrus is a writer, musician and arts administrator from Ōtepoti Dunedin. Her short stories have recently been published in *takahē*, and in the anthologies *Aftermath: Stories of survival in Aotearoa New Zealand* and *A Clear Dawn: New Asian voices from Aotearoa New Zealand*. She regularly writes programme notes for the New Zealand Symphony Orchestra. Find her on Twitter/X @febyidrus.

Gabrielle Amodeo (she/her) is a Te Whanganui-a-Tara-based artist and writer. Her drawing-based practice led to PhD research that proposes the essay as a form of expanded life-drawing. This research, titled 'Life-drawing: Trauma and intimacy in the essay qua drawing', earned her a place on Massey University's Dean's List.

Ghazaleh Gol is an Iranian-New Zealand writer, director and Fulbright scholar. Her book of essays *The Girl from Revolution Road* was published in 2020. She has contributed writing to anthologies *Ko Aotearoa Tātou | We Are New Zealand* and *A Kind of Shelter Whakaruru-taha*, and has written for various publications including *The Spinoff*, *Ensemble* and *Sauce*. She has a PhD in Media and Communication with a focus on Iranian diasporic cinema from the University of Auckland.

Golriz Ghahraman is an Iranian-born New Zealand politician, MP and author of the memoir *Know Your Place* (2020). The former United Nations lawyer was a child asylum seeker, and became the first refugee elected to New Zealand Parliament. Golriz is a member of the New Zealand House of Representatives for the Green Party.

Gráinne Patterson grew up in Ireland and has lived in Aotearoa for 10 years, settling in Te Whanganui-a-Tara in 2018. She is completing a Master's in creative non-fiction at the International Institute of Modern Letters and is writing a memoir based on her upbringing and experiences of supporting her mother through addiction.

Hazel Phillips is a writer and sometimes communications professional who is usually found somewhere near a mountain. She has published three books, including *Solo: Backcountry adventuring in Aotearoa New Zealand* (2022), and she holds a Master's with distinction in creative writing. When not working, she tramps, skis, mountaineers and dives. Her writing pursuits have so far caused her to wear out eight keys on her laptop keyboard.

Helen Rickerby lives in a cliff-top tower in Aro Valley. She's the author of four poetry collections, most recently *How to Live* (2019), which won the Mary and Peter Biggs Award for Poetry at the 2020 Ockham New Zealand Book Awards. Since 2004 she has run the boutique publishing company Seraph Press.

Henrietta Bollinger is a writer, performer and disabled community advocate. In 2022 they worked with Nathan Mudge as a co-editor of the guide 'Working together: Accessibility in Aotearoa theatre', published by Playmarket. Their first essay collection, *Articulations*, was published in 2023. They live in Te Whanganui-a-Tara Wellington.

Hinemoana Baker (Ngāti Tūkorehe, Ngāti Raukawa-ki-te-Tonga, Ngāti Toa Rangatira, Te Āti Awa, Ngāi Tahu, Germany, England) is a poet and performer who was born in Ōtautahi, and raised in Whakatāne and Whakatū. Her work is widely anthologised, and she has written four collections of poetry, including *Funkhaus* (2020), which was shortlisted for the 2021 Ockham New Zealand Book Awards. In 2015 she received the Creative New Zealand Berlin Writer's Residency and has since lived and worked in Germany. Hinemoana is completing a PhD in cultural studies at Potsdam University.

Iona Winter (Waitaha) is a widely published kaituhi. As the 2022 CLNZ/NZSA Writers' Award recipient, she completed a creative non-fiction project addressing the complexities of being suicide bereaved. In 2023, she launched Elixir & Star Press, a dedicated space for the expression of grief in Aotearoa New Zealand, in memory of her tama, Reuben Samuel Winter. Her preferred form is poetry, and she lives in the Tasman region.

Jackie Clark QSM is a New Zealand philanthropist and advocate for women. She established The Aunties, a charity helping vulnerable women and children who have experienced domestic violence.

Janie Smith is a former journalist and current communications advisor. Her interests include baking, cake decorating, cooking, knitting and quilting. If an Ultimate Grandma reality TV show is ever created, Janie will ace it.

Jazial Crossley is a writer who lives in in Te Whanganui-a-Tara. Her memoir-by-playlist 'Everyone I've Ever Loved & All The Songs That Remind Me Of Them' is published in monthly instalments on her Substack newsletter *All The Songs*. She has won several national awards for her writing as a journalist and holds a Master's in Business Administration and a journalism diploma.

Kate Camp is a poet and memoirist. Her latest books are *How To Be Happy Though Human: New and Selected Poems* (2022) and the memoir *You Probably Think This Song Is About You* (2020), from which her *Otherhood* essay is taken.

Kerry Sunderland is a freelance journalist, author, podcast host/producer and curator of the Nelson Arts Festival's literary programme. She has been published in *Headlands: New Stories of Anxiety* (2018), *Turbine | Kapohau*, *New Zealand Geographic*, *New Zealand Listener*, *North & South*, *The Spinoff*, *Stuff/Nelson Mail* and the *Byron Echo*.

Lily Duval is a writer and artist based in Ōhinehou Lyttelton. She is the illustrator of *Critters of Aotearoa* (written by Nicola Toki), published in 2023, and her illustrated non-fiction book *Six-legged Ghosts* was published in 2024.

Linda Collins (she/her) is the author of a memoir, *Loss Adjustment* (2019), and a poetry collection, *Sign Language for the Death of Reason* (2021). She was shortlisted for the Bridport Prize, runner-up in a national poetry competition in the UK and the Otago regional winner in New Zealand's 2023 national flash fiction competition. She has two Master's degrees from the International Institute of Modern Letters and the University of East Anglia.

Linda Rooney lives in Te Whanganui-a-Tara Wellington with her husband. She writes, among other things, a blog about life without children called *No*

Kidding in NZ. A former company chair, consultant, international marketing manager, and (junior) diplomat, she loves travel, languages, photography, writing, good food and wine and learning new things.

Lori Leigh (she/they) is a writer based in Te Whanganui-a-Tara. Lori has published with Palgrave MacMillan, Oxford University Press, Cambridge University Press and Routledge. Her work has also appeared in local lifestyle magazines such as *Capital*. As a scriptwriter, Lori has twice been shortlisted for the Adam NZ Play Award. Her drag musical *The Glitter Garden* won Playmarket's Plays for the Young Award in 2020 and the Wellington Theatre Award for Production of the Year in 2021. Their children's book, based on the play, was published in 2020. Lori has a Master's from Sarah Lawrence College in New York.

Lucy O'Connor (she/her) is a short-fiction writer from Te Whanganui-a-Tara whose first collection of short stories was published in 2024. Her body of work examines the way misogyny, power imbalances and modern technologies shape and influence contemporary relationships. Lucy got her fiction break after being published in *Mayhem*. In 2023 she was one of the 13 emerging writers selected for the New Zealand Society of Authors Mentorship Programme. 'Atmosphere' is her first non-fiction essay to be published in print.

Melanie Newfield is a writer and researcher who is based in Te Whanganui-a-Tara Wellington. She has a dog, two cats and dozens of tropical fish.

Michaela Tempany lives in Wellington with her husband. Her work has been included in *Turbine | Kapohau*, *Mayhem* and *Flash Frontier*. She was the recipient of the International Institute of Modern Letters' 2019 Prize for Original Composition, and first place winner of the 2019 Zephyr Short Story Competition. She completed her Master's in creative writing at the International Institute of Modern Letters in 2021.

Nicola Brown is a clinical psychologist, stand-up comedian, executive coach, writer and speaker. She lives in Ōtepoti Dunedin with her wife and son, and is currently working on a memoir. In 2021 she was awarded Dunedin Comedy's Best Storyteller award. Her website is www.nicolabrown.co.

Paula Morris MNZM (Ngāti Wai, Ngāti Manuhiri, Ngāti Whātua) is an award-winning novelist, short-story writer, editor and essayist from Tāmaki Makaurau Auckland. An associate professor at the University of Auckland, where she directs the Master's of creative writing, Paula is the founder of the Academy of New Zealand Literature and Wharerangi, the online Māori literature hub. She is also editor of Aotearoa New Zealand Review of Books and writes about television and film for the site KoreaSeen. She is the editor of the anthologies *A Clear Dawn: New Asian Voices from Aotearoa New Zealand* (2021, with Alison Wong) and *Hiwa: Contemporary Māori Short Stories* (2023).

Raina Ng was born in Malaysia, grew up in Ōtepoti Dunedin and lives in Te Whanganui-a-Tara Wellington. She spends much of her idle time pondering humanity and all the things that tie us together (or cast us apart).

Sam Orchard is a comic artist and illustrator who works on projects that celebrate difference. He has been drawing his autobiographical web comic Rooster Tails for over 10 years and is working on his first graphic novel. He's been on the Samesame But Different board since 2017 and is the assistant curator for cartoons and comics at the Alexander Turnbull Library, Te Whanganui-a-Tara Wellington.

Shaneel Lal (they/them) is the founder of the Conversion Therapy Action Group, the group that led the movement to ban conversion therapy in Aotearoa. They were named on the *Forbes* 30 Under 30 Asia List in 2022, and in 2023 was awarded Young New Zealander of the Year. Shaneel writes a weekly column for the *Herald on Sunday*, and in 2023 published the acclaimed memoir *One of Them*. They completed their law studies at the University of Auckland.

Steff Green, whose pen name is Steffanie Holmes, is the bestselling author of over 50 kooky, spooky romance novels. Her books feature clever, witty heroines, secret societies, creepy old mansions and swoony vampires who get what they want. Legally blind since birth, Steff received the 2017 Attitude Award for Artistic Achievement and was a finalist for a 2018 Women of Influence award. She lives at South Head on the Kaipara Harbour with her husband, a horde of cantankerous cats, and their medieval sword collection.

Acknowledgements

To our publisher, Massey University Press, including Tracey Borgfeldt, who first saw the potential in *Otherhood*, and the GOAT Nicola Legat, who nurtured it to life with her wisdom, experience and by answering emails even late on a Sunday evening.

Thanks to project editor Emily Goldthorpe, copyeditor Tessa King, designer Kate Barraclough, proofreader Jude Watson and the rest of the MUP team for their lovely work.

To all our essayists, including the ones we couldn't find space for in *Otherhood*, thank you for sharing your stories with us and trusting us to handle them with care.

To those who wrote essay samples to help us land a publisher, thank you for giving us your time and lending us your stories: Alice Soper, Bethany Rogers, Bonnie Etherington, Freya Daly Sadgrove, Hazel Phillips, Jazial Crossley, Kate Camp, Iona Winter, Nkhaya Paulsen-Moore and Penelope Whitson.

Thank you to the people who wrote letters of support towards *Otherhood*'s funding: Catherine Woulfe, Claire Mabey, Emily Writes, Emma Wehipeihana, John Cranna, Majella Cullinane and Zöe Meager. And to Chris Tse for his always sage advice. We may not have secured the funding, but we'll always have your words.

Thank you to Dr Tracy Morison for taking the time to share her expertise on reproductive decision-making for our prologue.

✹

Alie: It seems like a long time ago that I woke up to a notification that the author of *Not that I'd Kiss a Girl* had tagged me in a tweet about an anthology. I spent half a day wondering how serious this was because it was actually kind of a cool idea but it sounded like a lot of work. It has indeed been a lot of work, but if I'd known what wonderful friends I'd make in the process, I wouldn't have waited half a day. Kathryn and Lil have been a literary lifeline and a great solace as I moved to the other side of the world. I hope I continue to wake up to dozens of unread WhatsApp messages from them.

My thanks also to all the friends who were excited about this book. Your enthusiasm showed me how many people had been waiting to see their story represented and motivated me to keep going. And as always, to David, for being 'not fussed' about having kids, for reading my essays even when the rugby is on and for reminding me when I need to stop working and go do something nice.

✹

Kathryn: Thanks Alie and Lil for teaching me so much about editing, writing and life, to Pennie Hunt and my Literary Lunch critique partners for giving me a creative community, and to Tim Armstrong for building a beautiful life with me.

Some of my contribution to this collection was made while I was the University of Otago's Robert Burns Fellow, The Winston Churchill McNeish Fellow, and the recipient of the Hungarian Writers' Residency. My heartfelt thanks to the University of Otago, the Winston Churchill Memorial Trust NZ, and the Hungarian Writers' Residence for providing me with the time and space to write, edit, explore, think and dream.

✹

Lil: Firstly, thank you to my fellow editors Alie and Kathryn for giving me a positive association with the previously dreaded words: 'group project'. Deciding to embark on this wild idea with two near-strangers, and making two fantastic friends, has been one of the most rewarding experiences of my life. Thank you for listening to my rants, going along with crazy ideas and adding your own, talking me down off the ledge and supporting my own writing. I've learnt so much about writing and editing from you.

To Beth, for letting me write about her for the second book in a row, even though she doesn't like it.

And finally to my partner, Tanya: I love you. Thank you for making the space and time for me to work on this, for supporting me with baking and back rubs, and for always being the first to read my work and offer helpful feedback as well as far more positivity than the first drafts deserved.

❋

Thank you to the Boosted team, especially our mentor, Jess Covell, for giving us a platform to raise funds to pay our contributors.

Thank you to our sponsors and all the wonderful people who donated to the crowdfunding campaign, including our anonymous donors. We literally couldn't have done this without your support to pay our essay writers.

Our Gold sponsors

Rebecca Barrow

Our Silver sponsors

Emma Wehipeihana
Katija Vlatkovich
Leila Boyle
Tanya Johnson

Our Bronze sponsors

Elina from Storyo
Petronella's Bookstore
Schrodinger's Books

And all our other lovely donors

Abbey Allpress
Aimie Chapman
Aimee-Jane Anderson-
O'Connor
Alice Ingram
Alix K
Amy Russell
Angela Heape
Anjuli Muller
Anna Scanlen
Anne Kerslake
Hendricks
Anne T.
Anne Whittaker
Antoinette Hastings
Anuja Mitra
Bam Bialostocki
Becs Tetley
Belle Chance
Benjamin Lott
Briar Barry
Bridget Mooney
Brown Bread (Peg)
Bryony James
Bryony Skillington
Carole Beu
Carolyn Stebbing
Cat Waide
Catherine Robertson
Charlotte W
Chris Price
Chris Tse
Christina Wood
Christy Menzies
Clare Fraser
Clare McLennan-Kissel

Colleen Macdonald
Colleen Smith
Cushla Young
Dadon Rowell
Danielle Marshall
Divyaa Kumar
EeMun Chen
Elaine Lynskey
Eleanor Machiela
Ellen Boucher
Elouise Quigan
Emily Goldthorpe
Emily Nicholas
Emily Writes
Emma Bailey
Emma Barnes
Emma Christoffersen
Emma Neale
Emma Wood
Erin Webb
Estelle Best
Evelyn Scott
Feby Idrus
Fiona Campbell
Filomena Ng
Fran Caliari-Pearce
Frances Mountier
Graham Atkinson
Greta Yardley
Hana Craig
Hana Fahy
Hannah Harmon
Hannah Shell
Hannah Spyksma
Hannah Stanley
Helen Rickerby

Helen Vivienne Fletcher
Hilary Alcorn
Hilary Coffey
Hilary Cook
Isabel Bowler
Jackie Lee Morrison
Jacqueline Bublitz
Jacqui Smith
Jane Arthur
Jane Bloomfield
Jane Porter
Jess Keogh
Jess Young
JJ Lim
Joanna Wane
Johanna Barr-Beunk
John McCormick
Josie Shapiro
Jo Tracy-Inglis
Juliet Conway
Kat Ashmead
Kate Mackersy
Kate McDermott
Kate Newton
Kate Waltman
Katherine Wharton
Kathryn Hagen
Kirsten Mines
Kirsty Clarke
Kirsty Johnston
Kylie Etherton
K-J Dillon
Lara Liesbeth
Laura Hewson
Laura McNeur
Laura Volp
Lauren Anderson

Lauren Auty
Leigh Catley
Liesl Nunns
Lila Horrell
Lily Holloway
Lisa Schollum
Lucy Gardner
Maia Hall
Majella Cullinane
Marianne Elliott
Marilyn Velvin
Marnie Reinfelds
Mary Fawcett
Megan Ellis
Melinda Hickson
Mel H-T
Melissa Peterson
Michelle Beattie
Michelle Matheson
Muireann Heussaff
Naomi Arnold
Natalie Anderson
Natasha Evans
Nathan Joe
Nicola Cummins
Nina Hannert-Nimmo
Nouran El-Hilali
Olivia Egerton
Patricia Bell
Pennie Hunt
Phoebe Hunt
Polly Ralph
Rachael Kavermann
Rebecca James
Rebecca Leathem
Rebecca Marshall
Rebecca Williams

Robert Hurley
Robyn Hambleton
Rochelle Ivanson
Rochelle Jones
Rose Lu
Ruby Cumming
Sam Rodgers
Sarah Bassett
Sarah Benge
Sarah Borrie
Sarah Fitzpatrick
Sarah Naidu
Sarah Prestidge
Sarah Wells
Shirley Tricker
Sian Williams
Sophie Nielson
Steff Green
Stef Naldi
Stephanie Jones
Sue Worthington
Theresa
Thomas McLean
Tina Cartwright
Tom Frankish
Tracy Farr
Victoria Jones
@vivsternz
Yvette Merrin
Zadi Diedrichs-Farnan

And the many donors
who chose to remain
anonymous.

MASSEY
UNIVERSITY
PRESS

First published in 2024 by Massey University Press
Private Bag 102904, North Shore Mail Centre
Auckland 0745, New Zealand
www.masseypress.ac.nz

Design by Kate Barraclough

'My favourite girl', by Jazial Crossley, was first published
in *The Spinoff* in 2023; 'Why are there so many songs
about rainbows?', by Kate Camp, was first published in
You Probably Think This Song Is About You (Wellington:
Te Herenga Waka University Press, 2022); 'Departure from
the motherland', by Linda Collins, was first published in
The Short Story (TSS Publishing) in 2019.

Page 251: 'Another Birth', by Forugh Farrokhzad, translated
by Elizabeth T. Gray Jr., from *Let Us Believe in the Beginning
of the Cold Season*, copyright © Elizabeth T. Gray Jr., 2022
(translation). Published with permission of New Directions
Publishing Corp.

A catalogue record for this book is available from the
National Library of New Zealand

Printed and bound in Singapore by Markono Print Media

ISBN: 978-1-99-101674-4
eISBN: 978-1-99-101675-1